STEAMING EAST

STEAMING EAST

*The forging of steamship and rail links
between Europe and Asia*

SARAH SEARIGHT

THE BODLEY HEAD
LONDON

First published 1991
© Sarah Searight 1991
The Bodley Head, 20 Vauxhall Bridge Road, London SW1V 2SA

Sarah Searight has asserted her right
under the Copyright, Designs and Patents Act, 1988
to be identified as the author of this work

A CIP catalogue record for this book
is available from the British Library

Maps © Malcolm Porter 1991

ISBN 0-370-31497-2

The author and publishers gratefully acknowledge: the Witt Library
Photographic Collection for permission to reproduce illustrations of the
Searight Collection as well as the Victoria and Albert Museum where it is now
housed; Peninsular and Oriental for the use of their picture collection; the
Institution of Civil Engineers for pictures of Henry Maudslay and the
Stephensons; the Williamson Art Gallery and Museum, Birkenhead, for the
illustration on page 62; Ocean Group Shipping for permission to reproduce
the portrait of Alfred Holt on page 125; British Petroleum for permission to
reproduce illustrations on pages 232, 233, and 269; Faber & Faber for
permission to quote from T. S. Eliot's *Old Possum's Book of Practical Cats* on
p. 235; and HarperCollins for permission to quote from J. N. Westwood's
History of Russian Railways on page 177.

Printed in Great Britain by
Butler & Tanner Ltd, Frome and London

Contents

Illustrations

viii

Maps

Foreword and Acknowledgments

This is an account of how steam travel was developed in the nineteenth century over routes on land and at sea covering the world's great crossroads. Names such as Middle East and Central Asia are self-explanatory as crossroads; the Middle East is here taken to include what many in the nineteenth century referred to as the Near East – the old Ottoman Empire, Persia (Iran since 1935), and Afghanistan, while adjoining areas of Central Asia include the lands between the Black Sea and western China. To this one must add the crossroads of the Indian Ocean, their marine equivalent.

The outsider, whether writer, historian, traveller or politician, has always been fascinated by the comings and goings of people and goods at such a crossroads, myself included, whether in following the journey of a piece of lapis lazuli from Afghanistan to St Petersburg, a Kashmir shawl to the Victorian fireside, or a fragile glass bottle from Alexandria to an ancient cemetery near Kabul. The same routes were used for migration, for war and in the nineteenth century for steam communications.

For a hundred years, between the end of the Napoleonic wars and World War I, steam-powered European rivalries also followed these tracks. Geography dictated the route but steam introduced wholly new concepts of travel, time, speed and political power. In this book I have tried to describe how these concepts developed by sea as well as by land along the traditional routes to India, the source of such envied wealth, the goal of so many seeking to acquire it. The story begins peacefully enough, with hyperbolic enthusiasm for helping the darkened millions of the east in return for speeding up the trading of their valuable raw materials. It ends effectively with World War I. The war, much of it enacted in the Middle East with the help of steam, destroyed the crossroads; the victors drew frontiers, those behind the frontiers built them into barriers that only air travel – and not always that – could easily circumvent.

When I came to the story I was familiar with most of the terrain, though few of my personal travels have been powered by steam.

Exploring the development of steam technology, however, was as much a journey of discovery for me as it was for the first passengers a hundred and fifty years ago or less. Many helped to educate me in the technicalities of steam power, infecting me with their own enthusiasm, such as the acquaintance whose entire ground floor was covered with railway lines, even running through cuttings in the skirting boards, and another whose attic was given over to the railway tracks of an imaginary Indian Ocean island. They must forgive me where I may have failed fully to master their patient explanations.

Among those whom I would like to thank especially are Mr Jacob van Riemsdijk, Mr Adam Hall Patch and Mr Joe Room, all formerly of the Science Museum, Mr Laurence Beeching of the City of London Polytechnic, Mr John Blyth of the Stephenson Locomotive Society, Mrs Rossiter of the Marine Society, Mr Peter Bawcutt, Mr Frank Ludstrom at Cammell Laird, Mr Stephen Rabson of P.&O., as well as the patient librarians of the Science Museum, the National Army Museum, the London Library, the library of the National Maritime Museum, the India Office Library, and the British Library. Many thanks are due to my father whose picture collection, now in the Victoria and Albert Museum and used extensively here, so often reflects the *raison d'être* of Middle Eastern travel, and thanks also to its cataloguers and carers, notably Briony Llewellyn and Charles Newton. I thank my daughter for her patience in initiating the index, my son for initiating the maps and Mr Malcolm Porter for the final cartographic expertise. And I owe deep gratitude to my husband for his help with pictures and above all for tolerating my absence on ancient and sometimes remote routes between east and west.

Sarah Searight
January 1991

Note on spellings

This is always a contentious issue in any book on foreign parts, many of the names of people and places having been transliterated in a variety of ways over the years. I have mostly used the spelling which would have been familiar to nineteenth-century travellers and writers unless particularly unfamiliar to the twentieth-century reader, in which case I have used the generally accepted British Museum system of transliteration, omitting accents or diacritical marks.

I

The Power of Steam

The development of steam communications between Europe on the one hand and India and the Middle East on the other was inspired by the intensely covetable wealth of India. A succession of European wars in the latter half of the eighteenth century between Britain and France had their ramifications in India where the French, like the Portuguese earlier, were gradually driven into insignificant enclaves, leaving the British to reap the commercial benefits. India was suffering from the decline of Moghul authority, with dynastic squabbles degenerating into outbreaks of war in which the British increasingly found themselves involved, if only for the protection of a commercial empire ever more significant to the British economy. In the nineteenth century European powers became anxious to speed up access to that commercial empire, Britain as its jealous guardian, others – notably France, Russia and Germany – concerned to lessen the political power such wealth conveyed. Much of the rivalry between these powers occurred in and around the Middle East, and was powered by steam.

Early steam ventures were peaceful enough, advocated with an hyperbole that liked to draw on classical witnesses of earlier invasions, about speeding up communications and trade in order to help the darkened millions of the east. Herodotus and Arrian, even Gibbon, were called upon to boost these projects; volumes of decently expurgated *Arabian Nights* piled up on Europe's velvet-covered tea tables to divert at the evening fireside the imaginations of those who by day were doing their best to replace the fantasy with a smoke-begrimed familiarity. The hyperbole became more bellicose as the century wore on, adding to the intensity of Anglo–Russian rivalry that has become familiar as the Great Game, especially from the middle of the century when the locomotive started steaming eastwards through the Middle East and Central Asia. While the British, technically and industrially ahead of other European powers after the Napoleonic wars, always preferred the steamship and its naval ramifications, other European governments had a better comprehension of the steam locomotive's continental and strategic potential. Behind the moralising propaganda of German, Russian or French advocates of steam on land, there was a noticeably greater awareness of the strategic implications of railway lines than previously of steamship routes, though by the early twentieth century these too were regarded as part of an overall scheme of imperial cohesion. The last major developments in steam communications were under way just before World War I.

'Of all the inventions,' wrote Macaulay after returning from India in 1838, 'the alphabet and the printing press excepted, those which abridge distance have done the most for the civilisation of our species'. 'Nonsense', said John Ruskin: 'now every fool in Buxton can be in Bakewell in half an hour, and every fool in Bakewell in Buxton; which you think a lucrative process of exchange – you fools everywhere!'[1] Macaulay, having lived in India knew what he was talking about when it came to distance; Ruskin, who never left Europe, had a narrower perspective. Most of their contemporaries would have agreed with Macaulay. Whether for good or ill, steam travel introduced new concepts of speed and aroused the imagination far more dramatically than the imagination of the twentieth century was aroused by man's first landing on the moon.

When the actress Fanny Kemble was invited by George Stephenson to ride beside him on the bench of his 'steam-horse' the *Rocket* at 35 miles an hour ('swifter than a bird flies, for they tried the experiment with a snipe'[2]) and stood up with her bonnet off 'to drink the air before me', she was being presented with a wholly new experience. Steam was thrilling because it was obvious almost at once that it was going to give wings to ordinary men and women. People brought up to be stationary were bewitched by the movement, the sight and sound of a steam engine. This was why entrepreneurs leapt with more enthusiasm than understanding into plans to steam to India. Industrialists seized on its commercial potential, generals and politicians grappled with its strategic implications. Soon it was opening up continents, melding provinces into nations, shifting populations across the world – and also aiding and confirming military conquest. Man had discovered that he was born to go faster but when he did so he tended, unfortunately, to bump into other people.

This was particularly evident in the Middle East, the great crossroads over which merchants trading between Europe and India had made their slow way for thousands of years. Conquerors also swept across it, each depositing a rich layer of civilisation to amaze later Europeans, many of whom, standing at this junction of oriental and western influences, were beguiled by a cultural imagery easily extended to politics. Even before the nineteenth century, central authority imposed by earlier invaders often gave way to lesser local rulers whose rivalries interrupted the smooth flow of trade and communications further east. In the nineteenth century devout but also fervently political Europeans steamed into the vacuum, their firm belief in the partnership between moral improvement and material progress symbolised by these iron giants steaming eastwards towards the heathen loaded with bibles and manufactured goods. 'I wonder,' Charles Kingsley pondered in that year of revolution, 1848, 'whether, in the future ages, men will ever fall down and worship steam-engines, as the Caribs did Columbus' ships. Why not? Men have worshipped stone men and women; why not line iron?'[3] Those who were to gain from this traffic – who might therefore be expected to do the worshipping – were the millions who inhabited the benighted lands either in or on the way to India: Britain claimed benefits for India itself, Russia for the khanates of Central Asia, Germany for the inhabitants of Mesopotamia. The greatest benefits of all fell, of course, into the steam-borne laps of the claimants, their less high-minded territorial claims and rivalries emerging as the century wore on. In the process the crossroads suffered most.

Steam travel was such an adventure that it is unfair to accuse its early advocates of solely political ambition. Both France and Germany were devastated by the Napoleonic wars and initially lacked the capital to invest in technology. In Britain and the United States, where capital was readily available, technicians and mechanics in the first half of the century were often men with little formal education but an eye for inventiveness. 'There was once a man,' wrote Fanny Kemble of George Stephenson who clearly won her heart, 'who was a common coal-digger; this man had an immense constructiveness, which displayed itself in pulling his watch to pieces and putting it together again; in making a pair of shoes when he happened to be some days without occupation and finally . . . it brought him in the capacity of an engineer [to the House of Commons] with his head full of plans for a railway.' The pioneers of the steamboat and the locomotive were men of imagination and often great charm.

Quickness of mind could be cultivated under the apprenticeship system, a boy often travelling to the other end of the country or from one state to another to work alongside the masters. One of the most influential engineers in this respect was Henry Maudslay, who from his machine tool workshop in Lambeth in the early nineteenth century produced the first precision tools, innumerable marine engines and some pithy maxims to inspire his pupils, who included James Nasmyth,

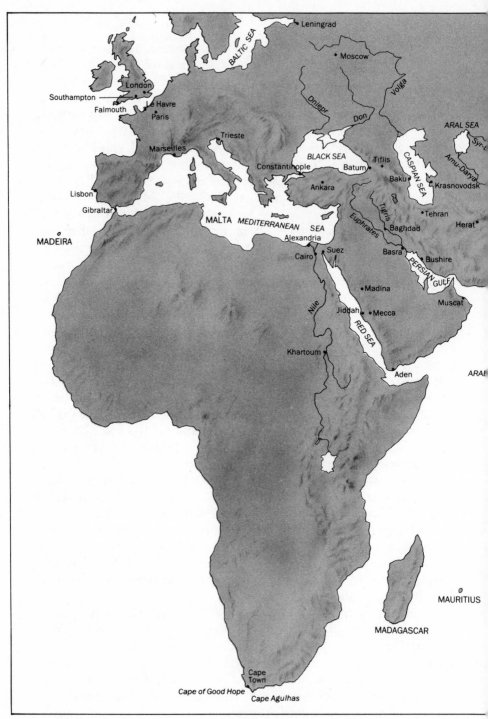

Map 1 From Europe to India by land or sea

nkent

ul

Delhi

achi

Ganges

Indus

Calcutta

Bombay

Madras

CEYLON

Point de Galle

Peking

INDIAN OCEAN

miles
0   1000
0   1000
kilometres

inventor of the steam hammer, and Joseph Whitworth the shipbuilder. Nasmyth's hammer went everywhere, including to Russia where it was seen at work in 1872 at the Russian naval base in the Crimea. It also helped to build the Nile barrage just below Cairo. These inventors knew each other well enough to develop a kind of camaraderie often at odds with the political and commercial rivalries their inventions aroused.

Steam transport developed from the outset along two distinct paths – on land and on water. Steam on land was the more expensive and needed the considerable skills of civil as well as mechanical engineers; a locomotive engine was more sophisticated than a marine engine, more economical in its use of space, weight and fuel, and its line was often expensive to lay. A railway demanded the organisation of the railway contractor and the persistence of the politician. By contrast water – even the stormy Bay of Biscay or the treacherous Agulhas Current off the Cape of Good Hope – made fewer demands and early marine engines could get away with being bulky, coal-hungry and relatively rudimentary. Rivalry at sea was gentlemanly compared with that on land, and most railway lines in and around the Middle East were built for strategic reasons.

Most early steam engines, notably that of James Watt, were stationary, for pumping water. But the impetus to apply steam to movement quickly grew, especially in France where communications on its wide tranquil rivers were already far in advance of those by land. Going upstream was to be the most admired achievement of all early steamboats. American inventors looking west and south over the untravelled wilderness of their continent were also realising the importance of river transport; the rewards for anyone who could discover a means of moving upriver as well as down would clearly be substantial.

It was in Scotland with its lochs, firths and inlets and difficult land communications that the first successful marine engine was designed in 1801 by William Symington and installed on the little stern-wheeler *Charlotte Dundas*. Among the audience of 'gentlemen' on board her maiden voyage was the American Robert Fulton, who in 1807 tested his paddle-steamer *Clermont* on the Hudson river; later that year he initiated a service between New York and Albany. Also in Scotland Henry Bell, a hotel proprietor 'cherishing a profound faith in the future potencies of steam,' commissioned the *Comet* on the Clyde in 1812 to provide the first regular steamer service in Europe; 'the elegance, comfort and safety and speed of this vessel require only to be proved ... the proprietor is determined to do everything in his power to merit

1   Henry Maudslay, pioneer inventor of precision tools, whose Lambeth works produced marine engines for early steam voyages

public encouragement.'[4] In the phraseology of the time the glorious day of steam had arrived.

With the huge expansion of shipping that arose from the growth of manufacturing and trade after the Napoleonic wars, shipbuilders soon had to change from timber to iron hulls. British boat-yards shifted from the Thames and Medway near the Kentish forests to the west of Scotland with its iron ore deposits. Here on the River Clyde the early iron shipbuilding industry developed, observers noting with pride that 'the sounds on the Clyde proclaim a mission of peace and goodwill among nations, for nearly all the ships constructed there are destined to carry to other lands the fabrics of our workshops and the products of our mills and with them the civilising and enlightening influence resulting from the skills and genius of our artisans.'[5] Most prolific of the Clydeside shipyards were those of the Napiers. Robert Napier, a blacksmith's son, began building marine engines in the 1820s, supplying engines for the East India Company's *Berenice* and *Zenobia*, and later went into shipbuilding. His cousin David originally had a Thames shipbuilding yard, but sold this when vessels outgrew the launching space and joined Robert on the Clyde.

The commonest early marine engine was Robert Napier's direct action side-lever engine, with two side beams, placed lower down than the old overhead beam engine, near the foundation plates of the vessel, thereby giving better stability as well as saving valuable head room. Joseph Maudslay's oscillating engine, patented in 1827 and improved by John Penn in 1838, was longer than the side-lever engine but low and compact. Later came the compound expansion engine involving the use of the expansive power of steam at different pressures in two or more cylinders.

The steamship's great advantage, particularly in communications with India, was its independence of seasonal winds. It was dependent, however, on the provision of fuel. This could be wood; towards the end of the nineteenth century it could be oil but usually it was coal. In the early days Llangannech coal from South Wales was the most highly prized, followed later by coal from the dangerous Risca mine in the same area. Welsh coal was exported all over the world, often at great cost, for locomotives as well as marine engines, although later adaptations of locomotives enabled them at least to steam on lower-combustion fuels.

The supply of coal was a major problem away from inland waterways. Marine engineers were badgered to produce engines of more modest appetite, by shipowners anxious to ensure reliable supplies of coal and by governments pushed into extensions of empire to ensure the security of those supplies. Coal consumption varied but in the early days of the Bombay–Suez run (first steamed by the *Hugh Lindsay* in 1830), a vessel would need over 500 tons, 380 of them consumed in the treacherous waters of the Red Sea against the prevailing wind. By mid-century, just before the introduction of compound expansion, consumption was reckoned at 4–5 lb. per horsepower per hour. Brunel's *Great Eastern*, launched in 1858, was designed for a voyage round the world independent of coal stops, with capacity for 12,000 tons of coal (not enough, however) as well as 4,000 passengers. Compound expansion reduced consumption immediately to 2.5 lb. per horsepower per hour, thereby relieving captains of the terrible disease of coal fever, a dread of not having enough coal to bring the ship into port.

As ship design overcame other obstacles to ocean travel so the establishment of coaling stations around the world became a top priority – well-entrenched settlements such as Aden or Cape Town, fed or fuelled from home or India. Whenever there was a war panic in the latter half of the nineteenth century, on several occasions fired for the British by the eastward advance of Russian railways through Central Asia towards India, the secure supply of coal hit the headlines. But alongside the politics of steaming to India was often an element of romance, for passengers as well as engineers. As engines became more efficient so the coal disappeared off the decks into the holds, leaving room above for deck chairs and rugs for the sedentary, deck quoits for the energetic, all regularly descending to eat gargantuan meals (except in the Bay of Biscay) or play interminable bridge in vast, mirrored saloons. Despite the affection which the steam locomotive still arouses, the British, as perhaps befitted an island race, had a far greater admiration for the steamship than for the steam locomotive, and echoing in the corridors of prosperity and power was Kipling's old engineer McAndrew, as he bawled out his splendid ballad in the cavernous engine room of his ship:

Lord, send a man like Robbie Burns to sing the Song o' Steam!
To match wi' Scotia's noblest speech yon orchestra sublime.
Whaurto – uplifted like the Just – the tail-rods mark the time.
The crank-throws give the double-bass, the feed-pump sobs an' heaves,
An' now the main eccentrics start their quarrel on the sheaves:
Her time, her own appointed time, the rocking link-head bides,

2   The 22,500-ton *Great Eastern*, designed by Brunel and Scott Russell, the largest steamer afloat when launched in 1857, propelled by paddle and screw

Till – hear that note? – the rod's return whings glimmerin'
   through the guides.
They're all awa'! True beat, full power, the clangin' chorus goes
Clear to the tunnel where they sit, my purrin' dynamoes.[6]

The locomotive engine was a more complicated development than
the marine engine. Its problem was not only fuel consumption; it must
also be as light and compact as possible and had to run on rails, the
laying of which was no simple undertaking. It is not surprising that
people were talking of steaming round the Cape and even as far as
India while Stephenson's *Rocket*, Fanny Kemble on board, was barely
on the rails. Comfort was also conspicuous by its absence from early
trains; passengers had to make do with glassless, often roofless coaches,
their design in Europe based on the old stage-coach. Engines were
small, their smoky funnels not much higher than the heads of their
passengers. But what a difference in speed once the locomotive got
going! No one was going to quibble about smuts. What is so amazing
about a locomotive is how little it changed from Stephenson's concept,
how quickly it developed and how fiercely the battles over its routes
were fought. And ultimately, how effective its role became in war.

Greater claims were made for steam trains than were ever made for
steamboats, and rightly so, given their greater sophistication. The claims
were more often made by Europeans and Americans, their keen eyes
on its transcontinental potential, than by the British, whose locomotive
development was soon overtaken by continental engineers – French,
Belgian and ultimately German. Stephenson's guest on the footplate
was ingenuous: 'I felt as if no fairy tale was ever half so wonderful as
what I saw,' she enthused and Stephenson and his backers firmly
believed that people and prosperity would follow in their wake, as they
often did. But public excitement in Britain over these monstrous engines
tearing up the countryside, showering it with sparks and cinders,
evoking hyperbole with decibels, was seldom matched by government
inspiration and it was continental developers – Americans, Russians,
Germans – who grasped the full strategic value of railways as a reliable,
cheap, high-volume system of transport for military as well as for more
peaceful needs. One of the greatest American locomotive builders was
Mathias Baldwin who began life as a jeweller in Philadelphia, decided
against spending his life making 'gew-gaws' and founded what became
the world's largest locomotive works; by the time it abandoned building
them in 1955 it had produced 75,000 locomotives, many of them sent
overseas. While the British steamed east, for war or peace, by sea,

3   George Stephenson and his son Robert with the *Rocket* locomotive completed in 1829, used to inaugurate the Stephenson-engineered Liverpool to
Manchester line in 1830

monopolising the best coaling harbours, others, occasionally and often
grudgingly admitted to Britain's ocean coaling facilities, steamed east
for the same reasons by land.

Railway tracks had been developed, before locomotives, in Europe's
coal, iron and tin mines. Simple stationary hauling engines powered by
steam evolved towards the end of the eighteenth century and by the
beginning of the nineteenth century there was hardly a coal mine that
did not depend on a steam engine – for removing water from the
workings or raising coal up the shafts. Small and under-powered, these

engines lacked the motive force, let alone the imaginative pull, to send them out over the open land. In 1801 Richard Trevithick, son of the manager of the richest Cornish tin mine, designed and tested a road locomotive; three years later his Pen–y–darran Locomotive was the first successfully to pull a train on rails. Trevithick also pioneered the use of 'strong' steam, at pressure well above that of the atmosphere, thus making feasible the light self-propelling machine. His grandson, Francis, was for twenty years the chief mechanical engineer with Egyptian state railways. Meanwhile Oliver Evans was at work in the United States, a wheelwright who persuaded his flour-milling brothers to back his designs for a steam carriage, a steam dredger and a high-pressure steam boiler. Steam power on a public railway first appeared in 1825 with George Stephenson's *Locomotion* on the Stockton and Darlington line built also by Stephenson in the same year. Four years later the Stephensons produced the *Rocket* for the Rainhill trials to choose a locomotive for the Liverpool to Manchester line. The *Rocket*, Fanny Kemble's 'curious little fire-horse', was chosen.

The fundamental design of a steam locomotive changed little thereafter. Its frame rested via springs on axle-boxes or the bearing blocks of the wheels. Slots in the frame allowed the axle-boxes to move vertically, while the springs of different axles could be connected by pivoted levers to equalise suspension. It was usual to have two double-acting cylinders, either outside the frames (as in the United States and most continental locomotives) or inside (as in Britain).

Soon locomotive depots were being set up all over the industrial world. British, American, Belgian and German engines were sent across the ocean, often on board sailing ships, including India's first which was sidetracked by storms to Australia. They came with their own 'erectors', in Russia often either German or the peripatetic Scots. British engineers and contractors worked on the continent, the French in the Caucasus, Germans in Turkey, everyone, including Swedes, Americans, French, British and Germans, in Russia which in the 1850s, before its own industry was developed, was importing engines from wherever it could buy them; later its main locomotive plant was at Kolomna south-east of Moscow. Stoking the engine demanded as much skill as driving it, to make the most of whatever fuel was available, and locomotive exporters in the early days liked to send home-trained teams to stoke as well as drive their engines in distant parts.

The way was as important in the development of steam communications as the engine that rode upon it. An excited public in Europe, the United States and Britain had to wait another five years after the

Rocket's public appearance for the first true passenger railways. In 1830 Stephenson's Liverpool to Manchester line was opened, its inauguration marked by the ex-President of the Board of Trade William Huskisson's tragic disregard of the new invention's speed potential; he had disobeyed instructions to stay in the carriage during a stop on the trial run and fell under the wheels of another locomotive. The same year the first section of the Baltimore & Ohio Railroad opened and the first section of the St Etienne to Lyons railway.

To steam long distances eastwards by land ultimately meant steaming over and through the Alps and the Caucasus, through the mountain passes of north-west India and Baluchistan, across the deserts of the Middle East and Central Asia. But even the bog of Chat Moss between Liverpool and Manchester seemed insuperable at first. Overcoming these physical obstacles was the achievement of civil engineers as much as of mechanical engineers. Often the desire to speed up track laying and to save money led to attempts to avoid too many tunnels, bridges and cuttings, thereby inflicting sharp curves and steep grades on the lines which ultimately restricted their capabilities. Lines were laid by railway contractors; they laid out the route, set the navvies to work, paid the wages, inspected the line and in the later nineteenth century sometimes came to promote the line itself. Some contractors became enormously wealthy and politically powerful. Sir Roger Scratcherd in Trollope's *Dr Thorne* is one of the best portraits of a railway contractor: 'he had become a contractor, first for little things, such as half a mile or so of railway embankment, or three or four canal bridges, and then a contractor for great things, such as government hospitals, locks, docks and quays, and had latterly had in his hands the making of whole lines of railway.'[7]

Materials were cheap and were used lavishly: iron, steel, bronze, brass, bricks and, above all, labour – men attacking the raw earth with pickaxes and shovels, carting away barrowloads of mountain and plain. These were the navvies, so-called from 'navigator', the men who excavated canals. Often on the strategic lines described in this account the labour was provided by railway battalions – semi-skilled labour from the army. At his best and when the earth was easy to dig, the navvy could move six cubic yards of it in an eight-hour shift. They operated in gangs, led by gangers, 188,000 of them at work in Britain in that year of continental revolution, 1848, and several hundred at least in France, where they were much feared as the nominal cause of a strike that year by French railway workers.[8] Samuel Peto and Thomas Brassey, the leading British contractors, took several hundred navvies to the Crimean War when the hideous exigencies of the Russian winter demanded an

4 Distinctive American locomotives on the six-foot gauge Erie Railway. By 1870 the US was criss-crossed by over 50,000 miles of railway.

improved supply route from the coast to Sebastopol. In India huge camps of labourers moved about the countryside, often decimated by disease, to the consternation of developers mainly concerned about the progress of their lines.

The speed of development was astonishing. By 1848 Europe was linked by rail as well as by revolution and most of the main lines had been built. In one year, 1870, R.M. Ballantyne calculated that some 307 million passengers travelled on the world's railway lines: 'it may help one . . . to know that if a man were to devote himself to count it, one by one – sitting down after breakfast, counting at the rate of one every moment and working without intermission for eight hours every day, excepting Sundays – he would not conclude his task until the thirty-fifth year.'[9] By the same year the Pyrénées were crossed at both ends, the Alps pierced at Mont Cenis and traversed over Brenner. Britain had 24,500 km (15,250 miles) of railways; Germany 19,500 km (12,100 miles), Russia and France 17,000 km (10,500 miles) each, and the United States 84,000 km (53,000 miles). Speeds were up to 36 m.p.h. initially, later improved to 60 m.p.h.; some of the fastest locomotives built by Thomas Crampton were capable of 90 m.p.h.

Channel tunnels, advocated as 'an heroic remedy for seasickness', posed as many problems for financiers and engineers in the nineteenth century as they do today.

'Verily we live in stirring times,' wrote the *Calcutta Review* in 1857, 'when ere many years are over we are borne along the Euphrates Valley Railway to England in twenty days, or along the "World's Highway" in ten, while our thoughts are flashed along the telegraph wires in so many minutes, we shall begin to feel ourselves so close to home that we shall cease to consider our separation from our mother country as an "honourable exile".'[10] The *Review* was over-cautious. Viewed historically, the separation was already beginning to look more like an umbilical cord that mother country and the 'exiles' were determined should never be cut. To the British, a chain of naval stations around the ocean, rather than railway stations through the Middle East, was looking a more reliable cord. Others, however, were sharpening their surgical scissors.

High Seas to India

Despite Britain's position as the dominant European power in India, few British were living there when the Napoleonic wars finally ended. Most of the British in India were employees, commercial or military, of the East India Company, established in 1600 with a monopoly of trade with India. As trade expanded so did the Company's responsibilities and by the early nineteenth century it administered a huge swathe of northern India, from the mouth of the Ganges to the banks of the Sutlej, and much of southern India, with the important exceptions of Hyderabad and Mysore as well as some smaller states. The expansion of the Company's authority in the late eighteenth and early nineteenth centuries highlighted the abysmal state of communications between India and Britain; there was no concept of home because those who went to India seldom returned. The Company's trading monopoly was abolished in 1813 and the growth of British commercial and political involvement in the country acted as a financial as well as psychological spur to the development of communications, in particular the steamboat. By the time India had become empire, home, thanks to steam, was easily accessible.

Political conditions permitting, ancient routes between India and Europe had generally been by land, merchants travelling to and from Aleppo, Cairo, Constantinople, the great market cities of the Levant, or across the Caspian. Anyone using those routes in the fifteenth and sixteenth centuries, however, was vulnerable to disturbances among the various peoples who sat astride them – Turks, Arabs, Persians and the semi-nomadic tribes of Central Asia. Some Europeans aiming for India struggled to reach it via Russia and the Caspian, Anatolia and Persia, or Syria and Mesopotamia, but their accounts discouraged all but the most intrepid. Meanwhile the small seafaring country of Portugal had launched new initiatives in ship design leading to a new route east. In 1487 Bartolomeo Dias battled his way round the Cape in his tiny caravel and entered the Indian Ocean.

The Indian Ocean is not a difficult ocean to cross; as with any other ocean a knowledge of its temperament can make for a relatively easy voyage although the most skilled captain could be hit by misfortune at any moment and the less skilled could make life miserable for his luckless passengers. By the fifteenth century the Arabs had come to monopolise the extensive commercial network of the ocean, finding their way by careful calculation and an encyclopaedic knowledge of the winds, currents and stars. The north-east monsoon blows (mainly north of the equator) in the winter months, giving way stormily around March to the stronger south-west monsoon, most forceful in July. Later sailors were to appreciate the advantages of letting the wind take one well to the west – almost as far as Rio de Janeiro – before heading south-east for the Cape of Good Hope. An Arab navigator, Ibn Majid, piloted Vasco da Gama from Mombasa to Calicut on the west coast of India ten years after Dias' voyage. For the next 320 years of European involvement in India virtually all communications were by the all-sea Cape route, but it was a long time before steam-driven vessels could rival the performance of those depending on the skilful use of winds and currents to cross that great expanse of ocean.

Before long the Dutch and the English were challenging Portuguese dominance in the Indian Ocean, their trading companies establishing links with the Mogul rulers of India, setting up their factories on the Indian coast and participating in a trade in spices, fine fabrics, precious stones and ivory, lucrative enough to justify the hazards of the journey and life in foreign parts. French nautical and commercial enterprise was delayed by internal wars until well into the seventeenth century; the Compagnie des Indes Orientales was founded in 1664 by Louis XIV's minister, Colbert. Commercial incentives inspired the spread of European settlement in India, primarily by the British who by the end of the eighteenth century had driven all erstwhile rivals either out of the country or into small coastal enclaves. Britain's possessions in India were the envy of her commercial rivals and their covetous glances, often stimulated in the nineteenth century by the potential of steam in bringing them closer to the goal, regularly sent tremors down the spines of successive British administrations in India.

Ocean travel in the days of sail was not for the fainthearted. 'No man would be a sailor, who had contrivance to get himself into a jail,' declared Dr Johnson, 'for being in a ship is being in a jail with the chance of being drowned.'[1] The voyage under sail to or from Calcutta could take four to eight months, depending partly on visits or adventures on the way but also on vital winds at the beginning and end of the voyage. Thomas Twining, aged sixteen when he sailed to India in 1792 (paying £100 for his passage including the cost of a privileged seat at the captain's table) was warned to take several sets of clothes with him to allow for growth.[2] The first East India Company venture to India – five vessels in 1601 – had to wait two months for a good wind to take it down the Thames. It could take a week to sail from Gravesend to Southampton. A friend of the well-travelled William Hickey, the scurrilous diarist who travelled many times to India usually to try to make a fortune, warned him from Calcutta: 'I scarcely ever knew a fleet or even a single ship go within fifteen days of the time first allotted.'[3]

Once on the open sea the passenger was often overwhelmed by a sense of helplessness as he or she tossed on its vast grey wastes, emphasised by the excitement of that call from the crow's nest, 'A sail! A sail!', which was only partly tempered by the strong possibility that the sail was hostile. Very few sailed the oceans, perhaps no more than 200 people a year between Britain and India in the later eighteenth century, and there was certainly no concept of pleasure behind a voyage. First there was the dependence on wind: 'we are in hysterics at the bare apprehension of a calm', noted the young Alexander Macrabie in 1774, when travelling to India as secretary to his uncle, the lawyer Philip Francis; 'people who pray for long life have it in their power to live as long as they think fit – they need only go to sea to turn seconds into centuries.'[4] Francis was a vociferous and dangerous critic of the East India Company governor in India, Warren Hastings, who was eventually impeached as a result of Francis' accusations. The food was repulsive, especially for the crew, and frequently led to devastating outbreaks of 'that horrible disease', scurvy. One solution to this was to carry live food, so that later passengers were liable to be woken by the farmyard accommodated on board: 'one cow, 50 Southdown sheep, 71 porkers and more than 600 geese, ducks and fowls,' wrote James Wathen, a surgeon travelling to India in 1811, complaining of their din at dawn.[5] Rats and cockroaches infested the cramped space between decks. Pirates were also inclined to sally forth from the many archipelagos of the Indian Ocean.

And there was the tedium. 'Oh the dull insipid system of a ship,' Macrabie exclaimed. It was only slightly alleviated by the routine of shipboard life: journal writing, music, games in a certain rigorous daily order, dominated, however, by eating, especially once the importance of fresh food had been established. 'No one seems to abstain from eating and drinking more than three hours together,' commented the Reverend George Trevor.[6]

Breakfast was more like dinner, the seventeen-year-old Harriet Atkinson marvelled, when she sailed to India as late as 1837: 'curry and rice is of course a standing dish but we have besides eggs and bacon,

5   Sunday at sea en route to India, on board P.&O.'s vessel, *Sumatra*, in 1875

ham, pork pie, tongue, fowl, duck hashes and stews of every description.'[7] And 'we have hot rolls every morning' – quite a change from the
interminable pest-ridden 'biscuit' of earlier voyages. Huge joints of
roast meat were occasionally supplemented by shark converted into
chowder, a highly relished sea dish, dolphin and other fish. Food was
washed down with wine, sherry, port and Madeira; a good supply of
'pipes' of this 'easy traveller' was picked up on route.

In between meals the passengers took their exercise, severely disci-
plining themselves to several turns round the deck. Or they wrote the
journals pressed into their hands on departure, the pages decorated
with trivia; 'smooth seas and fair winds afford little matter of curious
observation,' observed Macrabie a trifle smugly, while 'I believe if I did
not keep a journal I should never know the day of the month,' wrote
Harriet Atkinson, 'and if Sunday did not come sometimes I am sure the
day of the week would be equally unknown.' As for Sundays, services
on deck included hymns sung to those 'in danger on the sea', and
cautionary sermons were addressed to young men going to India. 'The
due observance of religious duties has here, as everywhere else, the best
effects,' noted Wathen, 'producing seriousness and reflection in the
mind, a reverence and awe of the Deity.'

Revictualling called for several stops en route. The most popular,
and often the first, was Madeira. The beauty of the island struck
everyone – 'the rich blue of the sea, contrasted with the dark brown

of the lofty rocks,' rhapsodised Lord Valentia in 1802, 'the rich scene of the vineyards ... the families looking out of their windows with a nonchalance that nothing but habit could give' – with only an occasional murmur about the tendency of the population to go about half naked and the pestering of 'the most indefatigable beggars in the world.'[8]

The next adventure was crossing the equator. Ladies discarded their bonnets and gentlemen took up straw hats; the punkahs were put up and worked all through dinner. Harriet Atkinson crossed the equator on her birthday and celebrated with plum pudding and Neptune's antics. Generations of sailing passengers, like those later on steamships, were subjected to an elaborate equatorial ritual – 'stale tricks', complained one of them who must have been ducked too viciously, but they did break the monotony. Old sailors would tease new by making them look through a telescope in which a hair had been placed between the glasses saying, 'Look, there's your equator!' The accompanying ritual involved the arrival of Neptune, the shaving of visitors fresh to his kingdom, dousing them in salt water, and liberal provision of grog to the crew. Being plunged backwards into a salt bath could be unpleasant, with ducking from the yard-arm another variant; Valentia's fellow passengers were all showered and ducked, except the captain's passengers, who bought their exclusion along with the privilege of eating with him. The ritual became more involved but also more sedate as the nineteenth century aged and the range of passengers grew; Neptune could hardly manhandle district officers returning home on leave with the same aplomb as a teenager such as Thomas Twining.

To sail to the Cape could take two months or more. After another two months tossing or becalmed on the Indian Ocean, weaving in and out of archipelagos, avoiding pirates and French vessels, stopping for a much needed break at Madras – and some four months out of Falmouth on a good voyage, often twice as long if the monsoon winds were missed – the ship might reach the Hooghly river, one of the many mouths of the Ganges, still to face a dispiriting voyage upriver to Calcutta. Only then could those journals be consigned to the bottom of the cabin trunks, their blank and now yellowed pages for the most part only containing a few hasty references to the weather thereafter.

Yet sailing vessels of the period were efficient, stable and safe, their massive hulls dominating the Deptford and later Blackwell riverside shipyards where so many of them were built. The largest could weigh as much as 1500 tons but most were around 700 tons. Shortages of timber in Britain in due course encouraged shipbuilding in India, especially by the Parsee community in Bombay with its great teak-forested hinterland. Teak is oily as well as strong and almost indestructible by the *teredo navalis* worm. In Britain the timber shortages were to lead to the development of iron hulls. With the great wooden East Indiamen speed was never an attribute but neither was it a factor in most people's consideration; East India Company standards were high and the reliability of these 'aristocrats of the sea' partly explains why it took so long for steam vessels to oust them from the Cape route. But as Britain's commercial and then political involvement in India grew, so did the pressure to speed up the links. In 1803, in the middle of the Napoleonic wars, the Marquis of Wellesley complained from India that 'in the present year I was nearly *seven months* without receiving one line of intelligence from England . . . so that I suffered almost insupportable distress of mind . . . Speedy, authentic and regular intelligence from Europe is essential to the conduct of the trade and government of this empire.'[9]

Steam navigation on inland waters had already been tested for several years on American rivers and lakes and in Scottish coastal waters before it ventured into the open sea. There was a wide gap in understanding between the early developers of steam – Fulton and Bell, for instance, who knew the sheltered waters of the United States and Scotland where their engines were designed to steam – and those nautical men who were familiar with the wide open oceans but knew very little about the strengths and weaknesses of the engines they clamoured to launch across them. Both engineers and sailors, ensnared in visions of ever speedier communications, thought that out at sea they could have the best of both worlds; so the American vessel *Savannah*, the first to use steam in crossing the Atlantic in 1816, was encumbered not only with bulky engines and huge low-pressure boilers but also with full-blown sailing rig.* In fact she sailed a great deal more than she steamed – 85 hours' steaming out of a total voyage of 27 days, 11 hours – and under sail her decks were cluttered by the paddle wheels, cunningly made collapsible and detachable to the frustration of the crew trying to raise the sails.

---

* All early marine boilers used sea water. This resulted in serious corrosion and accumulations of salt so that boilers had to be 'blown down' at frequent intervals, a dangerous operation if high-pressure steam was being used. This is one of the reasons why uneconomical low pressures were used at sea while high-pressure locomotives were commonplace on land. Samuel Hall invented his condenser in 1834 but the problem was not really solved until the 1860s, coinciding with the introduction of the 'Scotch' reinforced boiler which could withstand high pressure.

But the *Savannah*'s lesson was ill-absorbed. Sail might be a perfectly adequate means of trading over vast expanses of sea but fast communications were becoming essential to the elaboration of those economic ties which were to bind India and Britain so tightly throughout the century. Political developments, highlighted during the wars between Britain and France in the eighteenth century, and commercial expansion following the Napoleonic wars could not wait on correspondence and reactions that might be nearly a year old before they were received, two years old before a letter was answered. Steam must come to the rescue, and in 1822 a Steam Committee was set up in London to raise money for an experimental steam voyage to India.

One of its protagonists was Lieutenant James Johnston, a lively and optimistic sailor who had joined the navy at the age of sixteen in 1803 and had been present at the Battle of Trafalgar. At the end of the Napoleonic wars he was retired on half pay, and with little prospect of employment in Britain he headed, like so many, for Calcutta where he had friends. Calcutta in those days was a boom town and the owners of the handsome palaces proliferating along the Hooghly's banks, the British 'nabob' community, welcomed any innovation, such as steam communication with Europe, that might improve their trade. There is no record of Johnston joining in their speculations at that stage but in 1821 he was back in Britain where he was swept up by the enthusiasm for steam. Although opinion favoured a route through the more sheltered waters of the Mediterranean, by which a connection might be made with the less sheltered and unfamiliar Red Sea, an experiment on that route would involve at least two vessels, double the investment. One vessel would be enough for a Cape experiment.

Distinguished engineers on the committee aroused the necessary public backing. They included in particular Henry Maudslay, who from his machine tool workshop in Lambeth produced a succession of marine engines. 'First get a clear idea of what you desire to accomplish, and then in all probability you will succeed in doing it,' was one of Maudslay's maxims,[10] but his voice may not have been loud enough to counter the commercial speculations of his fellow members on the committee. Nor were they discouraged by the carping of a correspondent to the *Asiatic Journal* who compared the project with another to melt ice by transferring Mount Vesuvius to the North Pole: 'the details [Johnston] has furnished ... are so specious, and all the obstacles in the way of its success are so admirably disposed of, that it is astonishing the projector has not been deluged with contributions or subscriptions already, and that a steam vessel is not now unloading in the port of

Suez.'[11] Johnston paid no attention and with the committee's backing he sailed back to Calcutta to raise money, certainly gaining familiarity with the route.

British merchants there, formed by Johnston into another Steam Committee, saw steam navigation via the Cape as a way of sustaining an all-sea route to India (in other words to Calcutta) at the expense of the new and fast-expanding Bombay community whose eye was already fixed on overland routes through either Egypt or Mesopotamia. Bombay's case, which had some powerful supporters, rested largely on the fact that the route through the Red Sea via Egypt was far shorter than that round the Cape. Its shortness had been painfully brought home to the British by Napoleon's invasion of Egypt in 1798, an invasion which the French government and Napoleon himself viewed as a significant stepping-stone to India. In 1800 British troops dispatched to Egypt from India with the intention of helping to defeat the French, arrived too late, having had to sail from Bombay at the height of the monsoon. Napoleon's later intrigues to invade India, first via Russia and in due course also involving the Shah of Persia, again emphasised the relevance as well as vulnerability of Indian communications.

The Cape route favoured by Calcutta merchants was not a 'rash and hurtful speculation', the committee maintained not altogether successfully in one of several petitions to a reluctant governor: 'the contemplated undertaking involves no such serious risk as should deter government from joining us in the encouragement of the attempt.'[12] The Bengal government, more apprehensive, was indeed deterred, and described the scheme as 'fraught with difficulty and danger.' It refused all encouragement, pecuniary or otherwise. Later the government relented, to the tune of 20,000 rupees with a bonus of 100,000 rupees offered to whoever established steam communication between Britain and India on a permanent basis. This meant, it specified, completing two round voyages the first of which must be over by the end of 1826, with an average voyaging time of not more than seventy days one way.

Despite lack of encouragement from the East India Company, the indefatigable Johnston raised another 80,000 rupees privately, the committee advertising the fact that the project would 'halve the lengthened and heart-rending distance which separates the Husband and the Wife, the Parent and the Child.' Johnston returned to London to find an experimental steamer. One was already under construction at Deptford, traditional birthplace of East Indiamen, the *Enterprize*, a 479-ton wooden paddle-steamer, 120 feet long with a 27-foot beam. This was rather smaller than the average East Indiaman but a monster by comparison with most steamboats being built then. Maudslay, by far the best marine engine maker in the country, provided the two 60 horsepower side-lever engines; his huge 32-ton copper boiler, at £7,000 the most expensive item on the vessel, supplied steam at a pressure of about 3 lb. per square inch. Maudslay also contributed £2,000 to the cost of the venture – £43,000 in all. According to another enthusiastic member of the Steam Committee, James Taylor, whose advocacy of steaming to India later brought him to a tragic death at the hands of Mesopotamian Arabs, each of the boilers was heated by 7-foot-deep furnaces. Maudslay had also, Taylor told readers of the *Bombay Courier*, 'devised an ingenious method of changing the water in the boilers so as to prevent the rapid deposit of salt and sand,' which on board the *Savannah* had involved daily cleaning of the boilers. 'It is hoped,' wrote Taylor, 'that the great national benefit likely to accrue from the above measure . . . will induce the merchants of London to come forward in support of this undertaking with the same spirit that has animated those of Calcutta.'[13]

The *Enterprize* was the first oceangoing steamboat to be built in Britain and her size aroused the wildest speculation – a revolutionary engine, no stops for fuel, 'for every calculation that has been made it is expected that she will perform the passage in . . . about sixty days.'[14] Being independent of wind she would be able to cut hundreds of miles off the route taken by sailing vessels. The advantages of steam were obvious to some, but the reservations of others kept the experiment short of funds and its backers impatient to meet the East India Company's deadline. First-class coal from the Llanganech mine in South Wales was sent ahead to Cape Town; more was crammed on to the little steamer. Johnston was appointed captain. There was no time for trial trips nor was *Enterprize*'s departure timed to coincide later with the south-west monsoon in eastern waters. Seventeen proud and optimistic passengers boarded her at Gravesend, in itself three days' sailing from London or four hours by post chaise; among them, coyly noted the *Asiatic Journal*, 'were a number of females.' On August 16th, 1825, Johnston steamed down the Thames, round to Southampton, up and then down the Solent, his passengers heaving patriotic sighs as the Needles disappeared in the long summer twilight. Finally from Falmouth, first used as a packet (or mail) port in 1688 and the traditional departure point for India-bound vessels since it was far enough west to carry vessels away from the Channel, they headed out across the ocean.

They were a long-suffering party. The first test was the Bay of

Biscay, 'the seaman's hard trial', according to Thomas Twining. This was bad enough in a 1500-ton East Indiaman but must have been sheer misery in the 500-ton *Enterprize*, large as she may have seemed by contemporary steamboat standards. The passengers swung nauseously in wooden cots slung hammock-like from the timbers, notoriously difficult to get in or out of in a storm. On James Wathen's voyage through the Bay in 1810 even the cow was too ill to be milked. There was no such fresh food on board the *Enterprize*, however, no singing round the piano or post-prandial exercise. For the main problem of the voyage was coal. Under steam the *Enterprize* burned 10–12 tons a day in order to maintain an average speed of 6–7 knots. Every available inch was taken up with coal, which so weighed her down that she sat too deep in the water; in storms, however, her paddles were often lifted ineffectually out of the water. Crew members who should have been trimming the sails were kept busy stoking the engines. The coal, hand-picked for large lumps, had to be shifted from tanks into boxes beside the furnace, for much of the time in the terrible heat of the tropics; it took the whole crew to do this. So much coal was stuffed on board that sacks were even piled on top of the boilers where the coal accidentally ignited. The tanks were supposed to be filled with water as the coal went down; in fact the water was not heavy enough and Johnston had to

6   The *Enterprize*, the first vessel to steam to India, in 1825, taking 113 days

stuff sodden sails into them for extra weight. The lighter the vessel the more she tossed.

Such was the pressure of time that Johnston did not stop until they reached Cape Town, the first coaling stop. They even missed out Madeira, but there was no room on board anyway for the cargo of good Madeira wine, known for its excellent travelling qualities, which would have helped defray costs when sold in India. Johnston's shortage of coal obliged him to use his sails more than he had planned and the *Enterprize* entered Cape Town under sail, having had to add to the miles by sailing well to the south-west.

The Cape had been the most important stop on voyages to and from India for many years. Its strategic importance grew in the eighteenth century, paralleling that of India, and in 1795 a British military expedition occupied the settlement for the first time, introducing British social flutters to the stern Dutch community, settled in the Cape since 1652, with monthly balls at the castle sustained by visitors from passing ships. There was a second occupation in 1806 when a naval base was established, and British occupation was finally made permanent in 1814. Table Valley behind had fertile well-watered soil, good for growing the citrus fruit and vegetables which were already recognised as a preventive against scurvy. But in pre-steam days the rigours of Dutch Calvinism hung heavily over a settlement barely out of its tents and log cabins. In winter it often rained incessantly, turning the roads to mud and casting a soggy blight over the colony, yet it was in winter that sailing vessels usually reached the Cape, to time their departure eastwards with the arrival of the monsoon.

In the early days few people liked to anchor in the harbour of Cape Town itself, the focus of Cape Colony, because it was too exposed to the ferocious gales of the Roaring Forties especially strong in May and June. In May 1865 no less than sixteen vessels were sunk in Table Bay, after which an enclosed basin was built. Ships anchored either in False Bay or in Symonds Bay, an inhospitable stretch of coast, and passengers rode in from there, expecting a stay of at least two or three weeks to recover from the rigours of the first half of the voyage. British commentators on Cape Town in the early days were invariably rude. Macrabie lodged with a Mrs van der Lip – 'nothing can be colder or more comfortless than a Dutch house in winter' – who fed them at most unchristian hours, and at a concert at the governor's house he found the governor's wife 'fat but not fair and extremely rich in Diamonds.'

Coaling was always a filthy business; in 1825 it was also painfully slow, taking a day to load about 20 tons on board the *Enterprize*. In the permitted intervals between coaling Johnston took the governor and his officials for rides round the harbour. Maudslay's coal-hungry but powerful engines should have come into their own as soon as the *Enterprize* left the shelter of the Cape and ventured into the vicious Agulhas Current, the most dangerous part of the voyage. Many a vessel, steam as well as sail, has been shipwrecked on the rocks of Cape Agulhas, driven onto them by a frightening combination of wind and current caused by the meeting and mingling of hot and cold water.

7   Diplomacy in the later nineteenth century often hinged on securing coal depots for steam-powered navies, seen in the background of this 1898 cartoon

'Terrific seas' were noted by Thomas Twining in 1792, who felt both frightened and sick at the sight of these 'Alps of the marine world'. Sailing vessels occasionally found themselves carried right across the southern latitudes of the Indian Ocean even as far as Australia, as happened with vessels bringing the first steam locomotives to India. Early steam vessels were hardly powerful enough to make headway against a full-blown Cape storm although they could do so in steady weather. As it was, the little vessel had a hard time beating her way through the waves. By the time she reached the Indian Ocean she had missed the winds of the all-important monsoon, causing poor Johnston and his passengers more anguish and disappointment.

No more stops are recorded on the *Enterprize*'s voyage, though she may well have picked up more coal at Point de Galle on the southern tip of Sri Lanka, a relatively sheltered harbour that had been colonised successively by Arabs, Portuguese, Dutch and, since 1796, by the British. A substantial Dutch community lived in Dutch-style houses, packed within the massive grey walls of the fortress. Were it not for the pressure of time the *Enterprize* would have displayed her novelty at Madras, less prosperous than Calcutta but with its own nascent Steam Committee agitating for faster links with home. On she plodded, however, Johnston and his crew labouring night and day to speed her to the Hooghly river, the westernmost of the many mouths of the Ganges.

Here, finally, the *Enterprize* was in her element. The approach, through long ridges of sand, is particularly treacherous. The entrance to the river is a bleak, watery landscape, steamy and fever-ridden during the monsoon when the sailing fleet usually arrived from England. The river shifts its channel capriciously; there are unforeseen sandbanks, shallows, snags to ensnare the wiliest pilot; it was virtually impossible to get into the river with the wrong wind. Most vessels struggled as far as Kedgeree: 'nothing can have a more dreary and desolate appearance than the land about and below Kedgeree,' wrote one new arrival; 'the very sight is almost enough to bring on the ague, and the abominably filthy water of the holy stream heightens the feeling of disgust.'[15] Passengers were offloaded into 'budgerows' to be rowed for several days the 120 miles upriver. A passenger complained in the *Bombay Courier* in 1825, the year of the *Enterprize* voyage: 'I have had to sit all day long in a nasty little boat just large enough for six people, and we were seven exclusive of trunks, packages and parcels. The heat, the thirst, the hunger and the quarrelling – oh! I shall never forget it'.[16] Not surprisingly it was one of the first journeys in India to be improved by steam, with steam tugs much the same size as the *Enterprize* dispatched from Britain to tow vessels up to Calcutta.

And so finally, on December 7th, 1825, the *Enterprize* reached Calcutta, the sight of its palaces mushrooming along the river banks cheering the weary passengers. The 14,000-mile voyage had taken 113 days, of which 40 had been entirely under sail, 62 under steam and 10 at anchor loading coal. Not good enough, said the Bengal government and refused to give the reward. Steaming to India still had a long way to go, sighed the Calcutta Committee. The only compensation for the *Enterprize*'s backers was the fact that the government eventually bought the vessel from Johnston for £40,000, using her, for a while still under the faithful Johnston, to ferry troops to and from the Burmese war of 1826. And finally she was assigned to a mail run much more in proportion to her size between Calcutta and Bombay, already quicker than communicating by land.

The *Enterprize*'s voyage taught Calcutta merchants two lessons. The first was that existing marine engines were less suited than sail to long oceanic voyages round the Cape – a very different task from crossing the Atlantic; the second was how suited steam was to improving river navigation, in particular the horrible Hooghly stretch. This was 'an improvement of great importance to the trade of Calcutta,' noted Mr Davidson returning to Calcutta in 1840 for the first time since 1829. 'Anyone who has gone up and down this river, must be aware of the dangerous nature of its navigation, owing to the many mud banks, shifting sands, and the very rapid current.' He himself had the pleasure of overtaking, thirty-six hours out of Calcutta, three vessels going downstream that had left three weeks before. 'The mighty current of the sacred Ganges is now thoroughly conquered by all-powerful steam.'[17] But across the Indian Ocean the winds and currents remained supreme for a little longer.

3

The Overland Route

Many lessons were learned from Johnston's voyage, not the least being the difficulty of making an efficient sailing vessel out of a steamboat when the coal ran out or the wind blew. 'The sailing department cannot be economised,' Joseph Field, Henry Maudslay's partner, pointed out to a parliamentary committee investigating the potential of steam communications a few years later, 'while it is practically impossible to keep the engine expenses in a reasonable proportion to engine service.'[1]

But the cause of steam was not altogether lost. The *Enterprize* voyage up the dreary Hooghly was witnessed not only by the wealthy nabobs of Calcutta but also by a river pilot, Thomas Waghorn, who was immediately captivated by the ease with which the exhausted crew navigated the vessel through the changing shoals of the muddy river regardless of the shifting wind. Johnston's own enthusiasm, communicated, one would like to imagine, over pints of porter at Kedgeree and apparently undimmed by his experiences, inspired Waghorn with an equal determination to continue where Johnston, from lack of funds, had been obliged to leave off.

Thomas Waghorn was physically well-suited to stimulate interest in speeding steam communications between Britain and India. Over six feet tall and possessed of enormous energy, he dominates most accounts of the progress of steam over the intervening seas. He was not a successful businessman, lacking the discipline to make profitable ventures out of his dreams. But he was a superb publicist, extensively advertising the dreams by wild dashes through the Near East to fire the imagination of his own countrymen and others elsewhere to the potential of intercontinental movement – by steam. 'His ambitions and his hopes,' wrote Dickens ponderously but magnanimously, considering his own discomfort on a transatlantic steam voyage, 'were fused with the generation of the mighty steam forces that were to drive his steam ships across ocean and inland seas.'[2]

A strong case was already being mounted from Bombay in favour of the Red Sea and Mediterranean route, confusingly known as the Overland Route: only 250 miles of a total 7,000 between London and

Bombay were actually over land, through Egypt. Steam was seen as an all-powerful weapon with which to overcome the monsoon that effectively blockaded Bombay's communications between June and October, although it was in fact some years before marine engines were strong enough reliably to do so. Waghorn, however, arguing from a Calcutta standpoint, was still in favour of the Cape route. His 'singularly energetic appearance' offset his youth and lack of social standing and with the support of the Steam Committee he returned to England in 1827 to raise financial backing.

He was helped by the fact that despite Bombay's enthusiasm the Red Sea was not a popular channel with navigators. There were no charts in the early nineteenth century but a modern chart will show more dangerous pale water than safe dark blue. The pale disconcertingly invades the dark, and approaches to harbours along the way are dotted with reefs, sandbanks and islets which infect the charts like an angry discouraging rash. The winds are fickle, liable to drive even the most experienced helmsman on to the jagged coral. From the end of the eighteenth century the marooned were in danger of attack by tribesmen inspired by the puritanical Wahhabi movement of central Arabia to a fanatical hostility to 'infidels'. The land is hardly more inviting; on either side the coast is bleak and hostile, rugged mountains rising sharply behind occasional whitewashed villages often obscured by heat and dust. In ancient times it had often been used by Egyptians, Phoenicians, Greeks, Romans and Arabs; today the shattered relics of their traded artefacts still lie scattered over the mounds that cover the ancient silted ports up and down the Red Sea and along the south Arabian coast. The spread of Islam, based on its heartland in the Hijaz with its holy shrines of Mecca and Madina, effectively closed most of the Red Sea to non-Muslims, who were not allowed in the vicinity of the two cities. At the lower end of the Red Sea European merchants from the sixteenth century carried on a small though regular trade through Mokha, mostly in coffee; at the northern end, the chronic anarchy of Egypt during the seventeenth century and most of the eighteenth discouraged all but the most intrepid.

The Mamluk dynasty established a modicum of law and order in Egypt in the latter half of the eighteenth century when French merchants from Marseilles reopened trade with Egypt. The British were more reticent but various attempts were made to link India and Europe through Egypt, most forcefully by George Baldwin, a single-minded gentleman who hoped to make his fortune astride a thriving trade along that route and found some sympathetic friends in Cairo.

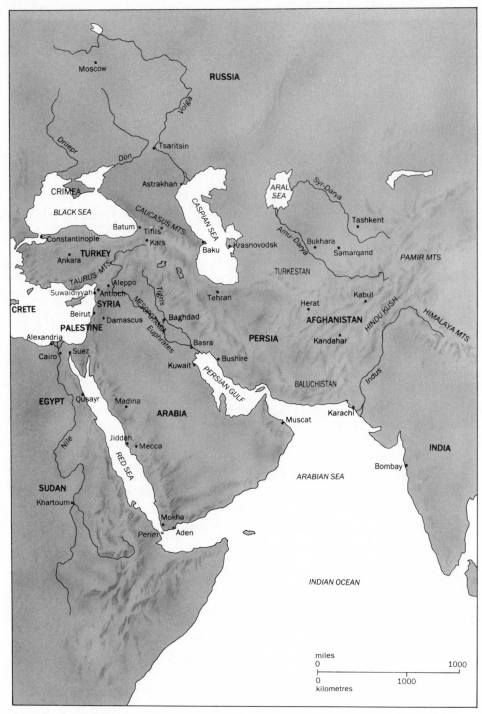

Map 2   The Overland Route and the Euphrates Valley

'We composed our bowl of the Ganges, the Thames and the Nile,' he wrote with characteristic exuberance in 1801.[3] In 1778 he proved his point by relaying news of the outbreak of the American War of Independence to India, thereby enabling the British to expel the French from India – or so he claimed. The news reached Madras sixty-eight days after leaving London.

The British in Bombay had responded swiftly to Baldwin's initiative. They were familiar with the Red Sea route; there were and still are age-old links between Bombay's Malabar coast and the Red Sea. India as well as Britain had taken advantage of the Mokha coffee trade, dependent always, however, on seasonal winds. Recognising the greater stability in Egypt they were soon sending vessels regularly up the Red Sea to Suez or to Qusayr, a more southerly harbour less subject to seasonal northerly winds. It was not a large trade but what cargoes there were, including mail, were carried by camel across to the Nile and downriver to Alexandria where with any luck other vessels might take them on to Europe. The hazards of the desert crossing to the Nile could be mitigated by following James Capper's travel hints of 1784, which included taking 'a Turkish dress, two coats, a dozen and a half of shirts, two dozen pair [sic] of common and one dozen pair of silk stockings, two pairs of shoes and other necessaries in the same proportion. This may,' Capper allowed, 'perhaps be thought a scanty allowance. . . .'[4] In Britain Egypt's enduring reputation for anarchy and disease discouraged greater interest despite frequent reports of growing French involvement in the country. Napoleon's expedition and conquest of Egypt in 1798 justified all Baldwin's labours and successive British governments never forgot the shock of being caught off guard by the French campaign. Bombay sent troops to guard the mouth of the Red Sea, first in midsummer 1799 to the waterless island of Perim, later to Aden and in 1801, the year of the *Charlotte Dundas*' maiden voyage, tacking against the monsoon to Qusayr and thence by land and river to Cairo. The intention was to meet up with a British force advancing through Egypt from the north; in fact the French were already defeated by the time the two armies met.

Various attempts were made in the early nineteenth century to chart the Red Sea despite Wahhabi hostility and even a few Bombay officials were choosing, at the right season, to return to Europe that way, among them Mountstuart Elphinstone on his retirement as Governor of Bombay in 1827. He chose it in preference to the Cape route because he suffered so desperately from seasickness. Besides, wrote a fellow passenger, the indomitable Mrs Lushington, who would not prefer to travel past the antiquities of ancient Egypt and Rome to 'devoting five long months to the monotony of a voyage round the Cape of Good Hope, in a ship crowded with passengers little known, or too well known, and distracted by the mirth or fractiousness of numerous children.'[5] But it depended on the time of year; a sailing vessel would take as much as three months just to reach Suez between June and October.

Bombay in the early 1800s was a very different place from that 'city of palaces', Calcutta. As well as spreading over the mainland, the modern city sprawls over an archipelago of seven islands, which were joined for the first time by the railway in the 1850s. At the earlier date, confined to the largest island, it was already overcrowded, unhygienic and smelly. The Portuguese had arrived in the early sixteenth century and Bombay became British in 1661 as part of the dowry of Catherine of Braganza when she married Charles II. 'An unveryhealthful island,' commented one of its governors all too aptly in 1706,[6] and certainly in the first half of the nineteenth century Bombay did little to dispel its reputation as one of the most noisome cities of the east. Cholera regularly took its toll, joined frequently by the plague in the latter part of the century.

Its British community was more pragmatic than Calcutta's, with its airs and graces. Bombay merchants were pugnacious in their pursuit of the Overland Route and demonstrated a streak of meanness in its exploitation. But they had no doubts whatsoever about the value of steam in promoting their trade and in narrowing the communications gap. Several officials, notably the Malcolm brothers, argued that not only trade was threatened by Napoleon; he had opened their eyes to a new vision of their political role in India. John Malcolm, as Governor of Bombay, commissioned Major Head in 1830 to report on the Suez route, which he did most enthusiastically, while his brother, Charles Malcolm, as superintendent of Bombay Marine, later the Indian navy, encouraged its acceptance of steam. The establishment of Calcutta's Steam Committee had been followed immediately by others in Bombay and also in Madras, the smallest of the three presidencies into which East India Company territories in India were then divided, and by the 1820s steam committees in all three communities were agitating for its development. 'Every mile of distance saved,' said the Madras Steam Committee in 1830, 'and every hour of time which brings them nearer in communication with all their soul holds dear, must stimulate them to active cooperation.'[7] There was no love lost between the presidencies: Bombay in particular was jealous of Calcutta and determined to make the most of its greater proximity to Britain, despite the problems of the seasonal tempests blowing across its access to the outside world. Bombay's claims were strengthened by the development of its sea communications with Calcutta, using little iron river steamers made by Laird's shipbuilding yard in Birkenhead as well as the *Enterprize*, returned from the Burmese war. If one great achievement of steam navigation was going upriver, the other was going against the wind, hence its appeal to Bombay merchants.

The *Enterprize* had barely moored alongside Calcutta's bulging warehouses before Waghorn was tackling the Steam Committee with his own theories on how the voyage to Britain could best be achieved. For Waghorn as well as Calcutta's merchants the Cape route was still the main objective, the ideal vessel for which, Waghorn told a sceptical East India Company Court of Directors when he eventually reached England,[8] would be given over exclusively to mail; it would weigh about 280 tons, just over half the size of the *Enterprize*, have two 25-horsepower engines and be loaded with fifty days' worth of coal. There would be no passengers, 'no lumber of any kind', and only one small nautical cabin for captain and crew. The voyage should be possible in seventy days. Steam enthusiasts in the 1820s and 1830s expected a great deal from their little vessels. Influential engineers such as Maudslay and steam enthusiasts such as Mr Goldsworth Gurney (later knighted) supported Waghorn; Gurney, a Cornishman inspired by Trevithick, had recently invented a high-pressure steam jet which he tested in steamboats and a steam coach. The Court of Directors, however, more sensitive to public scrutiny of its accounts than to Waghorn's missionary zeal, did not approve of risks and certainly passing through the Bay of Biscay or the Agulhas Current in a vessel of that size would have been an unpleasant adventure. Not surprisingly the Post Office, whose patronage was essential to the venture's success, was as discouraging as the Company and thought it 'a wild scheme to fit a vessel for so long a voyage with engines of the power of fifty horses only'.[9] It would be another thirty years before marine engines evolved that were strong enough to cope with the strains of regular oceanic voyages.

Determined to try its hand at steam navigation and disregarding the Company's reaction to Waghorn's Calcutta venture, the Bombay government turned to local talent to provide its own steamboat for the Red Sea route. The densely forested hinterland of the Malabar coast had for centuries supplied teak to the shipwrights of Bombay and elsewhere in the Indian Ocean. The craft was dominated in the nineteenth century by the Parsee community, foremost among them the Jamsetjee family. Ordering two 80-horsepower engines from Maudslay in London, to be sent out via the Cape, the government commissioned the *Hugh Lindsay*, a 410-ton steamer tactfully named after the chairman of the East India Company Court of Directors and in the mean time acquired the *Enterprize* and another little Laird steamer, the *Ganges*, from Calcutta. 'The government has given orders for the instruction of four Indo-British lads in the duties of steam engineers, with a view to their employment as such on the steamers,' reported the *Asiatic Journal* in 1829.[10] Other engineers, known as 'artificers', accompanied Maudslay's engines round the Cape. 'Although the expenses at the commencement will be so enormous that it will literally be burning rupees for fuel,' declared the *Journal*, 'still the undertaking is worthy a mighty nation, and the perseverance of man has overcome even greater difficulties'.

Interested parties in Britain were delighted to hear of Bombay's plans. If Bombay was going to send vessels up the Red Sea there must be a regular link to the northern shore of Egypt through the Mediterranean. That could also be achieved by steam; there was no need to wait in harbour perhaps for weeks for a starting wind, or the danger of sitting in mid-Mediterranean in a dead calm. Steam made a rendezvous possible. The project was encouraged by the relative tranquillity of Egypt, which had now been ruled for twenty years by the Ottoman governor, Muhammed Ali. Beginning his career as an Albanian soldier he had risen from being the commander of a small Egyptian troop at the battle of Aboukir via various military adventures to be governor of Egypt by 1806, a post he held until his death in 1848. With the help particularly of French technicians, he had worked hard to modernise the country, not least by welcoming foreign inventions.

The most ambitious suggestion for a steam rendezvous came from James Taylor, brother of Colonel Robert Taylor who as British Resident in Baghdad was a fervent advocate of yet another route to India, through Mesopotamia. Taylor proposed a private enterprise of 'a most gigantic nature'[11] – to establish a network of steam vessels both in the Mediterranean and up the Red Sea. To demonstrate its feasibility and hoping most optimistically to make a rendezvous with the *Enterprize*, the only part of the journey actually to be aided by steam, he undertook a dramatic dash in 1829 through Europe, reaching Suez via Marseilles and Alexandria only twenty-seven days from London. Sadly but perhaps not surprisingly given the poor communications between east and west which he was trying to improve, no *Enterprize* awaited him, only the sailing brig *Thetis* dispatched from Bombay up the Red Sea to lay deposits of coal for the *Hugh Lindsay*'s maiden voyage, which was expected any moment. To Taylor's disappointment the Bombay government was unenthusiastic about private ventures; with mail as the principal commodity it wanted to keep control of what might be such a vital link. Taylor was murdered north of Mosul soon after, while investigating his brother's Mesopotamian route.

No less determined and frustrated by the deliberations of the East India Company, Waghorn was not to be outdone and a week after Taylor crossed the Channel he was off himself, hoping also to reach Suez to find the *Enterprize*. 'This gentleman at least has the merit of perseverance,' commented Sir Francis Feeling, Postmaster-General, refusing to give Waghorn any Post Office mail but graciously allowing anyone else to hand over theirs.[12] Reluctantly the Company did so and Waghorn then raced from the Spread Eagle Inn in Gracechurch Street through five countries in five and a half days, pressing *The Times* into the hands of a most grateful British consul in Trieste 'which he told me had never been accomplished before that he knew of.'[13] In Alexandria the British consul, John Barker, much experienced in the ways of the Middle East as in the deliberations of the East India Company, cannily warned him not to be too sure of success. Waghorn eventually reached Suez forty-one days from London. There was still no sign of the *Enterprize*, which had in fact never left India, and after a series of mishaps Waghorn completed his voyage to Bombay aboard the same *Thetis* as his rival Taylor. Neither Waghorn nor Taylor was able to use the steam engine on land or on water to speed their journey; Waghorn's actually took nearly five months. But it demanded little imagination from the bureaucrats in Post Office and Company headquarters, let alone from the shipbuilders and engineeers, to see the potential for steam behind their endeavour, if only they could find some way of ensuring that link between Mediterranean and Red Sea.

The Red Sea rendezvous was by far the trickiest part of the endeavour. The problems of navigating that treacherous waterway were compounded by the difficulty of launching a satisfactory vessel, combining local shipbuilding skills with the huge engines then being made, that had to reach India via the Cape. Finally the *Hugh Lindsay* was ready for the experiment. By a strange quirk of fate Waghorn and Taylor missed her departure on March 20th, 1830, by one day. She steamed out of the magnificent Bombay harbour escorted by hundreds of lateen-rigged dhows that had been dependent on the winds of the Indian Ocean for so many centuries. The citizens of Bombay proudly saw themselves in the vanguard of steam navigation and the Calcutta *John Bull* generously extolled the venture: 'we hail her as the harbinger of future vessels of her kind who will waft us to our native shores with speed and pleasure.'[14] Her captain, John Wilson, gave up a good position in the regular navy because, so he later told a parliamentary committee, he was 'stimulated by a desire to be the first steam navigator of the Nile.'[15]

The voyage was not exactly pleasurable. Past the 'gloomy and thinly peopled coast of South Arabia' she steamed to pick up coal at Aden, a depressed outpost of the Sultan of Lahej whose permission Wilson had to seek to land. Wilson sent a boat ashore requesting permission; the local shaikh was away inland and his local deputy refused to take the responsibility. A message was sent to the Sultan, who insisted on seeing Wilson himself. Off went the captain and finally persuaded the Sultan to release the coal. The loading was a laborious business; it is already extremely warm in Aden by the end of March and two boatloads of coal a day was the most that could be achieved. Then they steamed on to Mokha, 'a spectacle of desolation', suffering four days' constant adverse gale between Mokha and Jiddah where they found the eccentric preacher Dr Joseph Wolff (a Jew converted to Christianity who led a missionary and nomadic career in the Middle East and Central Asia, describing himself as 'an enthusiast drunk with the love of God'), and on to Qusayr, the wind now so strong that they barely made 2–3 knots, decks awash and paddles snapping. The *Hugh Lindsay* took thirty-three days to reach Suez and return. Coal was once again the main problem. The designers of the hull, unfamiliar with the voracious appetite of contemporary steam engines, badly underestimated the fuel storage space. The *Hugh Lindsay* had room for five and a half days' worth of coal; but the longest leg of the journey, from Bombay to Aden where a couple of brigs including the *Thetis* had been sent on ahead with coal, was at least ten days away even with favourable winds – some 1,710 miles.

So the little 410-ton steamer, 'a rather heavy sailor' to put it mildly, had left Bombay harbour with coal piled up all over the decks, in the saloon and the passengers' cabins. Even so Wilson only made it back to Bombay by 'wetting and reburning' the ashes. Instead of her normal draught of 11ft. 6in. she was 14 feet down in the water and the engines so overburdened that they could hardly turn the paddles. Moreover teak, though proof against worm, is an extremely heavy wood. Of the thirty-three days spent on the voyage, twelve were spent coaling – four days for instance at Suez to load 100 tons, with the lighters bringing the coal alongside often hindered by onshore winds. An ideal vessel, Wilson told the Commons Committee a few years later, would be burning no more than 9 tons in twenty-four hours, still a near impossibility for an oceangoing vessel.[16]

In spite of these problems the steamer was greeted on its return with great excitement in Bombay and loud complaints from the *Bombay Courier* about 'the utter indifference of the East India Company towards the venture'.[17] The London *Times* joined battle: 'if the conduct of the East India Company in frustrating steam boat intercourse between this country and Bombay via the Red Sea be as represented by persons in the city the comment of the people of England need be only this: "Look to your charter, gentlemen".'[18] Captain Wilson addressing the Commons Committee pessimistically reckoned regular steam traffic up the Red Sea could never be commercially viable, but his exploit put paid for the time being to the alternative development of steam communications with India via the Cape.

While Bombay struggled with its monsoon and the Red Sea, the Mediterranean side of the connection was progressing more smoothly. Coaling stations had been set up at Lisbon, Gibraltar, Malta and the island of Sira in the Aegean. In the Mediterranean's relatively sheltered waters with notoriously erratic winds, steam was seen at its best. It was regular, reliable and punctual. Small steam packets were now a common sight in the western Mediterranean, patronised by both French and British navies. Here for the first time the forces of war led the merchants in the exploitation of steam.

Passengers on short-distance coastal and river routes just about produced a profit but any less frequented route was dependent at the outset on government subsidy, usually for carrying mail or naval messages. By 1830 the Admiralty had established a steam packet service between Falmouth and Malta. A similar and rather more useful French service between Marseilles and Alexandria was soon attracting a trickle of passengers. Behind the development of these communications lay a rivalry between the two countries for influence over the ailing Ottoman Empire which sat astride all routes to India. Viewed with the relative objectivity of hindsight, this was not quite as sick as its European neighbours made out. But its poor health was seen by French, British and also Russian governments as confirmed by the Egyptian invasion of Syria in 1833.

Meanwhile, a succession of parliamentary committees kept the issue of steam navigation to India alive, generally within the context of perennial criticism of East India Company affairs. One of the most significant of these, reporting in 1834, commented that 'a regular and expeditious communication with India by steam vessels is of great importance both to Great Britain and to India'.[19] The Company itself, acutely vulnerable to accusations of being spendthrift, was reluctant to embroil itself in what it considered a thoroughly risky venture, but in 1835 the Post Office came partly to its rescue and agreed to patronise a steam packet line from Falmouth via Malta to Alexandria. Clearly the Mediterranean was the safest section of the route and the easiest to organise.

British passengers preferred for reasons of speed and comfort to embark for Egypt from southern France, avoiding the Bay of Biscay and journeying for only six days from London to Marseilles by a succession of boats and diligences. Those who wrote about the experience seldom missed the opportunity to make snide remarks about France and the French. In 1839 Miss Emma Roberts recommended taking the French steamer *Phénix* from Tower Stairs to Le Havre, a fine vessel of its class, 'handsomely fitted up with vases of flowers in the salon' though its 160-horsepower engines were not strong enough to make way against a strong Channel head wind.[20] Miss Roberts, orphaned when young, sustained herself with her writing, publishing a number of books on India, including articles for the *Asiatic Review* on the Overland Route. Passengers, she advised, should continue from Le Havre to Rouen and thence part way up the Seine by river steamer, finishing their journey to Paris by train because the river was too shallow. (In due course they would be able to go the whole way by train, on a line laid in the 1840s by Thomas Brassey.) She advised against having too much luggage because of endless customs inspections; she confined herself to two portmanteaux, a bonnet box containing her bonnets, writing case and looking glass ('wishing to carry everything absolutely necessary for her comfort with her') and a leather bag containing her medicine chest (a cause of much French suspicion), a kettle, lamp and lucifer matches. From Paris one should proceed by diligence to Lyons where one boarded the steamer either to Arles or to Avignon and thence by land to Marseilles. One should allow 110 hours from Paris to Marseilles.

Marseilles, 'the handsomest and cleanest city we had yet seen in France,' was now risen from the impoverishment of revolution and war. It was slow to take to steam, the first steamboat arriving there from Naples in 1818, but soon appreciated steam's ability to counter the mistral, claimed to blow 140 days a year. The Bazin brothers, Charles and Auguste, were building steam vessels by 1830 and the French invasion of Algeria in 1830 led to increasing use of Marseilles port, making it by the mid-1830s the third busiest in Europe after London

8 Dioramic game of the Overland Route to India, from Southampton to Calcutta, printed about 1853 from contemporary watercolours

and Liverpool. A railway would connect it with the Rhône at Avignon in 1848. French steam packets to Alexandria were established well ahead of any British line, meeting the greater demand of the extensive French links with Egypt; Napoleon's expedition to Egypt in 1798 had included an army of 'savants', many of whom stayed on in Egypt and were joined by French technicians encouraged by Muhammad Ali to hasten Egypt's modernisation. 'Everything in Egypt is growing French,' complained Waghorn.[21] One French vessel advertised 'tous les agré-ments désirables', including a special ladies' room with a piano, and another offered the same culinary pleasures at sea as on land.

In general, however, packet boats at this stage were ships of war at heart and not particularly comfortable. By later standards they were small and cramped, noisy, dirty and shaken by the vibrations of their cumbersome engines. Emma Roberts with no great expectations found her *Megara* inclined to roll but otherwise well set up had it not been for a family with three children which meant they 'could not preserve the neatness and order which are so esential to comfort.' On the other hand young Samuel Bevan, going out to work as a clerk on the Overland Route in 1840, described the accommodation aboard the packet *Minos* as 'perfect and the discipline of the first order, and they are withal so strongly built, that they defy the ugliest weather, and are very rarely overdue'.[22] Punctuality was one of the many rewards of steam.

En route to Egypt ships called at Malta, a barren rock thriving not only on the new coaling business but also as a quarantine station. 'Malta is certainly not the most agreeable place to walk about in on a broiling hot morning,' Bevan wrote after his first visit, later spending many dreary weeks in quarantine there. Plague was still such a regular horror in the Near and Middle East, especially in Egypt, that most travellers in those parts were subjected to the strictest quarantine at one of the many stations ringing the northern shores of the Mediterranean. Malta was perhaps the busiest of them. Waghorn recommended the all-sea route from Egypt to Britain for the reason that it was long enough to act as quarantine in itself.

About two weeks after leaving Marseilles, depending on the length of stay in Malta, the India-bound passenger reached Alexandria, the Overland Route and, in the late 1830s, a warm welcome from Thomas Waghorn, who was still bursting with energy if somewhat disorganised. Seeing the significance of the *Hugh Lindsay*'s first voyage in showing how under the right conditions steam could be used to establish a connection with the Mediterranean, Waghorn had resigned from the East India Company's pilot service to devote himself to the Egyptian section, the Overland Route. He spent the winter of 1833–4 persuading the reluctant Egyptian governor, Muhammad Ali, already at odds with the British over his invasion of Syria, to smooth the onward passage of the mails through Egypt. To Muhammad Ali's credit, he did so. 'I do not know any European country where one may travel with greater safety than in Egypt,' wrote Dr Madden, erstwhile chaplain in Alexandria.[23] In 1835, 'with a sort of stigma on my sanity,' Waghorn set up as an independent agent in Egypt, offering to assist with mails and people travelling through the country.

'He only left Bombay yesterday morning, was seen in the Red Sea on Tuesday, is engaged to dinner this afternoon in the Regent's Park and (as it is about two minutes since I saw him in the courtyard) I make no doubt he is by this time at Alexandria or at Malta, say, perhaps at both.' Thus spake Mr Titmarsh, alias William Makepeace Thackeray, who was offered a free trip to the Mediterranean by P.&O. in 1845.[24] First impressions of the Overland Route and Egypt were not always favourable; Alexandria aroused some fierce reactions from those going to India, for it was here that many of them had their first glimpse of the east. The city looks imposing enough from the sea, Emma Roberts told her readers, 'but there is nothing in the landing place worthy of the approach to a place of importance.' It has never been a very prepossessing town, though pleasant European suburbs developed during the later part of the nineteenth century. Its streets are narrow and irregular, crowded with people and animals, and over all that extraordinary smell of the east – evocative only to those who know the east already. It generally lacks charm for those with no previous experience.

So most visitors left Alexandria as soon as possible, trundling on donkeys out to the Mahmoudiyeh Canal which linked up with the Nile. Emma Roberts had the good fortune to be looked after by Mrs Waghorn, who found her a servant and provided her with mattresses, pillows and quilts for the three-day voyage to Cairo, as well as a canteen equipped with tin saucepans, 'tea, coffee, wine, wax candles, fowls, bread, fruit, milk, eggs and butter, a pair of fowls and a piece of beef being ready-roasted for the first meal.' Travel between Alexandria and the Nile at Atfah had already been eased by the clearance of this old canal at enormous cost in lives but it was barely 10 feet wide and the long horse-drawn iron barges, later to be more smoothly pulled by steam tugs, were always running into the bank, the jolt sometimes pulling the horses into the water, and more rudely bumping into the water buffaloes wallowing in the canal. 'If they dig a canal,' explained Dr Madden, 'they use no shovels, no carts, no wheelbarrows, for nothing of the kind is known in the country'.[25] When someone complained of the canal's abrupt curves, Muhammad Ali is said to have replied that nature did not create straight rivers. As for the canal boat Miss Roberts declared she had never, in the course of all her travels, 'seen anything so forlorn, uncomfortable ... Dirt was now the predominant feature, and vermin, mosquitoes and flies came on board in clouds ... Cockroaches, as large as the top of a wine glass, made their appearance; we heard the rats squeaking around, and found the mosquitoes more desperate in their attacks than ever.' Judging by other contemporary accounts most passengers had similar experiences.

From Atfah on the Nile inessential luggage was usually sent direct to Suez using Waghorn's organisation to avoid Cairo; Waghorn had it loaded on to camels. Many other camels in the huge caravan carried coal for the onward voyage from Suez to Bombay; it was cheaper, Waghorn maintained, than sending it via the Cape. For the passengers themselves steam had revolutionised the next stage of the journey, on the Nile. The majestic local felucca could take five or six days to reach Cairo; steam took two, later one day. It was nothing like as comfortable but then comfort was never the most significant factor in early steam

9   A British deputation to Muhammad Ali, 1839. The British consul (third from right) is explaining the plans of Waghorn (second from right) to the Egyptian ruler. The artist, David Roberts, is last on the right.

travel. Steam was regarded as enough of a miracle in itself and those travelling under its auspices were supposed to tolerate the accompanying hardships. Space was usually at a premium, most of it taken up by paddle shafts and engines; noise and dirt were overwhelming.

The *Little Nile* steamer, 'fizzing at the quayside', waited to take the passengers up the great river to Cairo. Built originally for the Thames service, the *Little Nile* had such a hard time in the Bay of Biscay on the way to Egypt that her boilers came loose from their fastenings. Prior to her arrival Waghorn had used the diminutive *Jack O'Lantern*, said to be the smallest steamer in the world, with a draught of two and a half feet and described as having two and a half Cairo donkey power. Food was supposed to compensate on all these voyages and passengers spent much of the time eating, including on occasions 'a delicious breakfast of new bread, milk warm from the cow, coffee of the East, delicious grapes and cheese.'[26] But one's meal might at any moment be upset, as Samuel Bevan's was, by the vessel running aground. Sad to say the Nile was no diversion; Emma Roberts found it 'dreadfully disappointing' and read Wordsworth to pass the time.

Cairo compensated for the toils and tedium of travel. It still is a bewitching city, still able to strike horror in outsiders; those who came from India relished its atmosphere much more than travellers from Europe, although some of the latter put down roots and stayed to paint and write about its enchantment. Among them were J.F. Lewis the artist, John Gardiner Wilkinson, Egyptologist and historian, E.W. Lane, author of the still authoritative *Manners and Customs of the Modern Egyptians*. Baths, markets, of course the Pyramids, visitors helped to the top by obliging dragomans: there was never enough time for everything before Muhammad Ali's heliograph picked up signals from Suez that a vessel was waiting to take the travellers onward to India.

Bombay steam protagonists were anxious to make the Overland Route as smooth a journey as possible and from 1837 what little comfort was to be found on the dreary two-day desert crossing to Suez was financed initially by the Bombay Steam Committee. Waghorn got as far as finding some tents left over from a Scottish medieval tournament and erected them as an experiment in Ezbekiyah Square in Cairo; Samuel Bevan converted one into a beer shop 'much to the astonishment of Muhammad Ali who found half a dozen jolly tars recruited from the *Little Nile* smoking their clay pipes and discussing bottled beer.'

Waghorn's establishment of the Overland Route almost immediately exposed him to competition, and competition backed by better resources. Passengers looked for a little more tender loving care than

10 Ezbekiyah Square in Cairo, showing Shepheard's 'British Hotel', around
1860. The square was the centre of European activity in Cairo.

that provided by Waghorn's somewhat extempore arrangements for the
mail and his handling of passengers was soon taken over by Messrs Hill
and Raven, employers of Samuel Bevan, and long-time merchants in
Egypt. Hill and Raven acted for the Bombay committee and competed
with Waghorn for the patronage of the overland passengers, also,
somewhat savagely, for the available baggage animals; Waghorn once
managed to hire all baggage and carriage beasts, leaving his rivals
stranded. By 1841, however, the more powerful financial backing
provided by Bombay gave Waghorn's rivals the lead and he was obliged
to go into partnership with Mr Hill, by all accounts a genial gentleman.
They were in turn bought out by Muhammad Ali in 1843 when he set
up a new monopoly, the Egyptian Transit Company.

The desert sector of the journey was negotiated in a number of ways
including donkey chairs slung between two animals, a 'delightfully easy
movement' according to Emma Roberts though some would beg to
differ. She was much less complimentary about the primitive huts set
up across the desert to provide travellers with simple comforts, including
– horrors – warm champagne. They were managed by 'a mongrel sort
of Franks who have no idea of cleanliness, and are regardless of the

most unsavoury odours.' There were about half a dozen of these comfort stops, ill planned and executed, swarming with flies, poorly equipped and with little of the privacy which the nineteenth-century European woman considered as hers by right. Poor Mrs Griffiths in 1844 was dreadfully tired and exhausted by the journey and laid herself down in the cleanest-looking corner of the divan but 'I had no sooner taken up my position,' she wailed to her readers, 'before I was covered with flies from head to foot.'[27]

While homing passengers had the consolation of Cairo, outward-bound passengers had only Suez, 'always a miserable place of abode, hemmed in between the arid Desert and a boisterous sea.' 'Not a garden, not a tree, not a trace of verdure, not a drop of fresh water,' moaned the American missionary Edward Robinson in 1841. 'It can never be more than a mere place of passage which both the traveller and the inhabitant will hasten to leave as soon as possible.'[28] With coaxing from Waghorn and Hill it had acquired two hotels run by the two rival concerns, each as bad as the other. 'The bedrooms are few and the ultimate resort is the divana or large cushioned seat of the dining room, and the cold night air from the desert freely blowing on the sleepers from numerous broken panes of glass.'

What made Suez so unpopular was the fact that the connection with the Indian vessel was so poor. Here the parsimony of the East India Company made itself felt. The Company had committed itself to providing a monthly service between Bombay and Suez. Waghorn acclaimed the effort. 'Believing as I do, that the powers of the steam engine will, under Providence, be one of the means of bringing the unlettered and darkened millions of the East to Christianity, I hail with delight the forthcoming plan of steam intercourse with India.'[29] But the vessels used were wholly inadequate.

Like the British and French navies in the Mediterranean, the Bombay ships had two primary functions – war and mail. The Red Sea itself had been painstakingly and this time enduringly surveyed between 1829 and 1833 by Captain Robert Moresby and Lieutenant Thomas Elwon of the Bombay Marine; constantly going aground in their sailing vessels *Palinurus* and *Benares* on coral reefs, smitten by smallpox and dysentery, they nevertheless secured the route for safe navigation, especially when the advent of steam promised to remove a vessel's dependence on winds. That was the theory; in practice, when faced with the notoriously fickle winds of the Red Sea, as well as the ferocity of the monsoon, Bombay's vessels could not cope.

In 1837 the *Atlanta* and the *Berenice*, the latter suitably named after

the long-lost Roman port in the Red Sea, arrived in Bombay via the
Cape to join the *Hugh Lindsay* and the *Enterprize* (now used on a route
up the Gulf). The *Semiramis* arrived in 1839. The *Berenice* weighed 640
tons with engines of 220 horsepower by Robert Napier. The *Atlanta*,
built by Wigram and Greene in the Thames, weighed 661 tons with
engines of 210 horsepower by Maudslay. The *Semiramis* weighed 720
tons, with engines of 300 horsepower also by Maudslay; she ended up
as a coal hulk in Aden, anchored offshore so that ships needing coal
could tie up alongside. All three surprisingly survived the Cape voyage,
the *Berenice* completing it in eighty-eight days. Unfortunately the boats
turned out to be under-powered for coping with the monsoon and it
was beyond them to maintain the punctual service expected by Waghorn, Hill and connecting passengers in Egypt. The miracle of steam
navigation was the regularity – the fact that the Post Office in England
could tell its customers that mails would be leaving for India on the first
and fifteenth of every month, and leave they did. The same systematis-
ation could not be imposed on the little vessels struggling against nature
across the Indian Ocean and up the Red Sea. One found itself swept at
the height of the monsoon right down to Ceylon; another only reached
port by burning all spare spars and cables and even part of the deck.
The *Atlanta* caught fire in Bombay in 1840; she was eventually repaired
but meanwhile the service deteriorated further.

Above all the vessels were filthy. The tradition of donning white
garments in the tropics was well established but proved ill suited to a
constant shower of smuts. The boats were searingly hot, the outside
temperature aggravated by the proximity of the giant engines to the
saloon and hardly alleviated by the languid efforts of the punkah wallah
and his hanging fan. Emma Roberts, on board the *Berenice*, wrote
bitterly that 'the more I have seen of government ships, the more certain
I feel they are not adapted to carry passengers.... A week's baths will
scarcely suffice to remove the coal dust collected in the steamers of the
Red Sea'.[30] To make it worse, she warned prospective travellers, there
were no books on board 'except Bibles and Prayers'. Dickens listed
typical shipboard literature for an Indian voyage thus: '*Five minutes in
China* (2 volumes); *Forty winks at the Pyramids* (2 volumes); *Mr. Green's
Overland Mail*; *Toots' universal letter writer* (2 volumes); *History of the
Middling Ages* (6 volumes); *Kant's Eminent Humbugs*; *Bowwowdom: a
poem*; *The act of cutting the teeth*; *Miss Biffin on deportment*'.[31]

With such diversion the discomfort of the Red Sea section of the
journey became notorious. Passengers are grumblers by nature but their
gossip became gospel and in the early days of the Overland Route only

two or three hundred a year ventured through Egypt despite Waghorn's urgings. Most preferred to leave it to the mail. Sailing round the Cape was still a great deal more agreeable than steaming up or down the Red Sea. Nevertheless speed sometimes counted: in 1837 the new Queen Victoria was proclaimed Supreme Lady of the Castle, Town and Island of Bombay while Calcutta was still toasting William IV.

Waghorn himself was always more concerned with the mail than with disgruntled human beings. Thanks to his energy sixty-five days became the average time taken for the mail between Bombay and London; he once achieved forty-seven, with twenty-two hours for the Egyptian stretch. In 1845 Waghorn made one last demonstration of speeding the mail, this time through a wintry Europe. He always preferred the German to the French route (so, frequently, did the British government) and proved his point in bringing the Indian mail via Trieste and Vienna to *The Times* in London some fourteen hours ahead of its reaching the rival *Morning Herald* via Marseilles. But the effort cost him his health as well as the last of his funds. He never returned to Egypt after the race and the last five years of his life were spent pennilessly in London, writing unrequited pleas for pensions. 'The Overland Route was achieved by me without the assistance of her Majesty's Government,' Waghorn wrote beseechingly to the same government in March 1848, 'for truly, as my Memorial states, it grew into life, and to its present usefulness, through my own unaided toils, and this I can say without egotism'.[32] Waghorn timed his venture badly. Considering the fact that the British regarded Muhammad Ali as an enemy, his treatment of those living in or passing through his country was exemplary, but Waghorn had a hard task to persuade his countrymen that they were in no danger if they came to Egypt en route for India. Those who did come through Egypt – never very many before the opening of the Suez Canal – were also struck by the widespread French influence in the country's development and left more than ever convinced of the importance of British or, by inference, Ottoman, control of the routes to India. Waghorn died a pauper two years later, still waiting for recognition of his contribution even though the significance of the route was by then well established.

Recognition came, some four years after his death, from a foreign admirer. In 1854 Ferdinand de Lesseps, in Egypt to establish his Suez Canal Company, was staying at the Hôtel des Indes at Suez. It was still an unprepossessing residence but de Lesseps did think it worth his while to note down his dinner one evening. It included mutton from Calcutta, potatoes from Bombay, green peas from England, poultry from Egypt, water from the Ganges, wine from France, coffee from Mokha and tea from China. Quite a meal, considering the dust, the heat, the dilapidation of the little town where he ate it. De Lesseps had met Waghorn 'struggling with man and beast in the desert to carry his mails across' and later declared that this 'served as an example to him in after-life with the Suez Canal.' And so, sitting back in his chair at the end of his feast, he proposed a toast to the man who had made possible such a wide-ranging menu – Thomas Waghorn.[33]

4

High Road to India

Despite Waghorn's optimism and some brilliant navigation charts produced by Moresby and Elwon for the Bombay Marine, the Red Sea in the 1830s was an unpopular waterway, viewed by many British officials as too vulnerable to interruptions. Steam navigation still left a lot to be desired when it came to strong adverse winds; the *Hugh Lindsay*, for instance, could only steam between Bombay and Suez from November to March when there was no contrary monsoon wind. A year-round service still seemed out of reach. Nevertheless a new political factor, at least as potent as rivalry with the French, was influencing British plans for communications with India.

In 1830, a 'bold and adventurous spirit' sat down at the dinner table of the British ambassador in Constantinople, Sir Robert Gordon. Captain Francis Chesney, recovering from an unhappy love affair and disappointed with army life in England, had just returned from a sightseeing tour of Russian and Turkish positions in the Balkans. A year earlier the Turks had suffered a humiliating defeat by the Russians and at the Treaty of Adrianople in September 1829 had been obliged to surrender a number of Balkan possessions. Russia had nearly reached the gates of Constantinople.

Southward expansion had brought Russia up against the Ottoman Empire on several occasions since it was initiated by Peter the Great at the end of the seventeenth century. Between 1675 and 1812 Russia and Turkey had been at war seven times, with Russia finally gaining control of a great arc of territory from the Danube to the Caucasus, consolidating its dominion economically and militarily with a succession of new towns. Odessa developed into an elegant and thriving port for the export of the grain of the Ukraine; Sebastopol became a towering fortress to warn invaders off that fertile hinterland. In 1829, under the terms of the Treaty of Adrianople, Turkey ceded Georgia, eastern Armenia and all its Caucasian coast except Batum to the Russians, effectively turning the Black Sea into a Russian as opposed to a Turkish lake. Odessa, however, was felt to be especially vulnerable to the weakness of the Ottoman Empire. The greater its exports, the greater the fear that the

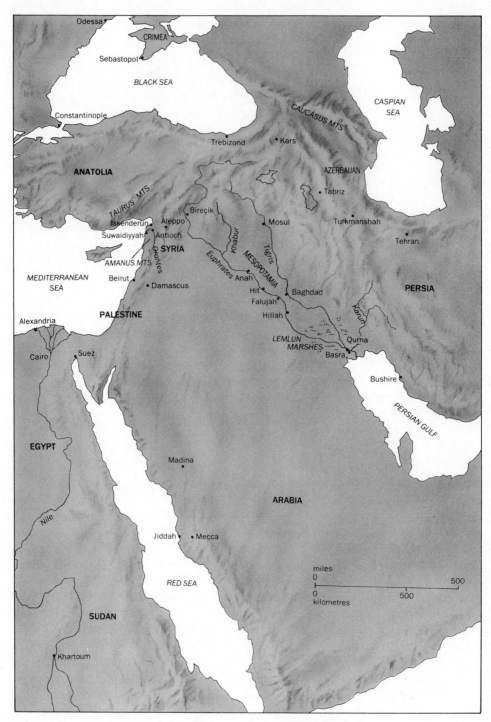

Map 3   High road to India

Dardanelles might be closed by Turkey's European allies. Russia was also beginning to be concerned that the British would extend their commercial hegemony in India to Central Asia.

Neither the British ambassador nor his diplomatic colleagues had enjoyed the prospect of Russia controlling this key waterway of the Dardanelles. The Russians were joining the French as the British bogey, their role confirmed in British eyes both by the Treaty of Adrianople and the earlier Treaty of Turkmanshah with Persia, which gave Russia jurisdiction over much of previously Persian Azerbaijan bordering the Caspian Sea. The stage was now set for the drama of Anglo-Russian rivalry that was to be played throughout the nineteenth and into the twentieth century, its advent speeded by the improvements in communications brought about by steam.

Like many foreigners in Constantinople, including the ambassador, Chesney was firmly of the opinion that the Ottoman Empire was sick almost beyond cure and the Russian bear was about to swoop upon the estate. The Russians did little to persuade anyone that their intentions were different. Chesney's account of his Balkan trip was grist to the mill of the scaremongers and he became a regular visitor at the ambassador's table where conversation about the Tsar's intentions played turnabout with unexciting games of whist. As an energetic young man he was hoping for rather more activity and before long persuaded the ambassador to send him on a tour of Ottoman Egypt and Asia. Better communications with India were to be the theme of his travels.

At this point Chesney was probably doing no more than looking for a diversion from the tedium of whist and dinner parties. His first serious pause, however, was at Alexandria. The consul here was John Barker, a man who had spent many years in Aleppo and his family many generations in the Levant. Barker, visited the year before by Waghorn, had just received from Thomas Love Peacock in East India House, London, a list of queries regarding the relative values of the Egyptian and the Syrian routes for mail communications with India. Would Chesney like to investigate them? asked Barker. 'Nothing short of absolute duty should induce him to throw up a mission fraught with such important possibilities,' replied Chesney, his mind 'intensely occupied with the subject of an improved line of communication with India.'[1]

Considerable controversy existed over the rival merits of these two mail routes at the time. Although Waghorn was far from alone in advocating an overland route through a peaceful Egypt, a substantial body of opinion favoured Mesopotamia and the Gulf, traditionally the oldest and most customary land and water route to India. Its attraction now was partly that steamboats had already proved themselves on rivers, hardly the case in such waters as the Red Sea with its navigational and seasonal hazards. The calmer Gulf was free of such impediments. Chesney also viewed Mesopotamia and the Euphrates as a potential barrier to Russia. Egypt was moreover smitten regularly by the plague which necessitated lengthy forty-day quarantines for couriers and extensive fumigation for the mail.

Chesney was able to spend most of the next two years, from 1830 to 1832, travelling in the region. He went through Egypt to Suez and down the Red Sea. He went across to and down the Nile (where he was converted to the idea of cutting through the Isthmus of Suez with a canal), up to Syria and over the desert from Damascus to the Euphrates. He reached here, full of Christian emotions, on Christmas Day. Following this he descended the Euphrates on a raft and travelled by means of various other craft to Falujah where he went by land to Baghdad, 35 miles away on the Tigris, to discuss plans with the British Resident, Colonel Robert Taylor.

Taylor was a remarkable man, rather more astute than his hare-brained brother James, Waghorn's rival. He was British Resident in Baghdad for thirty years after a military career in India, 'a most accomplished and profound Eastern scholar', profusely hospitable and deeply committed to British exploitation of the commercial and strategic potential of Mesopotamia (and equally to the prevention of anyone else so doing). He lived in a mansion overlooking the Tigris – a wide, brown and hypnotic river even from the dingy fish restaurants that today have replaced the Ottoman houses along its banks. There had been a British Resident in Baghdad since 1798, at first intended mainly to counter French influence. A previous holder of the post was the antiquarian Claudius Rich, a later one Henry Rawlinson, a prominent Russophobe who deciphered cuneiform. As a major entrepôt between East and West it was from mid-nineteenth century considered an important listening post but one singularly unpopular with the foreign community which, like the indigenous inhabitants, was regularly decimated by outbreaks of the most virulent plague. Steamboats would at least improve the chances of escape. Taylor had already organised a survey of the Tigris, both by a Lieutenant Ormsby and by his brother who not long before Chesney's arrival in Baghdad had been killed in a skirmish with Arabs north of Mosul.

Inspired by Taylor's political views Chesney continued down the Euphrates to Basra, over to Bushire on the Persian shore of the Gulf, up through Persia and finally from Tabriz to Trebizond. He eventually reached Constantinople in March 1832. It had been a hazardous and informative voyage, if a trifle breathless. He had a number of adventures on the way, mostly brushes with more or less hostile Arabs, but his optimism was contagious and a few months later the new British ambassador, the redoubtable Sir Stratford Canning, sent him back to London with the answers to Peacock's queries.

The Euphrates route which Chesney had by this time come to favour is one of the oldest land routes in the world, its antiquity attested to by ruined military posts and commercial cities along the way. Once free of the Anatolian mountains the stream of traders flowed through the centuries along its valley, rested and victualled by such caravan cities as Rakka and Resafa, Dura Europos and Palmyra. Pliny complained in the first century AD about Roman crazes for eastern perfumes, Indian gauzes and other extravagances imported by this route but trade was reciprocal; Roman wine went to India as did French in the imperial age, as well as glass and other luxuries from Alexandria. Traffic from the east came up the Gulf to Basra, by land up the Euphrates valley and thence across the Syrian desert to Antioch or later to Aleppo, once the greatest entrepôt of the Middle East. From the Mediterranean coast goods dispersed all over Europe.

Early European merchants travelling to India also investigated the route, knowing that it was well frequented by huge caravans of thousands of camels to which they could attach themselves. Some went with the caravans by land, others by river if they could, often in a small flotilla taking advantage of the spring flood. Dr Leonhart Rauwolff went downriver from Bireçik to Falujah in 1573, followed by Gasparo Balbi, an Italian jeweller who wrote a report on the river that was rather discouraging, to anyone except Chesney. Among a number of Englishmen using the route was Ralph Fitch, who spent two and a half days on a camel between Aleppo and Bireçik in 1583 and another sixteen more comfortably floating downriver to Falujah. The river tended to be safer and avoided the 'great weariness of the desert journey', but the customs posts were more extortionate; it was a question of weighing them against the thievery in and around the caravans on land. Advocacy of the Mesopotamian route was countered by tales of marauding desert tribes with little respect for Ottoman rule or Ottoman permits and European use of the route fell away almost completely from the mid-seventeenth century until the mid-eighteenth century. Sea via the Cape was slow but at least it was safe. By the end of the eighteenth century, however, that desire for faster communications was reviving interest in the

Euphrates route. It still took the better part of nine months for a letter to reach its destination via the Cape but it could take less, in an emergency, if the Euphrates route was used.

For centuries there had been an intermittent but far from rudimentary postal service between Asia Minor and Mesopotamia. The Persian emperor Darius is credited with having a messenger service in the fourth century BC between Ephesus and Susa and Herodotus wrote of the Persian system: 'neither snow, nor heat, nor gloom of night stays these couriers from completion of their appointed rounds,' an eulogy which is engraved on the façade of the General Post Office in New York City. Seleucids, Sasanians, Romans and Byzantines followed suit and Abbasid rulers in Baghdad had a well-organized system of communication across the desert, sustained later by the Mamluks from Cairo and the Ottoman Turks from Constantinople. Members of the East India Company living in Basra, a town at the head of the Gulf famous for its trade in spices and drugs, often found it convenient to use the Turkish system of *tatars*, dispatch bearers who could cover the 1,500 miles between Baghdad and Constantinople in twelve to thirteen days. There was also the pigeon post, the two most famous breeds of homing pigeons – Basra and Iskenderun – named after the two termini. The system was popular for communication between Aleppo and the coast but Europeans were wary when it came to the desert: who knew into whose hands the delicate messages might not fall?

The Company developed its own system of sending dispatches overland in the eighteenth century, between Basra and Aleppo. In general the desert route was used, running parallel to the Euphrates but a few miles west of it, to avoid bureaucratic delays in the small towns on the way. The Company also established a fortnightly service of packet boats in the Gulf – small vessels that could sail from Bombay to Basra in ten to fifteen days, less vulnerable to the monsoon than vessels using the Red Sea. The system was hazardous, 'fatiguing and rather dangerous,' wrote Colonel James Capper in 1784, 'and consequently will seldom be taken by choice, or for the bare gratification of curiosity.'[2] It was put successfully to the test, however, when the British in India heard of the outbreak of the Seven Years War with France in 1756 before the French did and took due advantage of the knowledge. In 1798 news of Nelson's victory at Alexandria was taken to India by Lieutenant Thomas Duval who rode from Aleppo to Baghdad in twelve days. He was received by the Pasha with the greatest consideration and managed to float down the meandering course of the Tigris from Baghdad to Basra in ten more days. Napoleon's dealings with Persia and Russia as well as his expedition to Egypt demonstrated, at least to the British in India, the vulnerability of their position to European threat. But in 1801 only the farsighted would have noticed the potential of the *Charlotte Dundas'* maiden voyage along the Forth and Clyde Canal.

Chesney found himself a person of considerable public interest on his return to London. Waghorn's advocacy of the Overland Route had not been wholly successful with the Post Office or with the government, hence his decision to set up independently in Egypt, and Chesney's alternative Euphrates route had clear advantages, not least the proven viability of steamboats on rivers. At sea, as the *Enterprize* and the *Hugh Lindsay* had demonstrated, coal consumption and paddle-wheel design still left much to be desired. The unpunctuality of the East India Company's service between Bombay and Suez reinforced its failure. Leading marine engineers were much happier with river steam, in particular the Birkenhead shipbuilder William Laird and his sons, one of whom, MacGregor, had joined an expedition with one of the family's little iron steamers up the Niger River. William's foresight led to the rise of the Birkenhead ironworks after he bought a few acres in 1824 on the banks of Wallesey Pool, later developed into docks. Laird's were the only builders of iron vessels of any experience in the 1830s. Other backers of Chesney included the Maudslay team, now led by Joseph, son of Henry, and his partner Joshua Field. Chesney was kept busy preparing memos to all and sundry as well as learning at first hand about steam engines and steam navigation. Mail, said Chesney, could be sent between London and Bombay in six weeks, up or down river. Moreover 'commercial steam, with peace restored among the Arab tribes, would soon alter the features of the country and cover it with peace and fertility.' Armed flotillas on the river, he argued with characteristic vehemence, would help keep the peace.[3]

Not everyone was in favour of faster communications; an East India Company director exclaimed, 'Ah but that is the very thing we do *not* want . . . No, no, now we write our letters, and get our answers every six months, and have peace and leisure between whiles; life will not be worth living if you get your way.'[4]

In 1832 the government was tottering, its health poorly since the passing of the Reform Bill that year. Chesney found it impossible to attract the attention of the one man whose support was essential to the undertaking – Lord Palmerston. The Foreign Secretary was reluctant, Chesney felt, to back a project that was at least partly aimed at forestalling a potential ally, namely Russia. For Chesney was fully caught up in the shifting pattern of European rivalries, stimulated by

Peacock who combined his writing of novels with being the Company's Chief Examiner and an exponent of the Russian menace. Peacock persuaded him to circulate his memoir on the Euphrates and brought it to the attention of William IV. The King was most concerned about 'the aggressive power of Russia in the East' and told Chesney so in an interview.

The result of this interest was a select committee of the House of Commons, set up in 1834 to investigate steam communications with India, including the possibility of sending an exploratory expedition to the Euphrates.[5] Chesney's plan, drawn up with the assistance of the Laird family and presented to the committee, was to take two steamers in pieces to the Syrian coast, transport them across land to Bireçik on the Euphrates and steam downriver, to establish contact with local Arabs who were likely, in Chesney's opinion, to be the principal difficulty, and to set up coal depots. Steaming downriver was thought to be potentially less of a shock to local Arabs than starting off by steaming upriver.[6]

Chesney also pointed out that the Euphrates route was shorter than that by the Red Sea (hence the frequent description of it, especially in later years, as the 'short cut' to India). A great asset of the Euphrates route, moreover, was that so little of it involved ocean travel, while the Red Sea as early as 1541 had been described by a Portuguese sailor as presenting greater obstacles to navigators than the whole circuit of the great ocean. The *Hugh Lindsay* had shown that steamboats were not yet powerful enough to beat against the seasonal winds of the Red Sea. Chesney concluded his evidence by reminding the committee that they must look beyond the mere speeding up of communications: the last but not the least consideration favouring the Gulf and Euphrates route 'is the prospect of introducing Christianity amongst the fixed and wandering inhabitants of Arabia.' Muslim eyes would be opened to the value of both trade and true religion.

The technical evidence submitted to the committee is an absorbing résumé of the state of steam navigation at the time, by some of those most closely involved in its development. There is a pleasant sense of clubbiness about the great steam developers, many associated with the Maudslays: Joseph Maudslay's partner Joshua Field, whose new Lambeth yard lay within sight of the House of Commons, giving evidence to the committee, Maudslay's engines going into iron boats at the enterprising Laird yard in Birkenhead, Maudslay's former pupil James Nasmyth in Manchester studying the problems of manipulating cast iron – a comforting vision of interlocking circles of technical cooperation, repeating itself in France and the USA.

An engineer with considerable shipbuilding experience was Mac-Gregor Laird. The Lairds were now leading the construction of iron ships, following on the pioneering *Aaron Manby*, built in 1822 for service on the Seine, demonstrating that iron vessels could be built with much shallower draught than wooden vessels. They could be built in England, MacGregor Laird told the committee, taken to pieces and reassembled wherever they were needed, thus avoiding an ocean voyage which they were still too small to handle. Laird himself had participated in an expedition up the Niger with one wooden vessel and one small iron steamer. Iron vessels were found to be cooler and less smelly because the bilge water was carried in a tank rather than a wooden cask; iron hulls could also withstand the vibration of engines better than wooden. Luckily for Chesney, Laird scorned the notion that there might be any problem carting steamboats overland from the Mediter-ranean to the river; he did admit that a good engineer was absolutely essential to the success of the expedition. The committee cross-examined Joshua Field about contemporary steamboat developments – paddle wheels, coal consumption, engine power, oscillating engines, iron versus wood, low-pressure versus high-pressure engines. William Morgan, a highly respected designer of paddle wheels, was questioned also about fuel, the plan being to take a certain amount out from Britain to supplement local wood as well as to try mixing it with bitumen from Hit, about half-way down the Euphrates. Chesney had experimented with burning a mixture of bitumen and wood while in Baghdad but no one really knew how successful a fuel this might be.

Chesney's main and most effective political support came from Peacock who reverted once again to the Russian menace, as he saw it.[7] 'It would be extremely easy,' he maintained, 'for Russia to follow the steps of Trajan and Julian, construct fleets in Armenia and float them to Bussorah [Basra],' voicing fears that have been echoed on a number of occasions over the intervening 150 years. Russia already controlled the Anatolian headwaters of the Euphrates through a recent treaty with Turkey and had been 'long supposed to have designs on Baghdad; they have had emissaries there a good while' and the Baghdad region would be a valuable possession. 'The Russians . . . now have steam-boats on the Volga and the Caspian Sea . . . They will do everything in Asia that is worth the doing, and that we leave undone.' Asked why he favoured the Euphrates route over that by the Red Sea Peacock maintained that it was less expensive, more navigable all the year round, politically and commercially of more benefit to Britain as well as to India. Above all, 'all our political interest, in the way of guarding against Russia, lies in the Persian Gulf, and not at all in the Red Sea where we have no business . . . of any importance whatsoever; the mere circumstances of steamers passing through the Gulf would accomplish one of the principal purposes for which the Bombay Marine is now employed, which is watching against the revival of piracy in the Persian Gulf.' Nevertheless Peacock ended up recommending both routes, the one supplementing the other.

Peacock's pessimism and Chesney's optimism carried the day. Chesney was asked one day, when lecturing on the Euphrates route, 'But won't there be difficulties with the Arabs?' 'Difficulties, Sir? Do you think I would have had anything to do with it if there had been no difficulties?'[8] Peacock's warnings about Russian expansionism seemed more than ever appropriate in the light of Russia's offer to help the Ottoman Sultan recover Syria from occupation in 1833 by his own powerful vassal, Muhammad Ali of Egypt. A substantial section of British opinion saw this offer as a kiss of death for the Turks rather than of life and began to wonder about the security of Britain's overseas commitments. Communications with India must be improved and not just via the Red Sea. The House of Commons voted £20,000 towards an exploratory expedition to the Euphrates; the East India Company followed with another £5,000. Not exactly riches but enough to be getting on with.

MacGregor Laird's advocacy of iron for river steamers won the day and Laird's Birkenhead Works was commissioned to build two flat-bottomed iron steamers. The larger, christened *Euphrates*, weighed 179 tons, and measured 105 feet by 19, with a draught of 3 feet. The smaller was christened *Tigris* and weighed 109 tons, measuring 90 feet by 10 with a 16–18in. draught. Maudslay's of Lambeth supplied the low-pressure engines. There was no shortage of volunteers from the army and navy and Chesney was able to recruit an able team of companions. One of the best accounts of the expedition was later written by Admiral Edward Charlewood who joined it as a young naval lieutenant and was sent to Laird's for training. Another member was Lieutenant James Fitzjames, 'the life and soul of the party', who later died with Franklin on his attempt to find a north-west passage. Artillery volunteers acquired practical experience in the wheelhouse of the Birkenhead ferries. Sappers were taught how to manage a diving bell and how to blow up rocks under water. Chesney left nothing to chance. Finally all was ready. Laird's assembled the boats for trials at Birkenhead, then took them to bits again and shipped them, with Chesney's team, to the coast of Syria. Here, Chesney had decided, the mouth of the Orontes river would give them the best access to the interior. The place was Suwaidiyyah, the ancient Seleucia which centuries ago had served as Antioch's port.

'We were wholly unprepared for the vexatious and almost insurmountable impediments which we subsequently encountered,' wrote Chesney later with a certain amount of disingenuousness in his *Narrative* of the expedition.* The obstacles facing them over the next 110 miles to the Euphrates were both geographical and political, in about equal proportions, and were so daunting that at least two-thirds of all accounts of the expedition are taken up with the difficulties of merely reaching the starting point. More than six months passed before everything was on the banks of the Euphrates, despite Chesney's reputation for never wasting time.

Suwaidiyyah is situated on a particularly beautiful stretch of the Syrian coast, at the mouth of the Orontes river which tumbles out of the Amanus mountains between the coast and the cities of the hinterland, Antioch and Aleppo. The Syrians call the Orontes 'al-Assi', meaning the rebel, because at times it seems to flow upsteam into the wild interior. As a rule the greater the beauty the more daunting the obstacles and in this case the maxim repeatedly proved true: the landing, across the sand bar at the mouth of the river, and the transport of everything to the depot set up on the shore and named Port Amelia after William IV's dead sister; the discovery, only now, that the river was not navigable; the struggle to make carts and hire beasts to cross the mountains, including the 'Hill of Difficulty', to a point just north of Antioch; the navigation of a lake and 'dismal swamp' rife with malaria and typhoid before reaching the relatively level plain across which the Euphrates flows. Ultimately Chesney hoped to avoid these obstacles by building a canal from coast to river or – a later scheme – a railway, and certain members of the expedition were sent off to investigate possible routes.

Political obstacles were both local and Egyptian. The local inhabitants were naturally reluctant to aid so strange a party of foreigners and

* Details of Chesney's expedition are taken from two accounts by Chesney himself, a biography of Chesney by his wife and daughter, and two other accounts of the expedition by two other members, William Ainsworth and Edward Charlewood. Chesney's first account was supposed to run to four volumes, of which he completed only the first two for publication in 1850; they contained detailed histories of the wider Middle East but never got as far as the actual expedition. His *Narrative* was published many years later, in 1868. Ainsworth's account, published in 1888, was highly critical of Chesney's rather verbose style. He is just as guilty, however, and the biography is much the most succinct as well as mildly critical account thanks to some careful editing by Stanley Lane Poole.

refused to hire out animals; Chesney realised too late that he would have done better to buy them. A far more serious problem was that of dealing with an occupying force. The Egyptians had invaded Syria in 1833, under the command of Ibrahim Pasha, eldest son of Muhammad Ali. The invasion was not unpopular in Syria, a province reduced to hardship by several decades of Ottoman misrule, but all Chesney's permits came from the Turks and these the Egyptians refused to recognise. Chesney suspected, probably with good reason, that Muhammad Ali had no intention of encouraging an expedition which if successful would remove profitable transit traffic from Egypt to Mesopotamia. Chesney also reckoned that the Egyptians were being encouraged in their opposition by the Russians, who in his opinion wanted to keep the Euphrates valley for themselves.

But at last the expedition landed. A boat overturned and the cask containing valves of both engines went to the bottom but was rescued by grappling irons. Somehow the party survived the snakes (young Lieutenant Charlewood was bitten by one in his bed) and the centipedes which infested its tents. The vermin were awful and one of Charle-

11 The shipyard of Laird's in Birkenhead, pioneer builders of iron vessels including the *Tigris* and *Euphrates* for Chesney's Euphrates expedition

wood's greatest luxuries was to find a stream, strip himself of his clothing, build a fire and smoke his clothes: the lice could not stand the smoke from green wood. Sickness was a serious problem, from malaria and typhoid. One of the officers overindulged in a local orchard and was smitten with dysentery. The engineers assembled *Tigris* and loaded her with parts of the larger *Euphrates* in the vain hope that she would be able to ascend the Orontes; the current proved to be too strong and she had to be taken to bits as well. The keels had to be dragged upriver; 'owing to their length they could scarcely pass the sharp turnings of the narrow roads.' It took four days to get them over the river rapids to the vicinity of Antioch. The small flat-bottomed rowing boats belonging to each steamer were put on wheels and dragged by land, assisted by a sail. Twenty-seven carts had to be built and a road opened. Thousands of hired camels carried the lighter materials and stores.

Half-way through his account Chesney paused, as if reliving the saga of that extraordinary feat was almost too much for him, and apologised for being repetitious. 'The narration of difficulties, which were so full of interest and excitement at the time, may now, it is to be feared, sometimes become tedious to the reader.' In fact his account is far from tedious; the reader is immediately involved in all his nightmares, logistical, mechanical and otherwise. 'Let it, however, be borne in mind, that in thus recording the trying difficulties met with in our transport service, the Commander is only endeavouring to do justice to the untiring exertions of his officers and men, whose persevering efforts were made at times almost against hope.'

The greatest resourcefulness was shown by Charlewood, who had the task of getting the 7-ton boilers over the mountains. On one occasion the guiding beam attached to the front axle of the cart snapped. Charlewood was at his wits' end: there was no timber available; the ox drivers, delighted at the unscheduled halt, unyoked their beasts and sat down to lunch. Charlewood set off for a nearby cottage to see if they had any food for him. It was a humble roadside hut but inside, as he flung himself despairingly on a cushion, what should he see but the roof supported by just such a beam as he needed for the cart. Just like King Bruce and the spider, he thought. No time for gentle persuasion, out with the purse and the startled shepherd and his family in mid-meal found they had sold their house, were being bundled out and were watching the roof being dismantled. They were, Charlewood insisted, handsomely requited.

At one point the burdensome boilers were stuck so fast in the mud (progress was at best no more than 100 yards a day) that even the forty oxen yoked to them could not move them, despite the efforts of their drivers. Accused by one officer of being 'effeminate', a driver came up at the end of the day with a pair of ox's ears, dripping blood, in his hand, torn off the beast in an effort to dislodge him. He flung them down at the officer's feet and demanded, 'Who will dare to call me effeminate now?' The *Tigris* boiler eventually reached Port William, drawn through a triumphal arch by 104 oxen and 52 drivers.

The expedition had landed in Syria at the beginning of April 1835. Chesney reached Port William, their winter base on the Euphrates just below Bireçik, traditional crossing point of the river and starting point of downriver journeys, at the end of July and sent messages for a steamer to meet him at Basra at the end of September with the Indian mails. Optimism, or perhaps malaria, had got the better of him; William Ainsworth, the surgeon and geologist to the expedition, recommended that the clang and clatter of construction work should be stopped to give him some peace 'but it was soon discovered that the stillness greatly aggravated my fever, while the sound of eight hammers hard at work gave me immediate relief.' In fact it was not until November and the onset of the winter rains that all the equipment reached Port William, while the expedition did not reach Basra until June the following year.

Bireçik is situated on a steep cliff above the river which at this point, released from the Anatolian mountains, spreads out among a number of islands and shoals. It was quite unsuitable for launching steamers. Chesney's expedition spent an uncomfortable winter assembling the boats below Bireçik and readying them for the spring flood. The local authorities were obstreperous, refused to give them bread and insisted on searching their stores for the 2,000 muskets they claimed were hidden there. Some members of the expedition were sent off by Chesney to make friends with local Arabs, to look for coal, and to have a look at the river lower down. Chesney, Ainsworth and one or two others went on a convalescing tour of the Taurus.

By March 1836 both boats were ready for launching, sideways, down the river bank. The river was in full flood and this, it was hoped, would save them some valuable fuel. The expedition had been joined by a German honeymooning couple, Dr and Mrs Helfer. Mrs Helfer appears to have been amiable but stupid, daunted perhaps by her husband's idea of a honeymoon, and her chief failing, shared with the interpreter Christian Rassam, was her stomach; the two of them always appropriated the liver when a sheep was slaughtered. Rassam also kept a pudding hidden among his possessions, which Charlewood and a fellow officer found and ate. Mrs Helfer was put in charge of the expedition's library, which included Addison, Johnson, Shakespeare and Gibbon; 'she revels in the idea of gliding safely and comfortably down the glorious river, well provided with food for the mind,' according to her husband's account which she later edited.[9] Coal and provisions were sent on ahead although the vessels would make use of local supplies of wood as much as possible; consumption would be low because they would be able to drift with the flood and the current but the supplies would be needed for subsequent voyages.

The *Euphrates'* engines failed the first day of trials but next morning, March 17th, 1836, all went well. 'There was the steamer proud in its iron flanks,' wrote Ainsworth, 'confident in its unspent force of steam, and manned with hearts zealous in duty while rejoicing in the spirit of adventure, and full of that ambition which, like the river itself, could not look back, but was ever urged onward with a strong swelling desire'.[10] Chesney was equally euphoric, steaming downriver imbued with 'the conviction that we had taken the first step in extending those commercial relations which Great Britain has so long maintained with her ancient ally the Sultan.' They left Bireçik to tremendous local excitement on either bank, 'and thus closed this eventful day, which formed the one bright spot between the toils and trials of the preceding eleven months and those which were still to be met during the further progress of the Expedition.' Might one detect a waning of that optimism?

Chesney himself saw his voyage down the Euphrates as essentially exploratory. From his previous experience aboard local craft he knew there would be difficulties, none of which he judged (more or less correctly) would be insuperable. The chief problem was going to be the local inhabitants and, provided one moved with caution and diplomacy and ample generosity, he reckoned, with fair accuracy as it turned out, that these could be reconciled to the project, at least as far down as Hillah. Corporal Greenhill out for a stroll, however, did have the misfortune to have his brass buttons cut off his jacket by one local who mistook them for gold; young Fitzjames, chief joker of the expedition, broke his leg in giving chase to the robbers and had a most painful recovery, with the juddering of the steamer causing the broken bones to grind against each other. On the whole their reception was moderately friendly, and certainly aroused curiosity among a stream of visitors who paddled around them on the local *keleks*. There were three tricky places to navigate on the way down but they proved passable, with the smaller *Tigris* usually sent ahead as pathfinder through the worst of the rocks, sandbanks and whirlpools. The boats went aground several times but only once seriously, when *Euphrates* was stuck for nearly three weeks just below Karkemish. But there was one event that, more than any other single aspect of the venture, damned it in the eyes of its distant audience: the great storm of May 21st.

It happened just below the junction with the Khabur tributary, about noon, after a clear morning and calm steaming. Both boats were quite close together. Quite suddenly, wrote Ainsworth, his self-satisfaction temporarily yielding to the full horror of the memory, 'the sky assumed an appearance such as we had never before witnessed, and which was awful and terrible in the extreme. A dense black arch enveloped the whole of the horizon, and the space beneath the arch was filled with a body of dust . . . whirling round and at the same time advancing towards us with fearful rapidity . . . The crash broke upon us like heaven's own artillery and the hurricane seemed as if bent upon hurling both steamers at once to the bottom of the river.'[11] Both ships tried to tie up in the face of the cyclone but the *Tigris* was caught too soon: in no time at all the wind had wrenched off the paddles, the waves had washed over the decks and in through the cabin windows which, even in dead calm, were only just above the waterline. Before the eyes of the horrified passengers watching from *Euphrates*, the *Tigris* stood up on her bows and sank. The midday darkness prevented men knowing which way to swim. Twenty-two people were drowned but Chesney was among those who managed to reach the shore, 'clearly in a pitiable plight, and utterly crestfallen, almost unconscious as to what was going on around him,' Charlewood wrote later. It was a terrible disaster.

But the expedition must go on. Chesney had already received discouraging news that the government wanted the expedition broken up but he was determined to persist, as were the remaining members. There was not room on board for all the *Tigris* passengers and they were dropped off a few days later at Anah, a large town made prosperous by the great caravans that assembled there for the desert crossing to Aleppo. The rest went on. Chesney had another bout of malaria but was cheered by Muhammad Getgood, the pilot from his previous rafting expedition, arriving just in time to guide them through the rapids of Karbala. At Hit they experimented with the use of a mixture of bitumen and earth for fuel, reasonably successfully apart from the smoke.

Below Hillah, a large town on the edge of the ancient ruins of Babylon (which they briefly inspected), they were steaming through more hostile country. Of the lower Euphrates Ainsworth wrote, 'no portion of the river left so painful an impression of former prosperity and present poverty as this lower part. Unprotected by a supine

12   The *Tigris* foundering in a squall on the Euphrates River, with the loss of
most of those on board

government, and harassed by lawless, plundering Bedwins, what was
once life, animation, and wealth, is now almost utter desolation.' In the
Lemlun marshes they found the local inhabitants 'unquestionably the
most wild, cunning, and untrustworthy of all the so-called Arabs we
met on the river.' Chesney had had trouble with them in 1830, when
they had removed most of his possessions; this time they directed the
Euphrates up a wrong tributary of the river, leading to a dead end where
she stuck in the mud and spent the night 'in a wilderness of waters and
enveloped in a cloud of mosquitoes.' The crew eventually extricated
themselves by backing the paddles. On another occasion a thief was
alleged by his victim, Mrs Helfer, to have tried to kidnap her and drag
her off the boat in the middle of the night; she was not popular with the
other members of the expedition, however, and there is a note of
scepticism in accounts of the event. Beyond the marshes, wrote
Ainsworth, in whatever direction the traveller moved he met with long
continous mounds of ancient dwellings now occupied by 'the present
degenerate hordes of tent and spear', though the party was suitably
impressed by the semi-nomadic lifestyle of the Muntafiq Arabs then in
those parts and the 'princely and patriarchal life' of their shaikh.

And so at last to Basra, where they arrived on June 19th, 38 miles below the junction of the two rivers. As Ainsworth pointed out, 'there are not many places gifted with so many advantages as Basra ... yet it is difficult to imagine a place more fallen.' Basra itself was not on the river in those days (it has since expanded to the river banks) but up a two-mile creek, enveloped in gracious date gardens. Creeks, now mostly filled in, flowed in all directions and boats were the principal means of transport though the arrival of the *Euphrates* caused some consternation. She only just made it to Basra before her fuel ran out; extensive flooding made it impossible for the crew to land to look for wood and they were reduced to burning anything they could lay their hands on. One can sense Chesney beginning to suffer from the dreaded captain's coal fever.

Basra has never been an easy place in which to sustain morale and Chesney by this time was neither an easy nor a sympathetic taskmaster. A later railway enthusiast, David Fraser,[12] would describe Basra ruefully as 'a place for optimists only.' Here the party split up. But for Chesney the task of the expedition – to speed up mails to and from India – was only just beginning. So far the voyage had been purely exploratory. Now the expedition had to secure the Indian mail, presumably brought up the Gulf on board the little *Hugh Lindsay*, and take it back upriver. But the captain of the *Hugh Lindsay*, impatient at waiting for the *Euphrates*, had decided to cut his losses and take his mail round to Suez in the Red Sea and send it via Egypt, returning then to India for further orders. *Euphrates* was in any case in no state to begin an ascent of the river. Repairs were essential and facilities available only at Bushire on the Persian coast of the Gulf. The vessel was not, however, equipped for even a short voyage across the open sea, one of the problems being that compasses had not yet been corrected for use in iron hulls; a correction theory did not emerge until 1839, calculated by Sir G.B. Airy. As a result the *Euphrates* was so nearly wrecked that Chesney had trouble persuading the crew to stay with him for the return trip. There was a feeling that Chesney had had a good run for his money but that the project might not be worth pursuing.

Moreover from Bushire Chesney now insisted on more diversions from the Euphrates, further delaying the mail project and prejudicing his chances of establishing the route. The stokers went on strike, not surprisingly given the heat of the Gulf summer, and the chief engineer fell sick. Eventually the *Euphrates* was towed back to the Shatt al-Arab, her deck split open and held together with chains lashed round the hull. Chesney spent the next few months investigating her potential on some

13   Bushire, a small but significant Persian port in the Persian Gulf which later in the nineteenth century became the British political and commercial headquarters

of the rivers of south-west Persia and on taking her up the Tigris as far as Baghdad, a painfully slow voyage as they were forced to rely on green wood for fuel. The Tigris, more tortuous and more temperamental than the Euphrates, ceases to be navigable for anything other than rafts about 40 miles above Baghdad; traditional river craft on the Tigris were either *kelek*, a raft on inflated skins used later by archaeologists such as Henry Layard to float their treasures down to the Gulf, or *quffah*, a kind of coracle. Luckily their arrival was 'one of the most triumphant moments in the progress of the undertaking'; the populace was invited to inspect the vessel and a special day was set aside for Muslim ladies who came heavily veiled much to the disgust of those on board. A second day of visiting was reserved for local Christian ladies, brought by Mrs Taylor the Resident's Armenian wife, who were delighted to shed their veils on venturing down to the cabins. 'To us indeed it was a very great treat' – Charlewood relished the memory – 'for with the exception of Mrs Helfer and the hags of Arab women on the banks of the Euphrates, we had scarcely seen a woman's face since we landed in

Syria.' Charlewood was not the only one to be impressed: Chesney's second-in-command, Lieutenant Henry Lynch, succumbed here to the charms of the Taylors' daughter and subsequently married her.

Back then to Qurna at the junction of the two rivers to try the Euphrates river again, having finally collected some mail from the *Hugh Lindsay* for onward dispatch to Britain. It was now the autumn, season of low water, which should have eased the upstream journey. But Chesney's luck, such as it was, now ran out. The locals had turned even more hostile – thanks to a German missionary who had been distributing biblical tracts – and even tried overturning the little steamer (a good indication of its size) when she went aground. Finally in the Lemlun marshes the end came. Three days were spent trying to drag the boat through the shallows but to no avail; on the fourth day the air pump for the port engine gave up the ghost and Chesney had to accept defeat. One of the officers, Fitzjames, was sent off across the desert with the mail and within a day was attacked by Arabs and had everything stolen, including the mail, while Chesney turned the *Euphrates* round and headed back to Qurna. There the expedition was disbanded and Chesney himself continued on board the *Hugh Lindsay* to India. He finally returned to England in August 1837, having carried the mails across the desert from Basra to Damascus in twenty-two days. He reached Italy just in time to learn of the death of his sponsor and principal supporter, William IV. It was the final blow to the project.

Chesney never lost his optimism and his report on the expedition made light of all difficulties. Enough was rumoured about his problems, however, to establish the Red Sea route as infinitely more attractive than the Euphrates and the Gulf. British progress with the marine engine on the open sea was outstripping that of any other nation and making land routes such as those through Syria and Mesopotamia even less competitive. The year of Chesney's return saw the launching of Isambard Kingdom Brunel's giant *Great Western*, a technological advance of such magnitude as to change the whole economy of steam navigation at sea.

Such progress may have underminded Chesney's ambitions for the Euphrates route for the time being but not all British politicians in India and in London forgot the political and strategic arguments that had inspired so many of the expedition's supporters. Chesney's was by no means the last project to propose steam transport for the exploitation of Mesopotamia. 'The unequalled position and resources of this region between the east and the west, with its great navigable rivers almost uniting the Mediterranean with the Persian Gulf and Indian Ocean, must ... again render it as rich and populous as it was when it formed the most important portion of the Babylonian, Assyrian and Persian Empires. I trust it may be the destiny of England to bring about that change, of such vast importance, of such incalculable benefit to peace, commerce and civilisation,' wrote David Fraser at the end of the century, when the viability of the Euphrates valley as a link between east and west was as topical as ever.[13] In spotlighting the potential of the Euphrates valley as 'a short cut to India', the title of Fraser's book, Chesney and his supporters initiated a strategy of communications which the British in India never wholly lost sight of, however secure the ocean seemed by comparison. The words of an old Arab shaikh whom Chesney met near the end of his expedition had a remarkable prescience: 'The English are like ants; if one finds a bit of meat, a hundred follow.' Over the next thirty years Chesney was to do his best to see that they lived up to their reputation.

5

Tender Loving Care

In 1837, the year the Euphrates expedition was wound up, Isambard Kingdom Brunel launched his magnificent *Great Western*. By contemporary standards she was vast. She weighed 1320 tons, was 236 feet long and 35 feet wide and her engines alone, built by Maudslay's, weighed 200 tons. She could accommodate 300 people including the crew. On her maiden voyage across the Atlantic the following year she consumed 43 tons of coal a day to maintain an average speed of over 8 knots and reached New York in fourteen days from Bristol. Such measurements and such a voyage changed the whole outlook of steam navigation. To the publicity surrounding the *Great Western* were added the voices of commercial communities in Calcutta and Bombay, always trying to narrow the enormous and expensive distance separating them from their families and their markets; the Red Sea stretch of the voyage alone cost £100–110 in 1834. Nothing like as many people wanted to steam east as wanted to steam across the Atlantic, most commodities were cheaper to send by the Cape and swift communications could only be sustained with the help of lucrative government mail contracts. Nevertheless the demand for speed was growing and Chesney's failure to convince the authorities of the validity of the Euphrates route meant it was no longer a question of which route to use to India but who could best develop the Overland Route through Egypt, and make it financially sound.

The same year that the *Great Western* was launched laboriously into the water of the Bristol Channel, yet another parliamentary committee was looking into the question of steaming to India.[1] The eastern stretch of the Overland Route was under particular investigation. A Captain Alexander Nairne reflected the thinking of members of the committee when he admitted that he had been very much opposed to steam nine years before but had changed his mind in its favour after being caught on board a small steamer riding out a storm. William Morgan, the paddle wheel designer, was summoned again and argued that any Asian service would need at least five vessels to allow the stokers time to recover from the heat of the tropics; Morgan knew of men having to be hauled out of the engine room even in the lesser temperatures of the Mediterranean and Adriatic. As the discussions droned through 1837 in the dusty corners of Westminister, not far away in the City of London two young men, Arthur Anderson and Brodie McGhie Willcox, were putting together the finance to found the Peninsular Steam Navigation Company.

Brodie Willcox had set up as a shipping agent trading with the Iberian peninsula in 1815 and soon after took on a twenty-three-year-old clerk from the Shetland Islands, Arthur Anderson. Anderson was a typical steam enthusiast, prepared to take the occasional risk on the grand scale. (He would also accept risk on a personal scale: he and his wife were on board the Company steamer *Don Juan* when it ran aground off Tarifa two weeks after P.&O. won the mail contract to the area.) Born in 1792 he was driven, like so many Scotsmen, to look for a fortune overseas, both in person (he was better travelled than his partner, the more shadowy Willcox), and in ventures that made the most of the new steam communications.

The principle behind the company's development was an early form of privatisation – to break down the Post Office monopoly of mail contracts on the grounds that his company could do it better. The mail contract was essential to making early steamboats profitable on many runs, since, quite apart from the cost of fuel, they cost more than twice as much to build as a sailing ship of the same tonnage. By the early nineteenth century the monopoly was subject to the familiar abuses of expense, delayed technology and sloth. Willcox and Anderson had argued for a private mail service to Spain and Portugal since the 1820s, underlining British trading links with the Iberian peninsula, and extended their operations to the Egyptian mail in 1837 using small steam vessels as far as Gibraltar where the mail was handed on to Admiralty packets for transhipment to Egypt and thence India. They proved the advantages of private mail contracts, not the least being the responsibility of ensuring that they made a profit, but these were partly offset by the disadvantages of having to change vessels. In 1840 the government was persuaded to allow the company to extend its services right through to Egypt.

At the Mediterranean end of the Overland Route, French steam packets had virtually monopolised passenger and mail traffic between Europe and the Levant through most of the 1830s. A regular mail service was established between Toulon and Algiers in 1833 and by 1836 the French government, through the Compagnie des Paquebots à Vapeur sur l'Océan et la Méditerranée, had a fleet of packets steaming

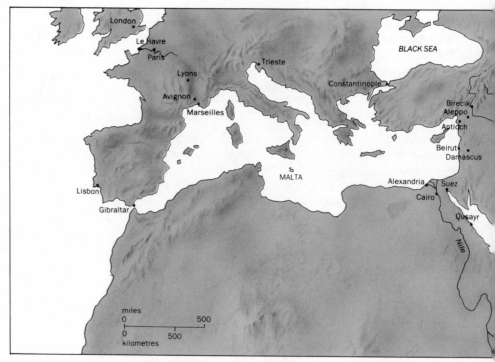

Map 4   Europe to India, mid-nineteenth century

round the Mediterranean. By the 1840s the Marseilles shipyard La Ciotat was beginning to turn out vessels for a regular link with Constantinople. Peninsular Steam set out to challenge this. Moving to the forefront of steam exploitation and taking a lead from the size of the *Great Western* the first two vessels introduced on its service to Alexandria – the *Great Liverpool*, bought by P.&O. from the Transatlantic Steamship Company and refurbished from the Atlantic run, and the *Oriental* – were huge wooden paddle-steamers driven by 450-horsepower side-lever engines, both built in Liverpool and each weighing over 1,500 tons. By the end of the 1830s ship designers were overcoming the problem of power versus weight and draught and these two vessels were a considerable advance, in capacity as well as comfort, on the company's previous vessels as well as on those of the French fleet. Coal consumption was down to 30 tons a day, 900 tons in all for the voyage to Alexandria and back. One way took fourteen days; by sail it had taken six to seven weeks.

Peninsular Steam now became the symbol for luxurious steam travel to Egypt. It cared tenderly for its clients, shepherding them through the

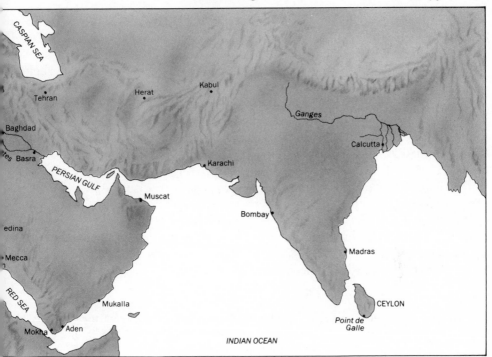

hazards of oriental travel, shielding them from the uncomfortable excesses of foreign peoples. Its success lay in a thoroughly businesslike approach to opportunities, characteristic of its founders Anderson and Willcox, who firmly believed that trade followed the facilities laid on for it. Some passengers embarked at Southampton, the company's home port, travelling there by train from London; despite the cold and smuts this was a great improvement on the journey seventy years earlier when Macrabie and Philip Francis went by post chaise from London to Southampton in 1774, reaching Epsom with 'every fatigue of body and mind', picking the bones of a thin neck of mutton at Liphook, being shattered by the price of nags to Portsmouth, finally facing the palaver of embarkation with a two-hour struggle against contrary winds to get out to the India-bound vessel. Others took a similar succession of steamers, trains and diligences through France to join the Peninsular steamer at Marseilles in the heartland of the company's principal French rivals.

Once on board passengers were bathed in the oriental splendour of chandeliers, plush upholstery (despite its unsuitability to warmer climes) and gilded mouldings; the strains of waltzes and mazurkas accompanied the gentle clink of glasses forever brimming with free alcohol. The *Oriental*, described as 'hermaphrodite' because in common with most of her contemporaries she used sail as well as steam power, had such luxuries as hot and cold showers, ice houses, bakeries and wine cellars with capacity for 400 dozen bottles. Charges were still high (£150 for a gentleman's and £153 for a lady's passage) but all-inclusive. There was the usual liberal allowance of alcohol, with champagne for dinner on Thursdays and Sundays. 'There was such waste in everything,' wrote Harriet Tytler travelling out to India in 1845 under the care of Mrs Moresby and her daughter who were going to rendezvous with Captain Moresby at Suez. 'I have seen the stewards pouring good whiskey into blacking bottles to clean the boots with.'[2] The company was a trailblazer in more ways than one. It even offered free trips round the Mediterranean in return for free publicity, most notably to William Makepeace Thackeray in 1844. The result, *Notes of a Journey From Cornhill to Cairo*, is not one of Thackeray's masterpieces but it served the company well.[3]

14 *Lady Mary Wood*, a P.&O. vessel launched in 1842 for the Calcutta–Suez run. Thackeray sailed on her maiden voyage as far as Gibraltar, seen in the background.

He was initially aboard the *Lady Mary Wood*, a small 570-ton wooden paddle-steamer being tried out in the Mediterranean before its dispatch on Far Eastern service.

Thackeray's coaling stops illustrate a revolutionised map of the Mediterranean, its outlines drawn in the wake of little Welsh colliers still for the most part sailing rather than steaming to the new coal depots strung along the principal routes. The coal was usually stored in discarded warships, dilapidated hulks anchored in an unfamiliar tranquillity. For most of the period of this book the Mediterranean was at peace, an unusual state of affairs which released a flood of prosperity over its shores. The French capture of Algiers in 1830 had eradicated the dreaded Barbary pirates who had done more even than war to interrupt and curtail trade in the western Mediterranean for nearly 300 years. Trade expanded as did shipping, and even freight was beginning to turn to steam at the time of Thackeray's voyage.

Thackeray's first coaling stop was Gibraltar, in British hands since its capture by Admiral Sir George Rooke in 1704. It had become a symbol of Britain's naval power, but despite this, and at least partly thanks to its coal stores, it had developed a thoroughly cosmopolitan character. 'Suppose all the nations of the earth to send fitting ambassadors to represent them at Wapping or Portsmouth Point, with each, under its own national sign-board and language, its appropriate house of call, and your imagination may figure the main street of Gibraltar.'[4] Thackeray was unimpressed by the charms of 'this great blunderbuss'; he found its martial airs too oppressive and thought it 'rather a release' when ordered back to his ship before having to endure a conducted tour of Gibraltar's military features. The next stop was Malta, the Clapham Junction of the Mediterranean sea lanes, British since 1803 and its stately harbour swarming with vessels of all nationalities as well as the British fleet. 'A half-score of busy black steamers perpetually coming and going,' he noted, 'coaling and painting and puffing and hissing in and out of the harbour.' Most opinions of Malta were coloured by forty-day quarantine incarcerations in the lazaretto, Thackeray's included, developed during his return voyage.

From Malta Thackeray's cruise took him to Athens, Smyrna and Constantinople. He told his readers that 'if they love the odd and picturesque, if they loved the Arabian Nights in their youth, let them book themselves on board one of the Peninsular and Oriental vessels, and try one *dip* into Contantinople or Smyrna.' The greatest sensation in Smyrna was a procession of camels – 'whole strings of real camels, better even than in the procession of Blue Beard. O, you fairy dreams of boyhood.' And yet, after descriptions of street scenes, bazaars and local life in either city, Thackeray has a note of warning. 'Wherever the steamboat touches the shore adventure retreats into the interior, and what is called romance vanishes. It won't bear the vulgar gaze; or rather the light of common day puts it out ... Now that dark Hassan sits in his divan and drinks champagne, and Selim has a French watch, and Zuleikha perhaps takes Morrison's pills, Byronism becomes absurd instead of sublime and is only a foolish expression of cockney wonder ... The paddle wheel is the great conqueror. Wherever the captain cries "Stop her," Civilization stops, and lands in the ship's boat and makes a permanent acquaintance with the savages on shore.' However, he concludes, no doubt after a great deal of thoughtful pacing on deck, it is much better to make piston-rods and furnace pokers than pikes and helmets, and commerce is stronger than chivalry.

Constantinople, he reckoned, was on a par with Drury Lane. He stayed at Misseri's Hotel in Pera, both owner and caravanserai made famous by Alexander Kinglake in *Eothen*(1844); he took a Turkish bath and made a long list of sights he *didn't* see partly because it was the Muslim holy season of Ramadan, but he did see the Sultan and the pigeons and the Turkish infantry exercising and finally the seraglio, 'a great town of pavilions' of which the kitchens were 'the most sublime part'. From Constantinople he steamed via Rhodes and Beirut (recently restored to Ottoman rule by a European alliance of Britain, France and Austria) to Jaffa. Here the passengers disembarked to go to Jerusalem, which Thackeray describes with due ecstasy. And so finally to Alexandria.

Passengers still received a rude jolt when dumped on the quay at Alexandria, forced to cope with the strains and stresses of the Overland Route. A clamour 'like a frog concert in a Carolina swamp', according to Harriet Martineau in 1848, beset the luckless arrivals.[5] She found her hotel full of Bombay passengers, hurrying over their letter writing and their tea. For passengers cushioned so gently through the Mediterranean such a state of affairs would not do; P.&O. was gradually obliged to intervene in the handling of the land route. A little twin screw tug, the *Atfeh*, now sputtered on the Mahmoudiyeh Canal and the company also encouraged the Pasha to build a lock between canal and river, obviating the tiresome loading and unloading process at Atfah. From Atfah and with the consent of Muhammad Ali (but rather to the disgruntlement of the genial Mr Hill who had taken over the running of the Overland Route from Waghorn) the company provided 'swift and commodious' iron steamers for the Nile stretch – the *Dahlia*, diplomatically renamed *Lotus*, followed by the *Cairo* and the *Delta*, each able to take seventy closely confined passengers, with gangways running along the sides of each vessel so that the crew could pass from one end of the boat to the other without having to push their way through the often recumbent passengers. The *Cairo* was designed with the Nile specifically in mind, with the lightest possible iron shell, 100 feet long and 14 feet wide and relatively fast: 12 knots in still water even with a hundred passengers on board. 'Hail! O venerable father of crocodiles,' wrote Thackeray, who was not greatly impressed by the river until he saw the Pyramids: 'Fancy my sensations . . .! two big ones and a little one!!! Several of us tried to be impressed; but breakfast supervening, a rush was made at the coffee and cold pies and the sentiment of awe was lost in the scramble for victuals.'

Cairo hotels were beginning to improve with competition; the best in the 1840s was reckoned to be Colombe's Hôtel de l'Europe but ten years later 'the English tongue', according to Trollope, who was in Cairo to renew a Post Office agreement and writing *Dr Thorne* in his spare time, 'finds its centre in Shepheard's Hotel.'[6] Thackeray stayed at the Hôtel de l'Orient, 'an establishment as large and comfortable as most of the best Inns of the South of France.' 'The court is full of bustling dragomans, ayahs and children from India; and poor old

15   *The Author's Entry into Alexandria*, sketched by Samuel Bevan who worked
in Egypt for Messrs Hill and Raven about 1840

venerable he-nurses, with grey beards and crimson turbans, tending little white-faced babies that have seen the light at Dumdum or Futtyghur.'

But here we shall leave Thackeray to his sightseeing, and donning our tropical outfits we shall continue east, mainly in P.&O.'s tender care. The more the company cosseted its passengers the more was demanded of it. Soon it was outdoing the lackadaisical Hill with some uncomfortable carriages, which at least freed passengers from the problem of finding a decent animal. The journey from Alexandria to the Nile now took about twelve hours, up the Nile another eighteen and across the desert, including comfort stops, another thirty-six; with a day's sightseeing in Cairo the journey from sea to sea need take only three and a half days. 'The day has gone by for desert travel,' wrote one traveller. 'All the urgent recommendations that people should provide themselves with camel-saddles, canteens, bottles of water, parasols, braces of pistols, green veils, carpets etc are, like the last comedy at the Haymarket, mere *Moonshine*.'[7] Eventually P.&O. had its own hotel in Cairo, its own sheep farm, and farms near Cairo and the railway junction at Zagazig to provide fresh eggs, poultry, vegetables and fruit; there was also drinking water and ice at Suez. Even with such attentiveness the overland stretch never quite matched the splendours offered on the ocean.

Peninsular Steam had been so successful in the Mediterranean that in 1840 it was given a royal charter, granted on condition that it establish a similar service in eastern waters over the next two years. The company had already been renamed the Peninsular & Oriental Steam Navigation Company – P.&O. – the 'Oriental' acquired with the extension of the service to Egypt. For the time being it was not allowed to operate from Bombay; the East India Company still clung to its difficult Red Sea service, at one point reduced to placing the Indian mail aboard a sailing dhow because all the Company steamers were out of action. (The dhow never reached Suez.) Disregarding competitors in India who were struggling to mount their own steam service, P.&O. extended its eastern services beyond Calcutta, establishing a main bunkering depot, stores and administrative offices there, to Singapore and China via Ceylon, later on to Australia and finally back up the Red Sea – but from Calcutta, not from Bombay.

Its grandest venture at this stage was the launching in 1842 of the *Hindostan*, followed a year later by the 1,974-ton *Bentinck*. Both were destined for the east, to ply between Calcutta and Suez. A normal fare for this stretch was around £140 for a gentleman, £150 for a lady, £60 for a European servant and £40 for a 'native' servant. The *Hindostan*, a wooden paddle-steamer with iron bulkheads driven by direct-action engines, was 242 feet long and weighed 2000 tons. She epitomised once again that yearning to improve others, now broadcast to the travelling, steaming world. Opening up the route 'will diffuse with magical rapidity the living radiance of knowledge over regions buried for ages in the night of ignorance ... The vast agency of steam must lead to the mental manumission of millions of our fellow creatures.'[8] To add to her prestige she was commanded by Captain Robert Moresby, who had painstakingly charted the Red Sea in the early 1830s. He had been so infuriated by the East India Company's handling of Red Sea traffic, as well as by their failure to promote him according to his self-esteem, that he had resigned their service and joined P.&O. So it was Moresby who took the *Hindostan* out of Southampton on September 24th, 1842, through a fleet of flag-waving well-wishers, heading round the Cape for P.&O.'s eastern run. Down the Solent she steamed, distinguished by her three masts and two tall white funnels, past Her Majesty's rural abode at Osborne, with 150 passengers on board, each of whom had paid a special fare of £40. Heaving sighs of nostalgia they watched as the Needles faded into the autumn twilight.[9]

Hindostan was the first of many luxury steamers commissioned by P.&O. At Southampton the passenger entered a world of *A Thousand and One Nights*, which in various expurgated translations was titillating the armchair-bound. Brocade settees, mirrored walls, chandeliers: the mystique of the oceanic odyssey was being established. Contrary to later arrangements, the cabins were grouped in the centre of the ship, with corridors down the sides 'forming, as it were, a street, having on one side the range of spacious side-ports and on the other the doors entering the private cabins'. The passengers would thus be more tranquil: 'the rush of water along the vessel's side will not, as in the usual plan, be heard close to the ear.'[10]

Indeed they soon settled into their routine. A piano was an essential in the ladies' saloons, the *Hindostan* no exception, and female passengers taking pianos to India were warned to wrap their own up carefully rather than expose them to salt and humidity by playing them on board. Ships' captains would soon try to ensure that a few members of the crew could play musical instruments, a custom leading to the great palm court orchestras of later first-class saloons. There were the usual gargantuan meals, with curry at every one of them including breakfast; the *Hindostan*'s sister ship, the *Bentinck*, carried a cook, pastry cook and

16   The *Hindostan* leaving Southampton in 1842 on her maiden voyage round the Cape to India, the first of P.&O.'s luxury steamers destined for the Calcutta–Suez run

baker. It was hardly surprising that accounts of voyages are heavily larded with days of queasiness. Games to help digest the meals were still sedate and included backgammon and cards (but never on Sundays), sack races and chess; the decks were still too cluttered with the paraphernalia of a sailing vessel to allow for the sporting activities of later voyages.

Colliers had been sent ahead to Gibraltar, Madeira, the Cape Verde Islands, Ascension, Cape Town, Mauritius, Point de Galle and Calcutta: there should be no dread of coal fever aboard the *Hindostan*. Madeira was their first port of call, as it had been for generations of sailing vessels; the *Hindostan* picked up ice, a novel luxury, as well as coal. The island was already acquiring a new reputation as a health resort for the aged or ailing; as early as 1836 Peninsular Steam was advertising that 'one or two of the vessels will also proceed in the Spring and Fall of the year to Madeira for the accommodation of Invalids . . . visiting that Island.'[11] The weather warmed up, the crew sweated over their furnaces, the piles of coal went down. Despite careful planning coal fever did set in even for the *Hindostan*, even for Moresby, between the equator and Cape Town. As the coal ran out Moresby must have been thankful he could still unfurl a set of sails, shuddering nevertheless at the ignominy of having to sail rather than steam into harbour. Once there, at least his supplies of coal were assured.

Cape Colony was well established as a coaling station. In due course it was to receive regular visits from Union Line's coal and mail service, originally between South Wales and the main ports, and operating to the Cape from 1857: forty-two days out and the same for the return. Their colliers were extremely economical to run with all available space taken up by coal: no bathrooms therefore until the 1860s and the cabins so cramped it was said a lady's crinoline would touch all four walls. From the moment of the *Enterprize*'s first stop for coal in 1825, British interest in the Cape was to revolve round its role as a vital coaling point on the route to India and later as a major naval link in imperial strategy. No dealings with foreign powers were involved, no bribery, no intrigues. Even in that desperate year of the Indian Mutiny, 1857, Palmerston at first insisted on sending soldiers via the Cape because, he said, using the Overland Route through Egypt might encourage the French to do the same. Passage of the Cape became known as the private thorough-fare of the British navy, unlike its later chief competitor the Suez Canal, which any foreign devil might take it into his head to close. While politicians at home extolled the Cape as 'the true centre of the Empire,'[12] the British living in India were happy to use it for holidays or convalescence; 'no situation in the [Indian] hills could have shown more merriment or better dancing' and more than one returned to India with a Dutch wife on his arm.[13] Not for another thirty years, however, was the Cape route commercially viable for steam vessels; as long as ships were powered by coal-hungry low-pressure engines too much space in their holds was taken up with coal to allow for the transport of freight.

The *Hindostan*'s passengers were committed to the new age of speed and appealing as the Cape's charms might be, they could be enjoyed only briefly as Moresby set off for Ceylon. Picking up more coal there at Point de Galle, dropping off a few passengers at Madras, where they were ferried to the shallow shore on unstable, unlikeable catamarans, the *Hindostan* continued north to the mouth of the Hooghly. Taking on board one of the famous Hooghly pilots she steamed between the shoals, her passengers able to stay on board for the tedious voyage upriver to a splendid reception on their arrival in Calcutta. On Christmas Eve that prosperous British community, employed in their traditional evening amusement of 'eating the air' – seeing and being seen on the esplanade[14] – had their show stolen by the *Hindostan* as she dropped her anchor. She was 91 days out of Southampton – 63 days at sea, 28 in port – quite an improvement on the voyage of the little *Enterprize*.

P.&O. now put the *Hindostan* to work on the Calcutta–Suez run, thus introducing to the Red Sea higher standards of comfort than the humble coastal steamers of the East India Company could mount, although it would still be several years before even P.&O.'s Red Sea vessels matched those in the Mediterranean. Passengers were still loud in their complaints; perhaps the *Hindostan*'s glories faded in the tropical waywardness of the Red Sea, for after that initial flourish round the Cape little is heard of P.&O.'s pride and joy. On other vessels there was still too little privacy, too many cockroaches and a film of coal soot covered everything. The number of passengers slowly grew, from 255 voyaging east in 1839 to 573 in 1840 and 800 in 1842. But in 1844 the *Great Liverpool* sailed with only 17 passengers on board, only three of whom crossed Egypt to pick up the *Hindostan* at Suez. Trade, as Anderson was fond of saying, follows not the flag but the facilities. Profits were meagre, the company skimped and the grumbles were soon bouncing like heatwaves off the barren cliffs of the Red Sea.

P.&O. was operating regular mail services from England to Alexandria, and from Suez to Ceylon, Madras and Calcutta as well as further east, including Australia, recognisably more efficient than the East India Company, whose only service was between Bombay and Suez. As so often it was a question of economy of size; P.&O.'s larger vessels were better equipped to stick to a timetable. Foreign competition was looming, in particular from a new rival, Messageries Impériales. In 1851 a French road transport company, Messageries Nationales, came to an agreement with the French government to take on the state-owned packet service to Levant ports. Two years later this was renamed Compagnie des Services Maritimes des Messageries Impériales. It was based at Marseilles and became a fierce rival of P.&O. on many eastern routes, often able, so the British felt, to offer cut-price freight and mail rates because of substantial government subsidies; by about 1860 P.&O.'s own all-important government mail subsidy totalled around £225,000 a year. Nevertheless Arthur Anderson reckoned his company could hold its own provided it kept up with the latest steamboat technology; Messageries was handicapped initially by having to make use of the state-owned packet fleet of obsolete paddle-steamers.

Meanwhile, Bombay's merchants, anxious to live as palatially and as efficiently as Calcutta's, winced at the Company's penny-pinching on the mail route (as they would have winced at any extravagance), lobbying all and sundry. 'It is notorious to those resident in Bombay,' said *The*

17   Calcutta after the great cyclone of 1864

Morning Post, 'that the conveyance of passengers and merchandise is a duty generally disliked by the officers of the Indian Navy, and very reluctantly performed by them'.[15] The Court of Directors in London finally surrendered their monopoly in 1852, and handed over all mail services to P.&O.

The efficiency of these services was greatly augmented a year later when the Great Peninsular Railway was opened, linking the Bombay islands with the mainland and the mainland with British India's other cities, eventually Calcutta. Now it was quicker to cross the subcontinent by train than to steam round Ceylon. The docks expanded, more land was reclaimed, the Bombay Coast and River Navigation Company, which took passengers north to Karachi, built a Mogul palace for its waterfront offices. The Apollo Bunder near the docks became a fashionable resort in the evenings and instead of the tents in which Emma Roberts maintained most passengers would set up home in the 1830s there were even two hotels. Passengers and the volume of mail grew, one load of letters about this time weighing 45 tons.

P.&O. launched its answer to the Mediterranean competition of Messageries Impériales in 1854. The *Himalaya* was the largest vessel afloat when it left Southampton that year – 3438 tons and 372 feet long – and combined all the latest technology with the ultimate in luxuries. The most dramatic innovations were the iron hull and screw propulsion. Both of these had been put to the test some years earlier after Brunel's commitment to them in his *Great Britain* completed in 1843. Brunel began his ship as a wooden paddle-steamer in 1838; a year later he was ordering an iron keel and just over a year after that he cancelled his order for paddles and placed one for a screw propeller. With the *Great Britain* Brunel went a good way towards converting the commercial shipping world to a belief in iron at sea. It was cheaper than wood, more buoyant and much stronger, as was demonstrated when the *Great Britain* withstood a winter's battering on the coast of northern Ireland when she was stranded there in 1846. The Admiralty was harder to convince, however, and those dependent on government mail contracts had to comply with government, in other words Admiralty, specifications. Few engineers were entirely happy with screw propulsion because of the inadequate power of the low-pressure engines to drive the propeller.

Anderson demonstrated his wholehearted conversion by ordering the *Himalaya*, not the first screw-propelled vessel ordered by P.&O. but certainly the largest contemplated by anyone for many years. Built at Blackwall, she boasted size and proportions sufficient to attract a regular crowd of sightseers and expert admirers. 'Time was when we could with truth and justice boast of our "wooden walls",' wrote the *Birkenhead Advertiser* in 1853, 'as an impregnable fortress . . . Now we may, with ever greater confidence, boast of our "iron walls." '[16] Her major problem was the inefficiency of those low-pressure engines – fine for driving paddles but inadequate for the faster-moving propeller – and her coal consumption made her thoroughly uneconomical. War, breaking out in the Black Sea in 1854 a month after the *Himalaya*'s maiden voyage, emphasised her unprofitability when the extra demand doubled the price of coal. 'The coal spectre,' Anderson joked with shareholders, 'assumed a very formidable attitude, was really very black to look at.'[17] Fortunately, perhaps, *The Illustrated London News* had already calculated that she could carry 3,000 men to Constantinople and the Black Sea and Anderson must have heaved a sigh of relief when the government asked to lease *Himalaya* as a troop ship, and an even deeper sigh when the government offered to buy it.

But before that she made one commercial voyage to Alexandria under the command of a Captain Kellock, carrying among others a group of East India Company recruits, who thoroughly enjoyed the trip. She was taken out of the dock by two steam tugs, with crowds of spectators lining the docks and a band playing 'Cheer, boys, cheer!' and 'The girl I left behind me.' Spinning yarns, playing cards, listening to the brass band helped passengers over their homesickness: one passenger, young William Adamson, declared he had never met with a merrier and more social set of people.[18] He himself was to be employed in Singapore. After the pomp and ceremony of assembling a suitable wardrobe for the east he was greatly relieved to discover that dressing for dinner and appearing fashionable on deck was all humbug; 'certainly they all dress as gentlemen and conduct themselves as such, also they consume half an hour before dinner in washing,' changing linen and so on (and Adamson's cabin was particularly well set up in having its own toilet), 'but they do not appear in dress coats or anything of that sort, neither is there any exclusiveness or keeping aloof on the part of anyone.' Everyone ate an enormous quantity of food; he never saw such good use made of knives and forks before. One tried to make room for the next helping of curry and rice by pacing seven times round the deck to make a mile. Even the acute pain of departure had yielded to a quiet sort of melancholy by the time they reached the Mediterranean, perhaps accentuated by those Sunday sermons to the young fellows going to India, warning and exhorting them on their course of life there. 'Tell mother,' wrote Adamson dutifully in his first letter home, posted in Gibraltar, 'I made use of my sewing materials this morning.'

The only black spot on Adamson's journey was Egypt. The travellers were almost torn to pieces by donkey owners on landing at Alexandria; 'a number of us got donkeys and rode about but I cannot say we were much delighted with what we saw.' The canal boat was small and dirty; Adamson had to sleep under the table 'with my bag as a pillow and my coat for mattress and blanket.' Cairo was all right, the Pasha's palace very gorgeous, with mainly French furnishings. There was nothing to be seen on the desert crossing except sand and camels live and dead – 'the latter very plentiful' – and vultures. 'This being our last post in Egypt,' he wrote from Suez, 'is to all of us a source of delight. I never was in a more miserable looking land . . . no ordinary inducement would make me live either in Alexandria or Cairo.' Adamson had little real cause for complaint; it had taken him only thirty days to get all the way from London to Suez.

It would take another thirty-one days to steam the nearly 5,000 miles

from Suez to Calcutta, sixteen to eighteen days for the 3,000 miles from
Suez to Bombay. Down the Red Sea Adamson's disgruntlement
continued. He was now on the *Oriental*, not nearly so well fitted up as
the *Himalaya*. There was plenty of jam and marmalade but the table
was not otherwise well supplied. The young amused themselves by
climbing the rigging; an old lady was unable to sleep for fear a cockroach
should eat her toenails; the apology for a library was in a wretched
condition, 'a few works of voyages and travels, some volumes of
Wellington's despatches and a number of Church of England prayer-
books.' At Aden, where Bombay passengers disembarked to pick up
their connecting steamer, everything was covered with coal dust. But
before he put his journal away on reaching Singapore, his destination,
Adamson demonstrated just what a difference to life overseas a mere
six weeks' journey rather than eight months meant: in a letter to his
father posted at Point de Galle in Ceylon he asked him to send out a
small book of songs he left behind, or any other book containing the
words of the popular songs of the day.

Sitting that same year in the fly-bedecked dining room of the Hôtel
de l'Inde at Suez was Ferdinand de Lesseps, thanking Waghorn for the
ingredients of his meal brought by steam to so godforsaken a spot. The
swift communication of pop songs did almost as much credit as de
Lesseps' Calcutta mutton and French wine to the efforts of steam
committees, parliamentary committees, Willcox and Anderson as well
as to Waghorn himself.

Nor did the glamour of steam travel fade or the Overland Route ever
lack publicity. In 1853, for instance, a certain Tom Taylor wrote a play,
performed in London and Manchester, set aboard a P.&O. Red Sea
steamer, the *Simoom*.[19] Most of the action is at sea, although in the last
act the ship has gone aground on one of those dreaded coral reefs.
Romance, villainy, flirtation, a touch of gambling and never a hint of
boredom for the London-bound passengers. There are comforts – food
of course, and drink, cabins, Venetian blinds, a handsomely decorated
saloon, chairs on the deck, four musicians playing the end of an
unspecified overture. Against a flaming tropical sky an amorous female
reads from *Don Juan* to an amorous male. What better advertisement
for steam travel could one possibly want?

6

War

The story of steaming east has hitherto been one largely of commercial impetus, with political considerations occasionally giving trade a little extra leverage. By the 1840s politics was beginning to have the louder voice, especially in the territories of the dilapidated Ottoman Empire.

The intricacies of European relations in the nineteenth century have been frequently and well described[1] and must always be borne in mind as one follows the development of steam routes eastward across and beyond Europe, both on land and on sea. In 1815 most of Europe was exhausted by the Napoleonic wars and with the exception of Britain, which emerged relatively unscathed, was too impoverished for some years to do more than wait for the wounds to heal. British statesmen retained a deep suspicion of continental powers as a result of the wars, but gained a head start in strengthening the maritime defences not only of the British Isles but also of India, the vulnerability of which it was felt had been exposed by Napoleon's expedition to Egypt in 1798 and his later negotiations with Russia and Persia, all aimed at India.

Major land approaches from Europe to India, for the first part of the nineteenth century, lay through the Ottoman Empire whose survival was therefore seen by the British as protecting those land routes. Within Europe the political concern with the well-being or otherwise of the Ottoman Empire became known in the latter part of the century as the Eastern Question; to the British in India, imbued with strong sporting instincts when it came to nomenclature even in the mountain fastnesses of northern India and Afghanistan, the extension of the Eastern Question into Central Asia became the Great Game, played against Russia. The name of the Game is often attributed to Arthur Conolly, possibly from a letter written in 1840 to Henry Rawlinson: 'you've a great game, a *noble* one, before you.'[2] It was not a lighthearted game to which he was referring. The more communications with India improved, the more jealously they were guarded by Britain and the more apprehensively they were eyed by France and Russia, wary of Britain's commercial and maritime supremacy.

Signs of British concern about Russian expansionism and Ottoman

18 Constantinople in the 1840s, showing paddle steamers at the entrance to the Golden Horn. The safeguarding of freedom of navigation through the Dardanelles was one of the causes of the Crimean War.

weakness were demonstrated in the political reaction to Chesney's ideas and the backing for his expedition in 1836. The concern developed slowly. An opportunity to reduce their vulnerability at the Dardanelles – 'the gates of our house,' the Tsar complained when other European powers badgered the Sultan to prevent Russia controlling the Straits – occurred for the Russians in the 1830s with the Egyptian invasion of Ottoman Syria. In desperation the Sultan turned for help to the European powers. Only one responded: Russia, in the process gaining virtual control of the vital waterways.

In the ensuing outcry certain characteristics of the Eastern Question emerged. Above all there was a deep unshiftable distrust between Britain and Russia, based partly on the question of freedom of navigation in the Black Sea, and more indirectly, emotionally and sweepingly on the question of those routes to India and Central Asia. Few British commentators travelling through or observing the Near East, Russia itself or adjoining lands, disputed the distrust. The Russians responded with similar defensiveness in Central Asia and around the Black Sea. The French, perhaps feeling they had less to lose and a great deal to gain, observed the distrust with disdain or amusement but were above all concerned that in the dismemberment of the Ottoman corpse their own interests should not be curtailed. The curtailer was most likely, in French eyes, to be Britain but from time to time British and French governments saw Russia as a common enemy. In the mean time the movement of armies amidst the development of communications went on. Steam was the motive force, for the British at sea, for the rest generally on land.

In the middle of the nineteenth century, political anxieties matured into violence. A simmering dispute over guardianship of the holy places in Jerusalem in the early 1850s grew out of hand when the Sultan, urged by the domineering British ambassador Stratford Canning, rejected the Russian demand to be recognised as protector of the Greek Church in the Ottoman Empire. 'Our passage to India depends upon our conduct in the present crisis,' declared Harriet Martineau in the *Westminster Review*.[3] In Parliament Palmerston fulminated against the sins of the Tsar; in the *New York Tribune* in April 1855 Karl Marx was to write that 'although John Bull can do a little annexation business himself now and then in India, he has no idea of allowing other people to do the same in other neighbourhoods in an uncomfortable proximity to himself or his possessions.'[4] In July 1853 Tsar Nicholas I ordered Russian troops into the Danubian principalities. In October fighting broke out between Russia and the Turks in the Caucasus, which was already viewed by Russia as a crucial link between Europe and Asia. In November the Russian fleet cornered the Turkish at Sinope on the southern shore of the Black Sea. In the ensuing battle the Turkish fleet was demolished, the Sultan turned to France and Britain for help and in January 1854 the allied fleets, which had been hovering round the Dardanelles since the previous summer, entered the Black Sea. War was declared in March.

Symbolically the news of the declaration of war was carried through the Dardanelles to the allied fleets on board the little steam packet *Banshee*. For their fighting vessels European naval authorities were hovering on the brink of accepting the new technology but still hesitant about innovation; the British naval and political establishment particularly believed that such radical change was tantamount to the destruction of Britain's naval superiority. In 1850 steam was used to power naval communications but not to power battles. Troop transports, little steam tugs towing as many as three ships of the line at once, and the electric telegraph between government and battlefield enabled the allies to transport whole armies from Europe to the remote peninsula of Crimea. But when it came to fighting vessels naval authorities had still not solved the problem of combining sail and steam or of devising new tactics to make the most of steam-powered mobility.

Fulton had built the first steam warship, the tiny *Demologos*, as far back as 1815 to defend New York harbour against the British. But it was certainly not designed for the open sea. In the twenty years or so following the Napoleonic wars, despite the public interest in steam for communications, naval authorities in Britain and France were pervaded by an economising mood that accorded well with their innate conservatism. For example in 1828 the Lords of the Admiralty felt it their bounden duty 'to discourage to the utmost of their ability the employment of steam vessels, as they consider the introduction of steam is calculated to strike a fatal blow to the supremacy of the Empire.'[5] Few ships of the line were suitable for conversion to steam as long as that was linked to low-pressure engines; there was simply not enough room between decks for broadside guns as well as boilers, engines and their coal. Paddles were liable to be shot off, the cumbersome machinery was above water and therefore also vulnerable. Moreover steam vessels were dependent on regular fuel supplies. The political establishment was no more eager for these so-called 'tea kettles': Palmerston characteristically warned his colleagues that 'steam navigation rendered that which was before impassable by a military force nothing more than a river passable by a steam bridge.'[6]

Nevertheless steam had its uses and both French and British navies had already employed small paddle-steamers as packet boats and also to tow ships of the line under sail. The first French war steamer was the diminutive *Sphinx*, launched in 1829 and later used to tow the Luxor obelisk from Egypt to Rouen. In 1837 the British Admiralty launched the *Gorgon*, a little paddle-steamer later involved off Acre against the Egyptians in 1840. The *Gorgon* was fitted with the first vertical direct-action engines patented in 1822 by Marc Brunel, father of Isambard. They weighed about two-fifths less than the old side-lever engines and were more economical of space, although still driving paddle wheels. She was used to tow fighting vessels but also lobbed shells from close inshore; it was probably a *Gorgon* shell that blew up the magazine of Acre fortress, killing over 1000 men. By 1840 the British navy could call on almost 700 of these little steamers, nearly a third of which had engines powerful enough to tow fighting ships, which were themselves still dependent on sail. The French had also been hesitant to adopt steam for their fighting vessels but faced with the chronic Anglo-French hostility of the 1840s gradually gave in. The marine steam engine and a revolutionary exploding shell invented in

1822 by the French General Paixhans placed the old wooden navies at a disadvantage; the Paixhans shell was particularly threatening to line-of-battle ships, producing an explosion in the timber or within the hull; it was to be used with devastating effect by the Russians at the battle of Sinope, where it helped them to wipe out the Turkish fleet. Such developments were viewed by certain French naval strategists as potentially compensating them for Britsh naval supremacy. In Britain they prompted the invasion scares of 1844 and 1852.

Neither country made substantial progress with steam in fighting vessels, however, until the advent of the screw propeller. Accounts of the screw propeller often make it sound as if it was immediately recognised as a revolutionary improvement to steam propulsion. This was far from the case; more accurately, as a French naval historian wrote, 'cette histoire est jalonnée de misère humaine, diffamation, procès, polémiques, revendications.'[7] The early propellers of Frédéric Sauvage, Francis Pettit Smith and John Ericsson, as well as of their many predecessors, were not very satisfactory when driven by low-pressure engines and these leading inventors had a frustrating time bobbing up and down French and British rivers and canals trying to convert their various passengers. The screw was particularly suited to war vessels, as it was below the water and thus less vulnerable than paddles, but naval authorities insisted on engines similarly sited below water level to drive it.

In 1837 Francis Pettit Smith, a Hendon farmer, had such success with a screw propeller on Paddington Canal that a syndicate was formed to back its application to a larger vessel. The *Archimedes* was launched the next year. At the same time John Ericsson, a Swedish engineer living in England, who had already designed a locomotive, the *Novelty*, and entered it for the Rainhill trials of 1829, also took out a patent for a screw propeller and even invited an Admiralty party out on the Thames in 1836 to convince them of its advantages, but without much success. The Admiralty was most uneasy at the idea of a hole in the stern of the vessel where the propeller emerged and they thought the screw might get in the way of the rudder. An American, Captain Robert Stockton, came to Ericsson's rescue, inviting him to demonstrate his theories in the United States, and in 1842 helped launch there the first screw warship, *Princeton*. Ericsson's second experimental vessel, the iron *Robert E. Stockton*, was built by Laird's of Birkenhead and demonstrated on the Thames before sailing across the Atlantic to work as a steam tug in New York harbour. Ericsson himself went on to invent the armoured gun turret.

Frédéric Sauvage was treated by the French Ministry of Marine with as much suspicion as Ericsson and Smith had been by the Admiralty, firmly told that the screw 'était impuisant sur une grand échelle.'[8] But the Ministry of Finance was cannier and asked France's leading shipbuilder, Augustin Normand of Le Havre, to design a packet boat capable of at least 8 knots. Normand was the founder of a family of prominent shipbuilders who worked in Le Havre for many generations; his grandson Benjamin was to develop the triple expansion engine there in the 1860s. In 1842, in collaboration with a British engineer named Barnes, Normand launched a small screw-driven packet boat, *Le Napoléon*. In 1850 came the launching of a far grander *Napoléon* designed by the great French engineer Dupuy de Lôme, with 900-horsepower engines, capable of steaming at 13 knots albeit with serious vibration; the problem of driving the screw still remained. This *Napoléon* became the fleet's flagship.

By now Brunel was changing his latest project, the 3,600-ton *Great Britain*, from a giant paddle-driven steamer to one propelled by a screw. It was finally launched in 1843; after a somewhat unhappy career, some of it spent grounded on the rocky coast of Ireland, it ended up as a coal hulk in the Falklands and was brought back to Bristol in 1971 to be restored. The British navy ordered its first screw-propelled vessel in 1842, again a small packet boat. But the final commitment awaited the results of a famous tug-of-war, staged in 1845, between two war sloops, the *Rattler* fitted with a screw propeller and the *Alecto* fitted with paddles. The vessels were tied stern to stern and both steamed full speed ahead. Soon the audience could see that the *Rattler* was towing its opponent. 'L'Amirauté anglaise a toujours aimé les matches et les décisions simplistes,' commented the French.

Some of the doubts of French and British naval authorities are understandable. Many different screws and arrangements in the stern were designed before a satisfactory speed was attained. The design of early screw-propelled vessels left much to be desired; one, the *Penelope*, was cut in two, lengthened by 65 feet and fitted with 650-horsepower engines to drive her screw but the changes left her floating so low in the water that wits dubbed her the porpoise of the British navy. Sterns were too rounded to allow a free flow of water to the screw; engineers had to learn to fine down the stern. This problem vanished when the multiple screw came into use. The design of the propeller and its shaft also went through a number of changes before the gearing, pitch, blade and screw size reached the right degree of compatibility and durability.

The other issue facing navies in mid-century was the question of timber versus iron for hulls. Laird's of Birkenhead worked hard to try to convince the Admiralty of the merits of iron, amply demonstrated in a succession of flat-bottomed river steamers, especially those used in India and China; they had built an iron steam tug, the *Robert E. Stockton*, as Ericsson's second experimental vessel, which was eventually dispatched across the Atlantic to New York harbour. But the Admiralty, wedded to its hearts of oak, was convinced that iron was not good at resisting shot, maintaining after shooting trials on a little iron steamer named *Ruby* that a hole in a timber hull could be more easily plugged. An iron bottom was also more prone to fouling and there were still problems with using a compass on iron oceangoing vessels. Moreover it was a condition of all government mail contracts that the vessels built to carry the mail should be convertible for military use in time of war. Much to Arthur Anderson's disgust, therefore, in 1846 the government prohibited the use of iron for packet vessels or potential troop carriers. Although a few years later Anderson was allowed an iron hull for the *Himalaya*, wooden fighting vessels continued to be built well into the 1870s. At the time of the Crimean War neither French nor British had a single iron fighting ship although the Russian victory at Sinope had demonstrated the all too devastating effect of the Paixhans shell on the wooden hulls of the Turkish navy.

Despite this vacillation over technology British and French fleets were vastly more efficient in 1854 than the Russian, dependent enough on steam to evoke nostalgia for the fading days of sail. 'Liners under canvas that once settled the fate of empires, are now considered "slow coaches", without the aid of the modern auxiliary [screw],' wrote 'an Old Man-o'-War's Man' in *Bentley's Miscellany*, 'and we are beginning to look forward with real sorrow to the day when the "white bosom'd sail" will be remembered amongst the glorious visions of the past. Black grimy stokers supply the place of neat sail-trimmers and active topmen, and the opening and shutting of a valve gives and takes away the motion of a line of battle ship.'[9] 'The power of bringing an enemy to close quarters, and avoiding long chases, is one of the greatest advantages a "screw" fleet possesses, and is, moreover, well adapted to our peculiar bull-dog mode of fighting.' There were notes of caution: 'but ... we must not blind ourselves to the fact that our "screws" are, up to this time, not only a novelty in war, but an experiment; they have not yet earned their spurs.'

Still, no one could deny the fact that, thanks to the little packet steamers, the allied fleets were more mobile. The allies dispatched over 200 steamers to the Black Sea, using them for communications and for manipulating the great sailing ships of the line. A small packet boat could tow two or even three ships of the line as well as transports. 'The smoke was for all the world like Staffordshire.' Most of the little packet steamers were built of iron, turned out as fast as possible by Laird's and Normand's shipyards. The Russian fleet, after its success at Sinope, spent the war holed up in Sebastopol harbour where the ships' ill-seasoned pine timbers were even more vulnerable than the French and British oak to the local underwater marine life.

Steamboats also made the allied armies more mobile. Troops entrained at Waterloo for Southampton or Portsmouth; special excursion trains were laid on for admiring and patriotic spectators (96 miles in three hours); paddle-steamers advertised trips around the fleet and the Queen came to see her army off from her steam yacht. In the Solent the troops boarded P.&O.'s handsome steamers; eleven of its best ships were taken up by the British government by the end of 1854 and the company had to close down its Australian mail service for lack of vessels to service it. Within a few months of young Adamson's voyage aboard the *Himalaya* she was commandeered by the government to transport British troops in a far less luxurious style to the Crimean War. In due course the British government bought the *Himalaya*, somewhat to P.&O.'s relief although for only half the £130,000 the company had paid in the first place; the company had over-extended its mail operations, and was also financially pressed by an unprecedented rise in the price of coal and the cost of updating its fleet from the old wooden paddle-steamers to powerful but coal-hungry vessels such as the *Himalaya*. But while the *Himalaya* was a luxurious liability for P.&O., she was a godsend to the government, able to transport an entire cavalry regiment on her first troop-carrying voyage, including all its horses and equipment. P.&O.'s steamboats alone carried some 62,000 soldiers and 15,000 horses in the course of the war and Alfred Holt of the Blue Funnel Line reckoned that the lavish freight rates which the government was prepared to pay resulted in the making of steam-borne freight business; a steamer could repay its capital investment in twelve months. Another life-saving venture of P.&O.'s was the use of its packet steamer *Vectis* to bring Florence Nightingale and her nurses from Marseilles to Scutari in November 1854.

The Crimean War was not of course a naval war, rather to the disgust of Captain, later Admiral, George Heath, who complained loudly of being ordered to transport troops rather than getting down to the meat of the business.[10] Even the Baltic campaign, fought on Russia's northern shore, was little more than a series of blockades with no engagement sufficiently heated to prove the value of fighting steam one way or the other. But many of those who fought the war on land were transported by steamboats, they were victualled, from time to time, by steamboats and they were taken to hospital by steamboats.

The vessels Heath commanded to transport the sick from the Crimea back to Florence Nightingale's care at Scutari were still basically sailing vessels, with auxillary steam that left him feeling stuffed with coal. Moreover the funnel got in the way of the sails although on some vessels it could be partially telescoped to get it out of the way. In Heath's opinion the only good thing about a load of coal was that when stacked carefully inside the hull it acted as protection against shot. But even Heath was finally converted to steam, despite the frequency with which the engines broke down, when captain of the screw ship of the line, *Sanspareil*. The inefficiency of her rickety engines, strained by driving a screw propeller, was indeed unparalleled, he wrote, 'but still she must be far better than any mere sailing ship.'

Many have described the Crimean War as a war which should never have been fought. Though it lasted barely two years, that was long enough to confirm the value of naval steam. The British fleet was divided between the Black Sea, where it was mainly involved in blockading Russian ports, and the Baltic, the latter a relatively shallow sea with long stretches of coastline inaccessible to the navy's deep-keeled sloops and frigates. The Admiralty's draughtsmen devised a flotilla of steam-powered screw-propelled gunboats which relied on their engines rather than sails and could scour the shores to destroy fortifications. Gunboats were supposed to be able to float in two metres of water and mount two 68-pounder guns; some 120 boats were on order by 1856, all engined by either Penn & Co. or Maudslay, Son and Field. They were also used in the Black Sea, and proved their value in the blockade of the narrow entrance to the Sea of Azov behind Sebastopol. Another innovation came into its own in the last major naval action in the Black Sea – powerful iron-plated floating batteries used to destroy the fortress of Kinburn at the mouth of the Dniepr. These later developed into the ironclads.

Within months of the outbreak of war the allies were concentrating on the Russian fortifications of Sebastopol whose massive strength, especially on the seaward side, were dangerously underestimated by French and British generals comfortably ensconced aboard their steam yachts, including that 'noble yachtsman' Lord Cardigan aboard his steam yacht *Dryad*. The men camped beneath the walls had no food, no clothes, no medicine, nothing even to drink; they wallowed in a sea of mud covering the seven miles that separated them from the inadequate supplies aboard the ships anchored in Balaklava Bay. In November a violent storm sank thirty-three ships bringing winter supplies, including fodder for draught horses. 'Ships were crashing and crowding together, all adrift, all breaking and grinding each other to pieces . . .,' wrote Fanny Duberley on board ship in the normally sheltered harbour.[11] 'By ten o'clock we heard that the most fearful wrack was going on outside [the harbour] amongst the ships at anchor.' Screw-driven colliers from Union Steam Collier Company had been commandeered to ship wooden huts to the Crimea but the materials could not be transported through the mud. W. H. Russell of *The Times* reported the misery, the sickness, the deaths decimating the forces;[12] *Punch* published cartoons almost as devastating to public opinion of the government as the winds to the men in their pitiful tents. Better leadership of the army would be provided by 'the great railway administrators and contractors,' Russell wrote, 'the men who manage lines of packets, who own and direct successfully the operation of whole fleets of merchant ships . . . men who, conducting their own operations with unfailing regularity, look with scorn on the miserable and repeated proofs of official blundering which has so grievously misdirected and wasted unbounded resources.' Well, said one of the greatest railway contractors of the period, Samuel Peto, turning to his fellow contractor Thomas Brassey, this surely is our challenge. When Peto and Brassey suggested that they should ship, build and run a railway line from sea to soldiers – at cost – the government leaped at the offer.

Railway development so far had been concentrated domestically, for economic and social reasons. This was its first venture into the political sphere, significantly enough in the context of the Eastern Question. The little Crimean line is hardly a fair assessment of the state of railway steam, 'an inefficient apology of a railway', according to E. A. Pratt, the historian of railways at war.[13] But it was quite an achievement in the circumstances. Never before had railways been used in war. But their potential was already being recognised and would be used in the future – much as steamboats in the Crimean war – to increase the mobility of armies. In some parts of the world, notably in the Middle East and Central Asia, this would be seen as their prime purpose. Light railways could be quickly built; there was no need to construct time-consuming embankments; the gauge was kept narrow to manipulate the line easily round contours; and the light locomotives used on them meant light ballasting for the track.

Within days of their offer being accepted Brassey and Peto had twenty-three steamers on the way to the Crimea loaded with men, 'great big English carthorses', engines and commissariat. Russell's publicity ensured plenty of volunteers even at navvy level, many of them hardened to winter by building lines in Canada; throbbing with patriotism *The Illustrated London News* described them as 'broad, muscular fellows, who are scarcely to be matched in Europe. Animated, too, by as ardent a British spirit as beats under any uniform, if ever these men come to hand-to-hand fighting with the enemy, they will fell them like ninepins.'[14]

Twelve days from the arrival of the first convoy (1,800 tons of rails

19   Railway works at Balaklava, organized by railway contractors Samuel Peto and Thomas Brassey to transport supplies to troops besieging Sebastopol

and fastenings, 6,000 sleepers, 600 tons of timber, engines, cranes, piling engines and so on) chief engineer Beattie had 7 miles of double line laid. Beattie was later injured when an overloaded train's brakes failed, and he died soon after from his injuries, much to everyone's dismay. Russell went off one day to visit front-line regiments and returned the next day to find a railway running across the courtyard of his lodgings. Despite a tendency to go on strike, 'the navvies in spite of the absence of beefsteaks and "Barkley and Perkins Entire" work famously,' wrote one Captain Clifford, 'and as I have mentioned do more work in a day, than a Regiment of English soldiers do in a week.'[15]

A total of 29 miles were eventually completed by the middle of April. For the first two miles from the coast the train was pulled by a locomotive, over the next stretch it was winched up an incline by a stationary engine, then came a level stretch, then two gullies which trucks had to run down and up under their own momentum and finally a section over which the train was drawn by horses. Later other locomotives arrived at Balaklava that were heavy enough to pull the wagons along the entire route. 'The whistling locos on the railway – the Alliance, the Victory – recalled to us the familiar sounds of Wolverhampton or of Swindon, and made us believe we were in a civilised country,' wrote Russell.

Food, water and clothing were soon reaching the troops. Sebastopol fell in September 1855 before another winter set in. Tsar Nicholas I, his forward policy in ruins, had died in March 1855, and his successor, Alexander, was obliged to settle for peace at the Congress of Paris early in 1856. Russia's southern expansion was halted for the time being and the British felt they had at least temporarily halted the great bear's threat to India.

Within a few months of signing the Treaty of Paris that ended the war British nerves were again set on edge by new movements in the Great Game. In Persia and Afghanistan each side was identifying certain sensitive points where any activity could be taken as a sign of aggressive intent. One such point was Herat, within the western border of Afghanistan. Commanding the lush green valley of the Hari Rud, Herat had been a major caravan city on the road between east and west, communicating to the west with the Caspian Sea and Mesopotamia and to the south-east via the Afghan city of Kandahar with India. Its heyday in the fifteenth century was a period of peace and prosperity; it became (and remained until the Russian occupation of Afghanistan in the 1980s) a city of enormous charm and beauty, embellished at that time by mosques, schools, palaces and tombs that were financed by the trade that passed through its gates. Herat has always been a place close to Persian hearts.

By the 1850s Persia had become a pawn in the struggle between Britain and Russia to gain control of the great thoroughfares of the region. A previous Persian attack on Herat in 1837–8, encouraged by Russia, had led ultimately to the disastrous British involvement in Afghanistan and the First Afghan War of 1842. The second attack on Herat in 1856 was again encouraged by the Russians, who hoped to take advantage of British involvement in the Crimea. This time the British responded elsewhere. When the ruler of Afghanistan, Dost Muhammad, appealed to the British to help him rebuff the Persian occupation of Herat in 1856, the British authorities in India dispatched a small but highly mobile expedition up the Gulf to attack Persia in the rear.

The Anglo–Persian War was brief and conclusive. Its effectiveness was largely due to the intelligent use of steam power. Troop transports, river steamers and gunboats were able to make their way upriver and attack the enemy's defences from well inshore. The expedition – some 14,000 officers, men and animals transported on P.&O. and Indian navy vessels from Bombay – moved so fast that its leader, General James Outram, in England at the time of his appointment, only reached his forces after much of the action was over. The island of Kharg was captured on December 4th, and Bushire five days later. Outram arrived in January, via the Overland Route, and the expedition moved swiftly up the Shatt al-Arab, some of it on board sailing vessels towed by steam packets. The shallow draught of the latter proved invaluable at this season of low water. The city of Muhammarah (now Khuramshahr), a few miles up the smaller Karun river, was soon captured; 'the war vessels did their work admirably; silenced the batteries in about three hours and then the troops passed up in steamers,' wrote Outram.[16] Part of the expedition was then sent further up the Karun river to follow the remnants of the Persian army. Despite their shallow draught the vessels frequently went aground. Another problem was shortage of coal; Outram was later blamed in some quarters for not pursuing the Persians more effectively but his dispatches include urgent appeals for more coal to be sent to Bushire. 'What a thousand pities we had not the means of following up the enemy; but without coal and cattle it is impossible of course.' British hegemony in the Gulf hereafter ensured that no such shortages would occur again. The Persians were soon suing for peace and a treaty was signed in Paris in March 1857. Outram was delighted that he would be able to get his men out before the heat really set in. But by June he was anxious for more desperate reasons.

He had received 'very startling news from Karachi,' he wrote on June 8th to Lord Stratford de Redcliffe (formerly Stratford Canning), ambassador in Constantinople: 'the native troops of the Bengal army in insurrection from Delhi and upwards . . . at Delhi Europeans had been massacred.' From India the governor Lord Elphinstone sent an urgent plea for Outram to return the troops from the Gulf as quickly as possible.

The outbreak of the Indian Mutiny in May 1857 in Meerut was far more traumatic for the British at home and in India than the little-noticed war with Persia. The news of the Meerut massacre reached London in thirty days, dispatched by steam via Egypt; Outram reckoned that his letter, sent by messenger to Stratford and thence by telegraph to London, probably brought London its first word of the mutiny. Despite the fact that the disaster coincided with the monsoon, troops were rushed from west coast to east, up and down the west coast and across the Indian Ocean, proving once and for all that steam was now able to supply strength and manoeuvrability capable of conquering the winds and currents of alien oceans. Reinforcements steamed in from Aden, the Cape and Mauritius, and Outram's men came from the Gulf, disembarking on monsoon-lashed coasts and marching to the relief of Lucknow and Delhi.

Transporting troops to India from Britain posed a rather more serious problem. The mutiny showed that Britain could not depend on holding its Indian possessions with Indian troops. There was considerable opposition to using the Overland Route through Egypt, not least from the indomitable Palmerston, who still commanded a dogmatic and somewhat xenophobic section of public opinion. When the British were fighting as allies of the Turks and the French as in the Crimean War, the Overland Route had served the British well and had been used to bring troops from India, some of them on sailing vessels so loaded with hay for the horses on board that it was difficult to shift the sails. Some passers-by had run up such excessive debts at Cairo's Shepheard's Hotel that the proprietor, Samuel Shepheard, chased them all the way to the Crimea to get his money back.

By 1857 the governor of Egypt, now Muhammad Said Pasha, was known to be much friendlier to the French than to the British, and one Frenchman in particular, Ferdinand de Lesseps, was already working hard at his favourite project to link Mediterranean and Red Sea by a canal through Egypt. The Pasha might well close Egypt to the passage of foreign troops, maintained Palmerston; even worse the French might copy the British and also decide to send troops on that route eastwards. The Cape route was fine; Britain after all controlled the oceans; and the first reinforcements went to India that way, taking three months to do so. Some sixty-eight transports were anchored in Table Bay in December 1857, including the *Himalaya* and the *Great Britain*; most of the rest were sailing vessels because there were few steamers large enough to carry both passengers and sufficient coal for the onward voyage to India.

Even when the government agreed to use the Overland Route, it took time for the diplomats on the spot to win Turkish and Egyptian authorisation for the passage of troops. P.&O. again came to the government's rescue in shipping the troops – some 6,000 of them eventually – all issued in Alexandria with regulation tropical gear of long smock frocks and white linen caps with long lappets to protect the neck from the sun. Part of the desert stretch was crossed now by a railway on which the troops were 'uncommon well fed with tea and coffee, Irish stews and all sorts of meat, bread and vegetables,' according to a young man with P.&O., Mr Kendall.[17]

That was only part of the crossing, however; when the tracks ended the journey had to be completed by the familiar assortment of vehicles and animals. 'Then came the fun of the day,' wrote Kendall, 'seeing the soldiers all mount their donkeys. The officers showed them how to mount first and the largest officer, a man about 6ft. 4″ and stout in proportion, mounted the smallest donkey he could find and rode around amongst the men, much to their amusement . . .' The unfortunate

20   Federal ironclads on the Mississippi during the American Civil War, such vessels developed from the stationary but floating iron gun batteries devised by the French in the Crimean War

animals – unless they broke down, as several did – had to carry the men
the whole 25 miles to Suez over a road where the hot sand was generally
over their fetlocks. Suez presented its usual lack of comfort and troops
were kept waiting on board the *Zenobia*, a kind of floating hotel
unpopular with its residents because of an earlier odoriferous incarna-
tion as a hog transport between Waterford and Bristol. There were
even murmurs of mutiny. But for the authorities it was worth it: sixteen
days to transport troops from Malta to Bombay had a stimulating effect
on imperial strategy.

The Crimean War established the validity of steam-powered navies.
Subsequently new ships of the line were universally driven by steam.
They still retained the old pattern of three towering gun decks and
were, for the time being, still built of wood; when they lowered their
telescopic funnels they looked much the same as the ships that had
fought at Trafalgar. The British government remained devoted to wood
and continued to order wooden war vessels up to 1860. By then the
French navy was rapidly being converted to ironclad construction,
threatening to make the entire British navy obsolete. The time had
come to change; Britain launched her first ironclad, the *Warrior*, in
1861.

Meanwhile the Mutiny, the Anglo–Persian War as well as the
Crimean War had all proved the value of steam in mobilising an
imperial army. Sea power made it possible to maintain relatively small
highly mobile armed forces. In the case of the Crimean War the security
of sea communications was seen as essential to the defeat of powerful
land forces. Britain was to depend on a steam-powered fleet to meet
perceived threats, especially from Central Asia, with a reliable and
flexible British army rather than dubiously reliable Indian troops. For a
while the military authorities in Britain toyed with purpose-built troop
ships and one, the *Serapis*, was commissioned in 1866; she was
extremely unpopular with those obliged to voyage in her, however, and
thereafter vessels were hired regularly from commercial shipping lines,
notably the Bibby Line of Liverpool. But military mobility was now
about to be enhanced still further, and the whole strategy, economic
and political, of steaming between east and west was to be drastically
changed.

7

'A Dismal but Profitable Ditch'

So said Joseph Conrad, recalling his application for a job as a pilot on the Suez Canal:[1] hardly a ditch, some might say, but dismal, yes, and profitable in the long run. The Isthmus of Suez is a bleak monotonous landscape, a stony plain interspersed with the swamps and marshlands of the Bitter Lakes and Lake Menzaleh, still the haunt of migratory birds that turn their backs on the monstrous cargo vessels gliding morosely along the narrow waterway. Yet the emptiness of that arid plain underlines the magnificence of the achievement, the canal's course marked by ships that hourly float like a mirage on the surface of the desert itself. The isthmus was ideally suited to the cutting of a canal between Mediterranean and Red Sea because of its featurelessness, and the engineers who directed its construction had very few complications to cope with. The problems were financial and political.

The story of steaming east so far has been largely about British enterprise. Now it moves to France. To British chagrin Egypt was very much a French preserve. In the early years of direct trading between the west and such parts of the Ottoman Empire as Egypt the French were less easily discouraged than the British by Egypt's internal anarchy and as British power further east grew, so commensurately did French interest in Egypt. Napoleon's expedition to Egypt in 1798, militarily a disaster but commercially and intellectually most successful, undertook a wide-ranging survey of the country with a view to its permanent occupation and the establishment of a French commercial empire to counter the British in India. Subsequent French influence remained predominant, despite British development of the Overland Route, and made possible Muhammad Ali's Egyptian renaissance. The Egyptian army, fleet, medical schools, Delta barrage and port facilities were nearly all planned and executed by French engineers, 'persons of great intelligence, of considerable activity and not particularly friendly to our commercial or political views,' Dr Madden had observed in 1829.[2] Powerful Marseilles merchants had long sustained French strategic and commercial interests in the Levant including Egypt and extended their

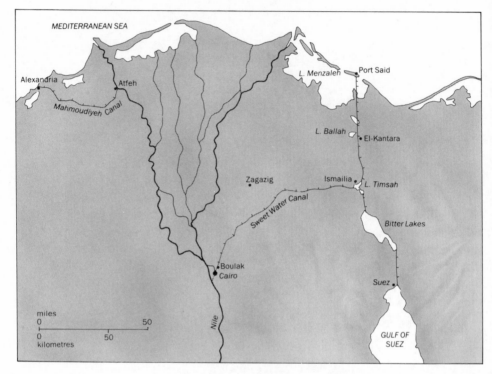

Map 5   The Suez Canal

power throughout the Mediterranean almost to a monopoly, demonstrated visibly in mid-century by the steamers of Messageries
Impériales.

All ancient canals to Suez linked the Red Sea with the Nile rather
than with the Mediterranean. Queen Hatchepsut ordered the digging
of the first canal for the import of myrrh about the fifteenth century BC.
A thousand years later the Pharaoh Necho of the XXVI dynasty built a
canal between the Delta and the Red Sea which was continued by the
Persian Darius and completed by Ptolemy II. A port, Arsinoe, was built
at the head of the Red Sea near the modern Suez. The canal was
revived by the Emperor Trajan in the first century AD and used on and
off until the Arab expansion of the seventh century, when it was used to
take Egyptian wheat to the Hijaz. The idea of linking Mediterranean
and Red Sea was current throughout the Middle Ages and Renaissance,
sustained during the years of Mameluk rule and misrule and revived by
engineers on Napoleon's expedition in 1798 who surveyed the neck of
land between the two seas. Haste and heat led them to conclude that

21 Ferdinand de
Lesseps, astride the Suez
Canal

the difference in height between them was too great to make a canal
feasible. Some years later, after another survey, Francis Chesney
maintained that the difference was in fact negligible; he may have
discussed his ideas with those in Egypt, among them Ferdinand de
Lesseps, then French vice-consul in Alexandria who later described
Chesney as 'the father of the Canal'.[3] But the ideas of a young army
captain were hardly likely to make a serious impact on his political or
military superiors.

Nevertheless by the 1830s many foreigners in Egypt were talking
about a canal. Merchants, British as well as French, were mostly in
favour, as were many of the French engineers now working for
Muhammad Ali, among them French engineer, Linant de Bellefonds,
who ultimately designed de Lesseps's canal. The French social idealists,
the Saint-Simoniens, took the idea under their wing and wrote poems
about it. De Lesseps showed no particular interest in the cause during
his vice-consulship but must have joined in the discussions. He actually
left Egypt in 1837 for other diplomatic posts and only after an early

retirement in 1849 did he begin to interest himself actively in the notion of the canal. Others, including Arthur Anderson of P.&O. who met Linant de Bellefonds in Egypt in 1841, kept the idea alive despite strong opposition from the British government whenever the subject was mentioned. In a memo to Palmerston Anderson pointed out not only the conventional wisdom of enlightening 'the ignorance and barbarism of the east' but in particular the advantages a canal would give to the movement of troops between Britain and India.[4] His point was painfully proved by both the Crimean War and the Indian Mutiny.

Muhammad Ali, the grand old patron of Egyptian modernisation, finally died in 1848. His successor was his grandson, Abbas, who was much less of an enthusiast for foreign technology and more inclined to listen to the British rather than the French. The idea of the canal was already being attacked in Britain, most vigorously by Robert Stephenson in the House of Commons: along with other British entrepreneurs and politicians Stephenson preferred a railway, a relatively modest idea which also appealed more to the cautious Abbas.

The idea of a railway had first been raised by Waghorn and a route surveyed in the 1830s by Thomas Galloway, a British engineer in Egypt who was much involved in Muhammad Ali's modernisation plans. Lack of funds and opposition by other European powers delayed its construction but eventually in the 1850s Robert Stephenson had laid a line, first from Alexandria to the Nile – much to P.&O.'s relief as it cut out the tiresome transhipment of passengers and their luggage around the Mahmoudiyeh Canal – and subsequently on to Cairo, much to the satisfaction of passengers. By 1857, when troops were in transit through Egypt on their way to the Indian Mutiny, the Cairo–Suez stretch was finished apart from the 25 miles of the donkey ride. It cost £11,000 a mile for its 140 miles and Stephenson was paid £55,000 for his pains. The line crossed the Nile at Boulaq on an ingenious floating bridge, one of Stephenson's triumphs, over which the train crossed in sections. The bridge was opened every other day for water traffic, the passage beneath it 'most exciting and pretty,' according to Lucie Duff Gordon, 'such a scramble and dash of boats.'[5] Stephenson was particularly noted for his tubular bridges, in particular the Brittania Bridge over the Menai Straits between Wales and Anglesey, the towers of which are decorated with 'Egyptian' motifs. He built two such bridges in Egypt, one over the Damietta branch of the Nile at Benha and the other over a canal at Birkah al-Saba. Both included a swinging span over the navigation channel but the railway ran on top of the tubes rather than inside as in

Wales. Construction of the bridge was facilitated by Nasmyth's hammer, adapted for driving piles.

Finally another line was built from Alexandria to Suez via the little Delta town of Zagazig, expressly for the Overland Route, making this route a rather briefer, brisker transit than, initially, the canal itself.* The system was run with oriental aplomb, a lot of dust and a disregard for timetables. On the whole British rolling stock stood up badly to Egyptian treatment despite an average speed of 10 miles an hour. William Russell travelled on it in March 1869 in the retinue of the Prince and Princess of Wales and complained that the train rattled incessantly.[6] On another occasion Russell travelled in the company of parties of Muslims setting off to make the pilgrimage to Mecca, who seemed to regard the 'Oriental hurly burly' at Cairo station as 'part of the sufferings to which the pilgrimage is subject.' Stephenson had had some elegant coaches and locomotives designed for Abbas' personal use but the viceroy (by the time of Russell's visit, Muhammad Said) had a tendency, according to Russell, to commandeer the whole train for himself or his soldiers, somewhat to the detriment of its punctuality.

Abbas, who died in 1854 before he could ride on his train, was succeeded by Muhammad Said, a plump bon viveur who immediately received a letter from the man who, according to possibly apocryphal tales, used to slip him forbidden sweetmeats when a boy – Ferdinand de Lesseps. The Viceroy summoned the sweetmeat donor, described as a man 'of untiring energy of both body and mind.' Lengthy discussions over desert picnics gave de Lesseps, 'who has made known to us the possibility of forming a Company composed of capitalists of all nations,'[7] a concession to set up such a financial company to build and operate a canal between Red Sea and Mediterranean.

Under the extremely generous terms of the concession no work was to begin on the canal until the Sultan's permission had been obtained. That was to be de Lesseps' biggest headache. French influence might be paramount in Egypt; in Constantinople the British had the ear of the Sultan and the British government wanted the railway and only the railway. It was cheaper and strategically safer. Despite the obvious commercial advantages of a canal it would clearly alter the geography of power in the context of the Eastern Question, already fluid enough with the Crimean crisis. From the engineering angle, the construction of the

* Alexandria–Benha–Cairo was built 1854–6; Benha–Zagazig 1860; Zagazig–Ismailia 1868; Ismailia–Suez 1868; Cairo–Suez 1868; Cairo–Assiut 1874; Assiut–Luxor–Aswan 1898.

canal presented no major problems and was given an engineer's blessing in the report of an International Commission published after their visit to the site in 1855. From the political angle, however, de Lesseps was to fight a grim battle against an array of constantly changing opponents, manipulated chiefly by the British, whose dislike of the project hung over it like a perpetual *khamsin*, the dreaded dust storm of Egypt.

British influence with the Sultan was powerful enough to forestall his issuing a firman (or edict) for the construction. This was not in fact issued until March 1866. After an inconclusive visit to Constantinople de Lesseps turned to London to arouse financial and political support for a project which would 'aperire terram gentibus,' he told Richard Cobden, the familiar theme without the Christianity.[8]

De Lesseps had a difficult time in London. The British government viewed the canal as potentially a second Dardanelles or Bosphorus. An interview with the ageing Palmerston was disastrous; each man regarded the other as a maniac. 'I found Lord Palmerston just where he was in 1840,' declared de Lesseps in his *Recollections*, 'full of mistrust and prejudices with regard to France and Egypt.' Palmerston maintained that the canal was a scheme 'which no Englishman with his eyes open would think it desirable to encourage.' Worse still, Palmerston went on, such a route 'being open to the navigation of all nations, will deprive us

22 'Locomotive-salon' designed for Muhammad Said Pasha, ruler of Egypt, by Robert Stephenson, a fierce advocate of railway rather than canal construction in Egypt

of the advantages which we now possess,' namely control of the world's oceans. In the House of Commons Palmerston insisted that it was 'one of those bubble schemes so often formed to induce English capitalists to embark their money upon enterprises which . . . will only leave them poorer.'[9] Stephenson, builder and backer of the railway, was even ruder in speaking of the proposed canal and was challenged to a duel by the enraged de Lesseps, who in due course won an apology from the man who in his younger days had been so bold in his development of new technology. Stephenson's opposition to the canal shocked even his biographer Jeafferson, 'the term conservative being by no means strong enough to express his abhorrence of innovation.'[10] The conduct of England 'has been pitiful in the extreme,' wrote a disgusted de Lesseps but there were consolations: *The Times* was firmly behind the project and so also, he thought, was Prince Albert. Why worry, George Delane of *The Times* wrote later: if the canal is ever finished, 'we can only say that [it] will be so far a British canal that it will be traversed by British ships, devoted to British traffic and maintained by British tolls.'[11]

The financing of the canal is an intricate story involving some fairly high-handed dealing by de Lesseps but not really part of a story about steam.* Much of the funding was precariously raised through European bankers; de Lesseps once said that if he was really desperate for money he would ask Palmerston to speak against the canal in Parliament and that would instantly fill his coffers with French money. He spent the better part of ten years negotiating finance and agitating for the Sultan's firman during the course of which he took the understandable decision to force everyone's hands by starting work.

Apart from finance, de Lesseps' other major headache was labour supply. There were three principal projects in the construction of the Suez Canal: a port at the northern Mediterranean end; a Sweet Water Canal from the Nile to Timsah, later renamed Ismailia, and the main ship canal itself. Where the Sweet Water Canal reached the bed of the main canal it turned south and was used not only to bring drinking water from the Nile to work teams on the main canal as well as to Suez but also for transporting men and materials. A service canal or *rigole* was also dug parallel to the Maritime Canal along which vessels were able to steam from Mediterranean to Red Sea before the main canal was open.

The canal stunned observers throughout its construction by the sheer

* More detailed accounts of the financing of the canal will be found in John Marlowe's *The Making of the Suez Canal* (1964) and David S. Landes' *Bankers and Pashas* (1958).

mass of material to be excavated, nearly 100 million cubic yards, much of it by hand. The traditional method in Egypt of gathering labour for public works was through the corvée, a system of forced labour that was almost a national institution. This was organised by the village headmen and worked quite satisfactorily for such seasonal local works, mainly connected with the Nile flood, as irrigation ditches and dikes. It was far less successful for such national projects as the Mahmoudiyeh Canal, excavated under Muhammad Ali's orders in the 1820s by some 300,000 Egyptian labourers who had been summoned from all over the country and in the course of which 20,000 are thought to have died. Labour camps were especially prone to the seasonal plague and cholera which could devastate them in no time at all. Labourers anxious to return to their fields at times of sowing and harvest were disciplined with the notorious rawhide whip known as the *corbash*.

The first project to get under way, in 1859, was the Sweet Water Canal from the Nile, the first 24 miles of which were navigable by February 1862. It required considerably less capital outlay than the proposed Maritime Canal and its water was essential for the labour on the main project. It was also possible to argue that the Sultan's permission was not required before starting work. A discreet decree went out from the Viceroy summoning the corvée on a large enough scale to meet de Lesseps' demand for urgency, and immediately attracted foreign, mainly British, criticism for its alleged brutality. Some criticism was disinterested, generated by the same social reforming zeal as British anti-slavery and labour legislation, but there was also a strong element of political expediency. The death toll of the Mahmoudiyeh Canal, though frequently commented upon, had aroused no particular horror nor had the number of deaths incurred in laying the railway lines that now criss-crossed Europe; this toll was also considerable, often resulting, as in Egypt, from dysentery and cholera. De Lesseps was on guard against any outbreak of disease, recognising the political as well as physical havoc it would cause, and despite a cholera outbreak he managed to keep the death toll among the Egyptian labour force well below that of similar construction sites anywhere else in Europe.

At the height of the corvée some 25,000 Egyptians were on site, usually for a six-month stretch. Another 25,000 then took their place. Given the time it took for them to travel between canal and home, at least 50,000 farmers might be away from their lands at any one time. Many also came of their own accord, attracted by good rates of pay and living conditions. This had a devastating effect on village economy. De Lesseps fought fiercely to retain the corvée and in the event the Sweet

Water Canal was three-quarters complete before the criticism began to take effect. De Lesseps' principal patron, Muhammad Said Pasha, died in 1863 and the new viceroy, Ismail, was more sceptical about the need for so vast a project offering so little advantage to Egypt itself. He therefore bowed to European pressure and withdrew the corvée at the end of 1863, by which time the Sweet Water Canal had reached the line to be taken by the main canal and the southern branch had been completed to Suez. De Lesseps was able to travel along the 40-foot-wide little canal as far as Ismailia in forty hours in 1862. But the scale of the main canal was much grander, and it was impractical to think of building it by human labour alone.

By now the construction of Port Said was well under way, perhaps the greatest achievement of the whole scheme. The place chosen for the port had been nothing but empty seashore – no shelter, no depth, just a desolate waste miles from any civilisation with a powerful current sweeping along from the mouths of the Nile. As late as 1865 the British ambassador visiting the site still found no sign of 'such a destiny as that suggested for it by the Canalists.'[12] But de Lesseps and the engineers he chose to work for him, first Mouguel, later Voisin, were undeterred. The marshes were reclaimed and the ground raised 10 feet above sea level. A town was built on piles. A long western breakwater, built of 250,000 concrete blocks manufactured on the spot, enclosed a vast area of water, the harbour destined to lie between two protective arms. Volumes of smoke and the clang of machinery hung over the desert. Yet in some ways desolation clung to it; the ramshackle settlement never quite discarded the notoriety of its squalor, poor living conditons (labourers were housed in wooden cabins brought from the Crimea) and indiscriminate brawling between the different nationalities employed in the original construction.

The route of the Maritime Canal was drafted by Linant de Belle-fonds. There were few technical problems. From north to south it was to run in a fairly straight line 99 miles from Port Said through Lake Menzaleh, Kantara, Lake Ballah, through the escarpment of El-Gisr (the highest ground on the route and a complicated eight-mile step of hard rock) to Ismailia, terminus of the Sweet Water Canal, through Lake Timsah, the Pharaonic ruins of the Serapeum, the Bitter Lakes (the ancient bed of the Red Sea), to Shaluf and thence to Suez, emerging into the Red Sea just to the east of the existing town. It was built between 1865 and 1869. With the dismissal of the corvée, de Lesseps appointed three labour contractors whose rates of pay soon attracted gangs of labourers from all over Europe and the Near East as well as many thousands of Egyptians who returned voluntarily to the site once they could be assured of good rates. A British engineer, Percy Fitzgerald, who wrote one of the best accounts of the canal's excavation,[13] found thousands of men employed on the Bitter Lakes crossing – Dalmatians, Greeks, Croats, even a party of navvies from Lyons, Nubians and Egyptians, superintended by Frenchmen and paid by piece work. The popularity of the wages left many Egyptian villages and farms more depleted after the withdrawal of the corvée than before.

'Not the least merit of this active and persevering man is the power he has of selecting and attaching to himself a staff of men of first-rate ability,' commented the British Consul-General Colquhoun.[14] Among them was the original surveyor Linant de Bellefonds, the engineer-in-chief Voisin Bey, and the principal contractor Alexandre Lavalley. The original single contractor Alphonse Hardon who had made a fortune building railway stations in France was replaced in 1865 by several – in particular Lavalley from Ernst Gouin's factory at Batignolles near Paris where some of the finest French locomotives had been made since 1846; Gouin also provided steam engines for the Suez project. Both Lavalley and his principal colleague Paul Borel were graduates of France's École Polytechnique. They represented a new generation of academically qualified engineers who combined mathematics with an innate ingenuity, especially in their design and use of hugely powerful machines for the canal. Borel died just before the inauguration of the canal, probably from overwork; Lavalley lived on to have two ships named after him. De Lesseps himself, with no engineering training but clearly a man with an enviable grasp of the issues and technology involved, was forever in attendance, often aboard his steam yacht, *Mathilde*.

Work on the canal actually began on April 25th, 1859, when de Lesseps at a well-publicised ceremony shifted some earth between two pegs; onlookers also had a ceremonial dig. Human labour was used initially to dig down to the water table; thereafter it was replaced by steam dredgers floating on the mud. Lavalley designed and adapted many of the machines, brought in gradually along the service canal from Port Said.

For centuries dredging had been a Dutch speciality, for ports as well as canals, and a Dutch engineer named Conrad was in charge of dredgers at Suez where the scale of the operations provided an impetus for a spate of new designs, 'mechanical devices ... of great originality and power.' These had a profound influence on dredging all over the world. Early dredgers had usually been horse-powered but about 1796

23   Excavating the Suez Canal with steam-powered dredgers, many of them
designed by the French engineer Bazin

Boulton and Watt designed the first steam dredger and in 1804 Oliver
Evans in Philadelphia designed a steam-powered bucket chain dredger.
Several European variations appeared in the first half of the nineteenth
century, including on the Clyde in 1824 and the Ribble in 1839. Many
of these new designs originated in the small Scottish town of Renfrew
under the inspiration of Henry Lobnitz, a Dane who had worked with
the marine engineers John Penn of Greenwich and John Scott Russell,
Brunel's rival.

'Difficulties prompt the means to overcome them,' according to Percy
Fitzgerald in his account of the project. 'No one who has seen an
ordinary dredger at its slow work in an English river could have an idea
of the bold fashion in which the principle was now applied,'[15] largely
thanks to Lavalley's ingenuity. One contractor, William Aiton of
Glasgow, with many years' experience of dredging the Clyde, was
virtually bankrupted by coping with the slimy ooze of Lake Menzaleh
although his seagoing hopper barges were useful in the Port Said
excavations.

The first steam dredger on the canal had an engine of 15 horsepower
and operated with a cloth band on a roller. It was soon superseded by
machines à couloir – some of them with a *couloir*, a chain of buckets, up

to 75 feet long, with engines up to 75 horsepower, ordered from France and Belgium and assembled on the spot. There were hopper barges, Goliath cranes, Scotch derricks, steam excavators, steam-driven hoists, winches and air compressors. At Port Said dredgings were taken out to sea in twin-screw barges. Further along the canal there was a special squirting dredger, a chain of buckets that delivered the mud into a high-level tank where it was mixed with water from a centrifugal pump before being squirted out over the canal banks some 30–70 metres, thus avoiding the need to dump the dredgings at sea. At El-Gisr another French engineer, Couvreux, installed in 1865 a land-based bucket dredger patented in 1860, described as the greatest labour-saving device on the canal. Bucket chains were driven by a 4-cylinder compound steam engine of 200 horsepower. Rams were lifted by hydraulic power, delivering 2–300 blows an hour. There was Bazin's steam-driven sand pump, a model of which was demonstrated at the 1867 Paris Exhibition. A *dérocheuse* was built by Lobnitz specially for Suez fitted with ten savage-looking rock cutters, chisel-pointed and each 42 feet long and weighing 4 tons that broke up rock in front of the chain of buckets. It was calculated to have removed 3 million tons of hard limestone from one shoal alone. Near the Serapeum the Sweet Water Canal was tapped to flood three large depressions, forming freshwater lakes on which dredgers could float.

Fitzgerald noted fifty dredgers in all, many of them built by the Société des Forges et Chantiers de la Méditerranée, founded in Toulon in 1855, several of whose vessels, built for Messageries Impériales, were to be among the first through the new canal. Barges from Ernest Gouin, Lavalley's old company, came out from France. Between them they used £40,000 of coal a month – 'this raw material which the genius of man has transformed into the world's main instrument of civilisation'. One could follow the line of the canal by the curling smoke from the dredgers' double chimneys. A combination of these remarkable machines removed in a month enough earth, as de Lesseps liked to put it, to fill the Champs Elysées to the tree tops, from the Arc de Triomphe to the Obelisk (also from Egypt, also shifted by steam).

By 1866 work was in progress all along the canal. At Shaluf, north of Suez, an outlandish combination of dredgers and Piedmontese labourers with experience from the Mont Cénis tunnel through the Alps, cut into a bank of hardened clay in which they found fossil remains of elephant and dogfish. Over thirty long trough dredgers were excavating in the main bed of the canal alongside some 8,000 European labourers and 10,000 Africans and 'Asiatics'. Indispensable also to the task were the 43,000 camels, 9,300 horses, 2,500 mules and 3,000 donkeys.

Port Said was now a town of 10,000 people with schools, bath houses, restaurants, market, mosques and mountains of coal. The dry sandy depression of Lake Timsah had become a shallow blue lake already attracting migrant flocks of pelicans and flamingoes. Ismailia, 'a toy city in the wilderness,' according to Russell, 'a pretty butterfly',[16] was a centre of European enterprise; de Lesseps lived there in a gabled chalet for the three years of the major construction works, solving by sheer force of personality the diverse problems of construction. The Khedive, (an official title granted to Ismail by the Sultan in 1867), had a palace just north of Ismailia at the junction of the two branches of the Sweet Water Canal, complete with domes and pillars. Constantly beset by finance problems, de Lesseps nevertheless kept the work going twenty-four hours a day; only when the canal tolls began rolling in would the project prove to be viable. A measure of his success was Arthur Anderson's public admission in London that simply rerouting P.&O.'s Indian ocean vessels through the canal would not in fact make full use of its potential; the company would need a new generation of vessels designed round the vastly more efficient compound expansion engine. The canal was at last an accepted fact.

It was far from complete, however, when opened with a tremendous fanfare in November 1869. Last-minute dredging of sand and scraping of rock ensured the grand procession of vessels could steam through but invited potentates had to be strictly warned about the draught of their vessels – a maximum of 13 feet at this stage. The stipulated depth was originally to have been 26 ft. 3 in. but this had been reduced by economy and haste to 17 feet by 1869 and in some places to less than that. There was a series of inaugurations in fact – a dress rehearsal with the Prince and Princess of Wales in March, the meeting of the two seas in August when the Khedive cut the dyke between them and finally the grand opening in November. A clever publicity move was to invite an advance guard of celebrities to ensure some high-flown hyperbole. Scientists and doctors, lawyers, photographers, members of Le Jockey from Paris, artists, including Fromentin and Gérôme, writers such as Gautier, Zola and Ibsen, all packed their bags for Egypt, many of them steaming across the Mediterranean on board P.&O.'s paddle-steamer *Delta*, the first British vessel to enter the canal.

Not all of them were satisfied with the programme laid on for their benefit but they were loquacious commentators on the festivities. 'It is a mad carmagnole they are dancing there in Cairo, with Kaisers and

Dervishes, Empresses and Almey girls, Patriarchs and buffons, Emirs
and engineers, Mussulman High Priests and Italian sailors all mixed up
helter skelter in the round . . .' sniffed *The Spectator*; 'the Suez Canal
may strengthen the hold of the West upon the East but the ceremonies
which accompanied its opening will not tend to make increased
authority additionally vivifying.'[17] Giuseppe Verdi was asked by the
French archaeologist Auguste Mariette to compose an opera for the
occasion but refused and only relented when it came to inaugurating
Cairo's new opera house two years later – with *Aida*, composed in little
more than six months and attended by Ismail and three boxfuls of his
harem on Christmas Eve, 1871.

Still, the inauguration was a grand display of the state of the art in
steamships. Vessels converged from all directions for the official
opening, bringing the 6,000 guests invited by the Khedive. A posse of
ironclads of various nations anchored off Port Said to greet the
celebrities arriving for the festivities. Apart from the rather old-
fashioned *Delta* there was the frigate of the Crown Prince of Prussia,
Messageries Impériales' *Péluse* with members of the canal's administrative council on board, the French warship *Forbin*, the Khedive's
magnificent yacht *Mahroussiah* – 'very comfortable' said Russell, 'but

24 The first convoy steaming through the Suez Canal, a parade of the most
up-to-date steamships in 1869

25   The Empress Eugénie with her cousin Ferdinand de Lesseps at the
opening of the Suez Canal, November, 1869

much of her space is occupied by great saloons full of gorgeous
furniture'. *Mahroussiah* was built by the Samuda brothers in London in
1865 and was over 400 feet long; as the world's oldest surviving steam
yacht and renamed *El-Hurria* she has been twice lengthened as well as
converted to steam turbine, is now used in Egypt as a training vessel
and was fit to steam across the Atlantic in 1976 to celebrate the US
bicentenary.

On November 16th – most impressive of all – France's Empress
Eugénie, a cousin of de Lesseps and longstanding supporter of the
canal, steamed into Port Said aboard her paddle-steam yacht *L'Aigle*,
the pride and joy of Eugénie's husband, Napoleon III, an enthusiastic
yachtsman. *L'Aigle* was a wooden paddle-steamer built ten years earlier
at Cherbourg. She was 90 metres long, 17 metres wide and was
powered with a 500 horsepower oscillating engine. A model is in the
Musée de la Marine in Paris. Napoleon's yachting enthusiasm encouraged another innovation not displayed at Suez; his yacht *Le Puebla* had
two 60-horsepower engines which in 1868 Henri Deville fitted with a
device for using liquid fuel, in other words oil.

Individual Britons cautiously praised the canal while the government
sent the British ambassador from Constantinople, Henry Elliott, to

attend the celebrations on board the 835-ton dispatch boat *Psyche*. 'The Queen of England has opened Holborn Viaduct,' scoffed the *The Saturday Review*, 'and the Empress of the French is going to open the Suez Canal.'[18] But the perspicacious Alfred Holt reckoned England would benefit most and two of his ships, the *Leith* and the *Blue Cross*, left immediately for India via Suez.

Queening it over all other guests was the Empress Eugénie, in one of her last moments of glory before deposition and exile the following year. Also on hand were the Emperor of Austria, the Prince of Holland, the Crown Prince of Prussia, numerous ambassadors, African and Asian potentates. Port Said was transformed, its normal atmosphere of a low-living frontier town yielding momentarily to a stately ambience for European and oriental nobility. The more honoured guests attended a sermon at Port Said by the Pope's representative, Monsignor Bauer, who paid the customary lip service to that ubiquitious theme of nineteenth-century communication: 'one of the most formidable enemies of mankind and of civilisation, which is distance, loses in a moment two thousand leagues of his empire; the Orient and the Occident were now one world.'[19]

Inevitably a few last-minute hitches developed. A fire threatened to destroy not only the fireworks stored at Ismailia for the celebrations but the entire settlement. An Egyptian corvette ran aground, blocking the canal, and was only with difficulty refloated. Questions of European protocol tormented the gathering. Who should precede whom? The Russian vessel missed her place in the line and lost precedence to the British ambassador's *Psyche*. But on November 17th a vast procession of boats led by *L'Aigle*, followed by Ismail on board his *Mahroussiah* and the Emperor of Austria on his *Greif*, steamed between two colossal wooden pyramids erected either side of the canal entrance and set off for the Red Sea – 99 miles away, no locks intervening, along a canal whose minimum width was 492 feet at the surface but only 72 feet at the bottom. Tension mounted as the vessels proceeded along the canal, for the Port Said to Ismailia section was known to be the trickiest. Passengers hung anxiously over the railings to hear the first crunch along the bottom. Fortunately none came and that night was spent at Ismailia.

Here the chaos was appalling – lost luggage, missing sleeping quarters, upset stomachs – indescribable confusion, confessed Fromentin, turning from brush to pen for the occasion and struggling long and hard to describe it all.[20] The town was garlanded with greenery. At a palace built specially for the occasion a feast was prepared by 500 cooks and served by 1,000 waiters but not until one o'clock in the morning; one unhappy guest, the Austrian Chancellor Monsieur de Buest, started off on foot for the party after his carriage failed to turn up, but getting stuck in the sand he was only too pleased to complete his journey on a small black donkey. The banquet of twenty-four dishes included 'Poisson à la Réunion des Deux Mers' and 'Crevettes de Suez au Cresson'. Soup kitchens were provided by the Khedive for lowlier attendants. A ball to work off the effects of the feast was attended by 3,000 men and 200 women. Meanwhile in London they were dancing the Suez Quadrille.

Next day, somewhat the worse for wear, the procession reached the Red Sea, with a moment of anxiety as it steamed over a shallow patch at the Serapeum where a layer of rock was still defying the dredgers. Sure enough Messageries Impériales' *Péluse*, with twelve directors of the Suez Canal Company on board, did go aground here. Several others had problems with the canal's bends. The first vessel to reach Suez was a private yacht, Mr Ashbury's *Cambria*, surely an example of *lèse-majesté*. Participants rejoiced at the grand backdrop of the Arabian mountains, bathed in the light of the setting sun, after the monotony of their earlier surroundings. One observer in a fit of enthusiasm described Suez as the Marseilles of the Red Sea; Eugénie was sufficiently enchanted to stay on an extra day. The passage of two P.&O. liners, a British troop ship and a Turkish frigate demonstrated some of the uses which the canal in future would serve. After a night at Suez the procession went back up the canal, reaching Port Said fifteen hours later.

And quietly, at the end of the ceremonies, de Lesseps unveiled a statue of Waghorn at Port Tewfiq, the new canal port just to the east of the old town, his tribute to the man who did so much to prepare the ground for the canal.

8

Posh

Users of the canal and the Red Sea were quick to appreciate the strategic significance of both. The question of who would control the canal – or prevent another from controlling it – immediately exercised the European powers. Periodically bitter negotiations between the British, the French and the Khedive ensued, while in the Red Sea the French and the Italians, jealously aware of Britain's advantages in possessing Aden with its excellent harbour, coaling facilities and guardianship of the entrance to the waterway, tried to secure similar positions for themselves in suitable harbours along the African coast. Steam boosted these rivalries, enabling the powers to move troops swiftly to the scene of their strategic or imperial ambitions.

The inauguration of the canal inspired some magnificent hyperbole about the benefits of commerce to the benighted barbarians of the east but once the festivities were over it was back to work for most of those involved in the canal. There were many forecasts of disaster. Portions of the canal were not deep enough (hence the tension with which de Lesseps hung over the rails of *L'Aigle* with his cousin Eugénie); the buoys were not in place; bends and sidings, known as *gares*, were unfinished. Passage seemed interminable, because ships could only move by day until the introduction of lighted buoys and ships' lights in 1887; by being obliged to tie up at night vessels could take three days to navigate the length of the canal compared with the twenty-four-hour Overland Route between Alexandria and Suez which P.&O. was still using. Vessels often went aground and tolls were high. The main reason for such shortcomings was lack of money: tolls nowhere nearly covered the continuing expenditure. Political problems were aggravated by squabbles over rates, only solved after an International Commission laid the basis for international tonnage measurements. Their report published in 1873 backed the status of the canal as an international waterway; a sudden spurt in traffic resulting from the assurance established its status permanently.

Yet the canal's success was ensured not by documents, not by the tireless dredgers, not by de Lesseps' continuing energy and optimism, but by some revolutionary developments in ship design and propulsion systems. These included the compound expansion engine, the efficient use of the screw propeller, and hulls increasingly built of iron and later steel, breaking away from the design limitations imposed by wood. None of these developments was foreseen by de Lesseps yet his magnificent venture might well have been a failure without them. Paddle-steamers were almost as unsuited to the canal as sailing vessels. 'The whole of our Eastern trade has been revolutionized by the Canal,' said Sir James Elphinstone in 1871. 'The ships in which we placed so much pride . . . are improved off the face of the earth. Trade with India, right or wrong, must fall into steam trade.'[1]

Much of the inspiration and finance for these new developments came from Liverpool, its wealth founded on the cotton trade. The East India Company's monopoly of trade with India came to an end in 1813 and Liverpool merchants were among the first to try to take advantage of the new opportunities. Exports of Indian raw cotton to Lancashire mills swelled enormously following the Napoleonic wars and concomitantly exports of British cotton goods back to India (817,000 yards in 1814, over 7 million yards in 1819, over 23 million in 1824 and an amazing 52 million in 1832). The first Liverpool ship to trade directly with India, sailing in 1814, belonged to Gladstone's father. Most raw cotton entered and most textiles left Britain through Liverpool, with its easy access to Lancashire mills, and the city lived, moved and had its being in ships and shipping; everyone talked ship. The 1830s, 1840s and 1850s saw a steady stream of steam developments to speed up the trade, many of them originating in Liverpool or across the Mersey in Birkenhead.

The iron screw steamer was slow to be accepted. Shipbuilders were reluctant to abandon the paddle on large vessels; even when a satisfactory propeller had been devised large vessels still needed more power to turn it than that provided by the low-pressure engines currently in use. In due course the extra power was provided by the simple expansion engine. The first experiments with compound engines were made in the United States as early as 1824 but their dependence on a high-pressure boiler meant waiting for boiler technology to improve. This it did in the 1860s and 1870s, enabling compound expansion to come into its own. John Elder had already begun building the compound expansion engine in England, as had the Normand family of Le Havre in France and the potential speed and economy of the new engine was spotted by Alfred Holt four years before the Suez Canal was opened. As steam pressure increased, two or more cylinders were introduced to expand the steam in stages. So the triple expansion engine evolved. Through the 1850s the freight-carrying trade had converted gradually to steam, helped by lavish freight rates paid by the British and French governments during the Crimean War that offset similarly steep rises in the cost of coal. The same steep rises resulted in the acceptance of the compound expansion engine, which finally gave the freighters the cargo space they needed to be profitable. The more powerful engines provided the necessary drive for the screw propeller.

Holt was a Liverpool railway engineer turned shipowner given to calculated risks, who demonstrated the first successful combination of engine and propeller when his *Cleator* steamed round the Cape to India. The *Cleator* had already had a worthy life. Built for Holt in 1854, leased to the French government during the Crimean War and with the proceeds refitted by 1864 with a new compound engine, it was so successful in its trials, including steaming the 8,500 miles to Mauritius non-stop in thirty-seven days, that Holt laid down three other vessels, the *Ajax*, the *Agamemnon* and the *Achilles*, each 2,280 tons and fitted with compound engines and blue funnels. These were the founding vessels of Holt's Ocean Steam Shipping Company, later known as Blue Funnel, registered in Liverpool in 1865.

The narrowness of the canal also influenced the shape of ships, and widespread acceptance of iron as the building material made the changes possible. Long and low in the water, ships had come a long way from the high-prowed sailing vessels of less than fifty years earlier, or even the wooden paddle-steamers of only a few years before; for practical reasons the length of wooden ships rarely exceeded five and a half times their breadth, but there is virtually no limit to the length of an iron vessel. There ensued a mania for lengthening vessels, which meant cutting them (usually at a point a third of the way back) and adding a central section, raising the ratio of length to breadth from about 7:1 in 1852 to as much as 11:1 in the early years of the canal. The canal was by no means the easy straight line originally envisaged, and negotiating its eighteen curves caused great problems for these lengthened vessels. By 1880 some shipowners were agitating for the canal's enlargement, others for a parallel canal and others for an entirely new canal. Eventually in 1882 the British government accepted the recommendations of another International Commission that the existing canal should be made wide enough for two steamers to pass at any point. This meant a channel 230 feet broad at the bottom on the straight parts and 262 feet broad on the curves. The canal was also to be deepened to a minimum of 9 metres throughout.

26 Alfred Holt, founder of
the Ocean Steam Ship
Company (also known as
Blue Funnel) and promoter
of compound expansion
marine engines

By 1875 steamers were in the majority on all routes except the
Australasian, many of them Holt's on their way to China. Once the
Suez Canal was open, cutting the route to China for instance by 3,000
miles and the voyage time by ten to twelve days, the route was opened
to competition, not a problem on the Cape route where few foreign
shipping companies had the coaling facilities available to the British for
the long voyage. Efficiency of design became all important, as was the
technology for navigating the canal and a new generation of coal-
efficient steamers caught Europe's imagination as had the technology
for excavating the canal itself. 'Coal, the stored-up sunlight of a million
years, is the grand agent,' declared the author of a eulogy of the canal,
Our New Way Round the World. 'Liberty lights the fire and Christian
civilisation is the engine which is taking the whole world in its train.'[2]
Holt himself was no starry-eyed idealist; he calculated his gamble
carefully. 'There was no novelty, no invention, in the proper sense of
the word,' he wrote in 1870, 'but merely an application of long-
enunciated ideas to appropriate purposes.'[3] The application of steam to
the freight trade of the world was akin to a revolution which only those
who had been involved in it could appreciate. But Holt did not
recommend shipowning as a business. By and large, he said, it was a

bad trade for those engaged in it. 'The perpetual progress of invention has made good vessels unprofitable while still new ... In fact the only person to profit by the change has been the over-idolised idol of these later free-trading days, the consumer.'

So the canal began to flourish. The British, having failed to prevent it, turned it to their advantage. Nearly 500 vessels steamed through the canal in 1870, its first year, three-quarters of them British. The number had trebled by 1875, again mostly British. Sir Charles Dilke had warned in 1867 that France 'would only find she had spent millions on digging a canal for England's use,'[4] although the first vessel to go to China via the canal was French – Messageries Impériales' *L'Impératrice Eugénie*. But Eugénie was about to lose her empire. France was laid low by war and revolution almost as soon as the empress returned to Paris from the canal's inauguration and the French were slow to develop the shipping interests to profit by the canal. Up to World War I over half the vessels using the canal were British.

The control and defence of this vital link with India became now and henceforth the linchpin of British attitudes to the Eastern Question. It was of particular concern to Benjamin Disraeli, whose policy in the 1870s concentrated on the protection of the routes to India. Dressing this up in the new language of imperialism he bequeathed to many of his political successors an obsession with the vulnerability of India and with the alleged greedy glances of Britain's rivals in Europe. Thanks to Disraeli, British interest in Near Eastern approaches to India shifted from Constantinople to Egypt. Public opinion was also losing its sympathy for 'the sick man of Europe'. Thus the political and diplomatic energy of the canal's principal patron came to be focused on securing Egypt and essential bunkering stops *en route* to India, to the detriment of those still pressing for a land route to India via Mesopotamia and the bolstering of the Ottoman Empire which such a route demanded.

At first, physical control of the canal was fundamentally French since most of the non-Egyptian funds for its construction had come from France. At the same time the Khedive Ismail, its largest single shareholder since 1863, was desperately in need of funds and the low ebb of his credit prohibited further borrowing. Rumours began circulating that he was contemplating using his shares in the canal as security for a French loan. The British were unhappy with the prospect and firmly said so. In 1876 therefore the Khedive disconcertingly offered them to the British government for £4 million. Disraeli, Prime Minister at the time, hesitated momentarily – what would the French say and where does one find £4 million? The banking family of Rothschild came to the rescue and Britain thus became the principal shareholder, the whole transaction taking a week. The shares were shipped to England aboard the little P.&O. steamer *Malabar*. 'This action can only be to the effect,' de Lesseps wrote in November 1876 to the British ambassador in Paris, perhaps a little sadly, 'that England will abandon her long-standing attitude of hostility towards the interests of the original shareholders of the Canal.'[5] Disraeli, challenged in Parliament by Gladstone to defend his action, declared that Britain was 'getting a great hold and interest in this important portion of Africa' and securing 'a highway to our Indian Empire and other dependencies.'[6] To Queen Victoria he exclaimed gleefully, 'you have it, madam!'

A similar excitement inspired the increasing numbers of passengers who were now steaming through the canal, many of them on board either P.&O.'s great black-funnelled fleet mostly built by Caird's of Clydeside or the vessels of Messageries, demoted from Impériales to Maritimes since the 1871 revolution but still the largest shipping company in the world, from Toulon and Marseilles. In 1871 P.&O. ordered its first iron screw-propelled steamer, the *Khedive*, designed for the canal, from Messrs Caird, with accommodation for 164 first-class and 53 second-class passengers as well as holds for 2,000 tons of cargo. She averaged 10 knots, and burned 32 tons of coal a day, powered by the revolutionary compound expansion engines – two cylinders, however, rather than the three which soon became the standard and stayed so for many years. Passenger traffic, mainly British, steaming east to service the expanding ramifications of the empire, grew as dramatically as cargo. With India so much closer and more accessible because of the canal a new aura began to envelop the voyage: adventure and mystery for the masses in the lower classes and with ever more elaborate rituals accompanying the first class in their passage from one world to the other.

Fares for some fell (although women were still charged more than men) as passengers began to be divided into different classes. Oh the misery of travelling by a class beneath one's self-esteem, sighed the frustrated wives of civilian and military officials. Those in first class hoped to steam 'poshly' (port out, starboard home), so that their portholes would be shaded from the blazing sun. From England there steamed the annual 'fishing fleet' of young or not so young ladies aiming at the hearts of British India. British and French living in India and South-East Asia could now escape the heat of the summer by a trip home: 'even our hill stations,' wrote one observer in India in the 1870s, 'are losing their summer visitors – drained off by the absorbing Suez

Canal.'[7] Competitive pressure between Messageries and P.&O. reduced some of the frills for economisers – that unlimited provision of alcohol for instance – while increasing those for the affluent, including Edward Lear (who was invited by Lord Northbrook, Viceroy in India, to 'purSuez Eastern journey further').[8] Luxury appeared as soon as the coal could be cleared off the deck, leaving space for deck chairs and deck games while below deck first-class passengers ate ever larger meals in vast glittering saloons hung with velvet. P.&O. laid on special trains to take their passengers from London to Marseilles or to Brindisi to catch their steamers.

How merry was the new sea voyage, wrote W. J. Loftie in his *Orient Line Guide*.[9] A sea voyage offers a vista of entertainment and attainment (all those competitions) 'and to be ignorant of these is to be ignorant of a mode of travelling which is happily now rapidly approaching perfection.' A steamer voyage would provide an exquisite microcosm of human society. 'The rush and worry of modern life has promoted the creation of luxurious floating hotels on the sea . . . excellent for the health of the healthy as well as for that of invalids.' But – a dire note of warning – beware of indigestion, constipation, that dread ill of the Victorians with their passion for regularity, for which the remedy was to eat less and pace the deck more; and seasickness, the latter to be remedied by moderation, wrapping a wide sash round the loins, fresh air and 'courage to sit down at table.'

Loftie was the perfect all-round guide. What a contrast between his list of essentials and that of Emma Roberts thirty years earlier. Choose clothes wisely, he advised – thin flannel suits, sun helmets (a special boon when landing at Port Said), slippers and pyjamas for the essential exercise of pacing the deck, although for alternative exercise there was cricket, tennis, quoits, curling, bowls, hopscotch, and gymnastics on the ropes to combat the indigestion and constipation. There was never an idle moment let alone time for those journals. Evenings were spent in dancing and theatricals (dressmaking for the ladies), fancy-dress competitions and the chaplain's choir. The activity was essential, of course, if the voyage was to live up to its reputation for healthiness. Meals were still prodigious: tea and biscuits between six and seven a.m., breakfast equal to Scotland's with porridge, chops, steaks, curries, fricassees, omelettes and jam, tiffin at noon with cold meats and garnishings, dinner between five and seven – the 'great event of the day at sea' – a series of soups, fish, meat entrées, curries, puddings, pies and desserts, tea and toast around nine and finally 'grog', at which solids yielded precedence to liquids. *Punch* lyricised:

> We mould our minds to suit the East;
> We stuff our brains with MURRAY;
> And school our baser parts to feast
> On curious forms of curry.[10]

Passage of the canal never lost its novelty; even those travelling through the canal in the last days of long sea voyages in the 1950s remember it with awe and nostalgia. Neither Port Said, nor Ismailia nor Suez, nor the canal itself had much charisma yet de Lesseps' achievement always caught the imagination.

Port Said was the drabbest of introductions, the sleaziest of canal towns, its principal characteristic its coal. For the first few years of the canal, coaling was in French hands, in particular two Bordeaux companies, Bazin and Hippolyte Worms. But before long the coaling had been taken over by the British Port Said & Suez Coal Company, itself owned by the Ocean Coal Company of South Wales, and from South Wales most of the coal came – in the 1860s, for instance, nearly 3 million tons a year. Best Admiralty Large, Best Seconds, Best Dry Large – these Welsh coals were famous for their high calorific value and ability to generate heat and therefore steam quickly. Much of it was stored on coal hulks moored offshore for convenience, around them clustering grimy low-lying lighters, 'and up and down the improvised gangways from them to the ship, and back again, an ant-like stream of basket-carrying figures, dark brown, grimy, turbaned, petticoated, barefooted, swarmed endlessly,' wrote a surgeon on board a P.&O. vessel in 1911,[11] egged on by Quranic calls to Allah from a white-turbanned imam who would station himself at the head of one of the gangways. 'Coaling is a nightmare,' he complained. 'Plug your ventilators, fasten the doors of your cabin, screw up your ports hermetically and yet the coal dust gets in.' One forgets how grimy steam travel always was.

A steamer docking at Port Said to collect coal would be beset by swarms of pedlars come to sell fake antiques, exotic perfumes, trinkets and baubles to the captive passengers. On shore, Port Said was notorious for its sleazy restaurants and bars. Just as British shipping predominated in the passage through the canal, so British influence gradually permeated its entrance at Port Said. In the 1880s George Royle, Director of the Canal Company and 'king' of the port, improved its facilities and reclaimed land to the west of the port for more salubrious residential areas; his wife devoted her days to improving the health, morals and manners of the natives and foreigners about her. A Protestant church was built, a sporting club, the Minerva baths and the

Khedivial theatre. But no amount of British decorum could change its raffishness. 'A sand-bordered hell,' wrote Kipling in *The Light that Failed*; 'there is iniquity in many parts of the world, and vice in all, but the concentrated essence of all the iniquities and all the vices in all the continents finds itself at Port Said.'[12] On shore sailors were as liable to be fleeced as guileless passengers, bewitched by stout Egyptian ladies in ramshackle brothels flanked, now that Egyptology was all the rage, by crude paintings of Isis and Osiris. 'There is nothing so sad and so unsightly as these commonplace cross-roads which have no existence of their own, and live only by the continuous passage of strangers in search of amusement,' wrote the Frenchman André Chévrillon; 'there is nothing here but a little European scum flung down upon the edge of the desert.'[13]

The voyage along the canal inspired passengers by its historical associations but seldom by the surrounding views. Their vessels were usually piloted by Frenchmen who boarded at Port Said: 'the excellent manner in which the different lines are conducted and navigated by Frenchmen,' condescended the historian of merchant shipping, W. S. Lindsay, 'is the best answer that can be given to the old saying that the French never were and never will be a maritime people.'[14]

It is a dreary landscape of hot yellow gravel wavering in the heat except in the sunset-draped evenings, swamps and marshes occasionally cheered by flocks of migrating pelicans and flamingos. Passage through the canal, according to Captain John Steele, required 'the most circumspect steering.'[15] Progress was slow because of strict speed restrictions enforced by shallows and curves. Hard sides on the bends could damage screw or stern post; the deep-water channel was only about 80 feet wide, slightly less at the Suez end; there were awkward currents set off by a vessel's wake, the *gares* carved out of the banks for letting another vessel pass or for spending the night were particularly awkward to handle and the worthy captain warned colleagues not to pass them at more than 3 knots, never more than 4 knots when laden. At first only mail boats were allowed to steam at night, carrying red lights to show they had the mails on board; other vessels had to tie up in one of the many sidings as darkness fell. When the surgeon J. Johnston Abraham steamed through the canal in 1911 his vessel was held up for several hours by a lighter sunk under its load of stores. ' "If England were at war and I were an enemy," commented the Captain, "the first thing I'd do would be to block the Canal. It's as easy as falling off a log." '[16] The canal was indeed most effectively blocked during the Suez crisis of 1956 and took several years to unblock.

Having received clearance that nothing was coming the other way, the vessel steamed slowly through the monotonous landscape to Ismailia, which from a distance looked as if it were riding on the gravelly plain itself. Despite the glamour of the inauguration Ismailia now had little more cheer to offer than Port Said; instead of charmless coal it had malaria, so seriously that it was almost abandoned. The town had failed to live up to de Lesseps' expectations. Except in the small Arab town to the west of the European quarter, it remained a garden city amidst a sea of sand, empty of the raffish vitality that sustained Port Said. Only in 1882 did it acquire a momentary breath of life when Sir Garnet Wolseley made it his headquarters in the campaign against the nationalist revolt of Colonel Arabi. 'The siroccos blow the sands of the desert on the paved streets of Ismailia,' wrote an American visitor in 1871, 'and there is neither men nor money to sweep them out.'[17]

As for Suez, it had had its years of glory before the canal was built. It later suffered from being a few miles west of the mouth of the canal despite giving its name to de Lesseps' achievement. Only elegant Arab dhows frequented the old harbour, the indolence of their crews a sharp contrast to those on board the great steamers donning their tropical whites and solar topees as they emerged into the clear waters of the Red Sea. A new port complex was built on reclaimed land alongside the entrance, Port Tewfiq, but it never became as important a coaling station as either Port Said or Aden. The roulette tables mouldered unused: 'rien ne va plus,' whispered the greying merchants, packing up their bundles and moving to more prosperous surroundings.

So out into the Red Sea, unscrewing posh ports and setting ventilators to the wind, shaking out tropical outfits from Thresher's waterproof trunks. Awnings and deck chairs (best to bring your own, advised Loftie) covered the decks. Dashing young officers vacated their cabins to sleep on deck, risking being swabbed down early in the morning as the decks were washed by lascars, the mixed-blood crews of the Indian Ocean. In the warm embrace of the night passengers hung over the rails to marvel at the phosporescence, the souls of those who had died at sea, said devout Muslims, themselves now on their way to the tomb of the Prophet aboard little Jiddah-bound steamers. 'The Pilgrims' P-and-O-gress,' commented *Punch*.

The shores of the Red Sea were still unfriendly, with Wahhabi Muslim fanaticism on one side and wild, untameable Africa on the other. But unlike their predecessors a mere fifty years earlier, passengers now could be as blissfully ignorant of these local disturbances as today's airline users often are of life beyond the airport perimeter. More to the point in the context of the Eastern Question, though hardly of pressing interest to most of those steaming through those translucent waters, Europe had carried its rivalry for empire into the Red Sea. Egypt and the Ottoman government followed suit. Grand themes of imperial expansion were enacted tentatively along these arid coasts and the occasional steamer apprehensively steering between the reefs caused havoc among inexperienced African spectators. Ventures into the interior all too often led to disaster but along the coast European rivalries were making themselves felt. The British acquisition of Aden in 1839 was partly offset by the French acquisition of Obock on the Somali coast in 1862; later the French developed Djibouti on the other side of the same bay. In 1869 Italy bought Assab on the inhospitable Danakil coast for 6,000 Maria Theresa dollars, 'to introduce the thin end of the wedge of European civilisation and order.' 'It seemed to be a law of nature,' Captain James Mackenzie had written with foresight after returning to England through the Red Sea in 1838, 'that the civilised nations should conquer and possess the countries in a state of barbarism' and thus extend the blessings of knowledge, industry and commerce among people hitherto sunk in 'the most gloomy depths of superstitious ignorance.'[18] The choice of words rankles today but the

27   *Homeward bound at Yuletide.* More economic compound expansion engines freed the decks of coal, leaving room for deck chairs and Blind Man's Buff.

captain was not far wrong: thanks to position and the steam engine both Aden and Djibouti thrived.

A trickier venture, with long-term implications, was the British expedition into the highlands of Abyssinia in 1868 to rescue a group of European hostages imprisoned by the Emperor Theodore. Among them were the son of Christian Rassam, who had been on Chesney's expedition, as well as the British consul from Massawa on the coast, a Captain Cameron. The expedition was mounted from India, another tribute to steam, while some 6,000 mules were collected at Alexandria from all over the Mediterranean and sent on down to Obock. Extra coal had to be laid on – 30,000 tons at Bombay, 10,000 at Aden, the main base of the expedition and communications centre for the army. While the ships were at anchor in Annesley Bay, their engines were used to desalinate water for troops and animals. Chinese labourers laid a 12 mile railway from the coast inland; their materials (carried by elephant) were seconds from India, as were the small worn-out locomotives. Bombay forgot to send the spikes to fix the rails and the rolling stock turned out to be obsolete. The line was ready just in time to handle the expedition's evacuation. In the end the prisoners were recovered and the Emperor killed at the siege of Magdala. The anarchy in Abyssinia which followed the Emperor's death encouraged the Khedive Ismail in Egypt to try to extend Egypt's control of the Nile valley southwards, a policy which would subsequently ensnare the British in the same region in the 1880s. But now, as Kipling versified:

> Be'old a cloud upon the beam,
>   An' 'umped above the sea appears
> Old Aden, like a barrick-stove
>   That no one's lit for years an' years.[19]

When Marco Polo visited Aden in the thirteenth century it was thriving on the sea route between India and Egypt. Its economy had declined in the eighteenth century partly because of the falling coffee trade, partly because of the rise of aggressive and unsettling Wahhabism in the Arabian interior. By the beginning of the nineteenth century Aden had become a desolate straggling village with barely a thousand inhabitants. Its nineteenth-century prosperity was built on coal. 'The American who said if he held prosperity both in the place unmentionable to ears polite and in Aden, that he "should part with his Aden holding and live in Hades for choice", was guilty,' reckoned the telegraph engineer J. C. Parkinson, 'of a coarse exaggeration in which it is the fashion to speak of this well-abused corner of the world.'[20] To the

British, as well as to disgruntled imperialists of other nations – in particular the French and the Italians – it symbolised British hegemony in the Red Sea; in 1883 during the French war in China, the British even had the nerve to forbid Aden's coal to the French, who were led to develop the port of Djibouti.

Aden occupies a magnificent site on a peninsula formed by the crater of an extinct volcano, well protected from monsoons and with a deep easy channel. Its climate for much of the year roasts its inhabitants as thoroughly as any volcano. But its potential as a British staging post between Britain and India had been spotted as early as 1802 by Lord Valentia who, eyeing French designs on Egypt, prophetically called it the Gibraltar of the East and recommended its fortification. Valentia produced an impressive report on Aden and the Red Sea in his three-volume *Voyages and Travels in India, the Red Sea, etc.* (published in 1809), taking only six months to write it; it was illustrated by his companion on his voyage, Henry Salt, artist and subsequently consul-general in Alexandria and ardent collector of antiquities. Valentia's tour was upset, however, by quarrels with the captain of their tiny vessel; midsummer in the Red Sea is not conducive to good temper. In due course Bombay's enthusiasm for steam communications with Egypt led to Moresby's charting of the Red Sea in the 1830s and in 1837 the British consul-general in Egypt was recommending to the Foreign Office the development of Aden as a coaling depot. Socotra had been mooted but was disqualified by the absence of a suitable harbour and the prevalence of malaria. The same year an Indian vessel, the *Duria Dowlat*, was plundered near Aden and its passengers outrageously mistreated; several high-ranking Indian ladies on their way to Mecca were insulted – most shocking to the British public. Commander Haines, who was sent to investigate the incident, mentioned in his report what an excellent sheltered harbour Aden possessed. The East India Company offered to buy it from its owner, the Sultan of Lahej; when their offer was spurned Haines was ordered to occupy it, using the *Duria Dowlat* incident as a pretext.

The British occupation of Aden established a peaceful haven in a peninsula where law and order had otherwise disintegrated. Although it remained in a state of semi-siege from hostile Arab neighbours, by the mid-1840s Aden had grown to a thriving settlement of 16,000 inhabitants. This compared with the 1,300 that Haines had found in 1839. By the 1880s there were 30,000 inhabitants. Haines received small thanks for his efforts, which included importing water as well as soil from Bombay with which to grow vegetables; after struggling for several years to govern the colony despite Company parsimony and lack of interest, he was dismissed because of a deficit in the accounts and ultimately imprisoned for debt. The Bombay government was only interested in Aden as a coal depot, in the Red Sea as a highway, and wanted no greater involvement.

The settlement's new commercial prosperity was largely the creation of Bombay Indians – craftsmen, builders, blacksmiths and coolies as well as the soberly dressed father figures of the Parsee community. Ottoman expansion down the Arabian littoral of the Red Sea and Egyptian expansion down the African littoral aggravated British fears for its communications with India but this tightly knit community was not daunted; it used every opportunity not only to corner the coal trade but also to extend its own trade throughout the area. The opening of the Suez Canal and subsequent developments in the size and design of steamships resulted in the abandonment of Aden's Front Bay, facing the breezes of the Indian Ocean, in favour of the Back Bay, dredged deeper in the 1880s and more sheltered for the bunkering on which Aden was to thrive. Its commercial and military importance gave Aden nearly a century of prosperity.

Generations of Cowasjees and Muncherjees sent boats out to the steamers to enquire after passengers' needs and satisfy them at their well-stocked emporia on Prince of Wales Crescent. Occasionally pass-engers had the luxury of a night ashore – staggering on their sea legs to carriages that whisked them across the narrow isthmus to the town, situated in the sun-scorched crater, along the blown, blistered Esplan-ade to the Crescent Hotel overlooking the dusty but indubitably imperial parade ground of Aden's hard-worked garrison. When the Brassey family arrived in their famous yacht *Sunbeam* in 1878 they were treated with style, the Parsee merchant Mr Cowasjee sending his private carriage to meet them and conduct them to his store, 'an emporium for every conceivable article', and thence to the Hôtel de l'Univers. *Sunbeam* was owned by Sir Thomas Brassey, son of the railway contractor, who took both yacht and family on several notable voyages including one round the world described in 1878 by his wife Anne in *The Voyage of the Yacht Sunbeam*, during which they visited Aden.

But coal was Aden's prime commodity. Compound expansion engines ate less coal but owners of the vessels in which they were installed wanted to save every available inch of space for valuable freight, which made frequent fuelling stops imperative. Most of Aden's coal still came from Wales, usually sent by the cheaper Cape route and offloaded into the decaying hulks of ignominiously retired steamers anchored in Back

Bay or off Steamer Point. Coal deteriorates if kept too long in hot climates and Aden's hot winds caused gas to evaporate, hence the importance of keeping supply routes secure; oil, to which Winston Churchill switched the British navy just before World War I, can at least be stored. Large steamship companies such as P.&O., Messageries Maritimes and the British India Steam Navigation Company had their own coal depots and fleets of colliers. Once emptied, the little colliers continued east to fill up with rice, jute or cotton for the return journey.

Coaling was filthy and passengers were advised to disembark during the process; it speeded up considerably with the introduction of steam-driven machinery in the 1880s – 8 tons a minute by the end of the century, compared with the *Hugh Lindsay*'s 100 tons in four days in 1830. Coaling coolies were usually Somalis, forty of whom could coal a steamer at a rate of 30 tons an hour. Somalis were also taken on board steamers as stokers, as they were reckoned to be suited to withstanding the heat of the furnace in the tropics. Arnold Wilson, a young political officer stationed in south-west Persia, worked his way home as a stoker in 1913: 'I soon found out how to wield a shovel and how to spread the fine coal over the length of the grate. I learnt how to time my stroke to follow the heavy pitch or roll of the vessel, and when and how to rake the bars. I took my turn at the ash-shoot and my watch with three other men, clad only in a pair of rope shoes to save the feet from being burned by hot ashes.'[21] P.&O. warned its stokers never 'to indulge the inexcusable and filthy habit of lying down on their bunks in their working clothes.'[22]

More coal was stored on the nearby island of Perim, guarding the tricky straits of Bab al-Mandeb at the entrance to the Red Sea which the British just managed to occupy ahead of the French. Perim had undergone a number of foreign occupations over the years, one of the most notorious being that of a band of British pirates in the eighteenth century, among them the British freebooters Avery and Kidd who tried to establish a base there but were defeated by lack of water. It is a hardship post to this day: often obscured by squalls and mist, yet a waterless rock with barely a glimmer of shade, not even for its Russian guardians, whose presence in cold war days sent shivers down western spines similar to those touched off in the French by the British – and vice versa – 150 years ago.

Garrison morale for the British was bolstered when Perim was made the terminus of the British–Indian telegraph link in 1870. The Abyssinian War of 1868 and crises triggered by the Russian advance in Central Asia led to a demand for better telegraphic communications

28 *The stoke hole.* Aden as a major coaling station attracted many African
labourers, seen here stoking a steamer's engines.

with India, and two years later Aden became a cable station on the
British–Indian telegraph linking Bombay and Europe. In Europe the
telegraph initially developed alongside railway lines, with telegraph
officers in every railway station. In less stable parts of the world such
lines were vulnerable to local unrest, as proved to be the case in Persia
and Mesopotamia. Less vulnerable were the sea routes where the cables
were unreeled across the oceans, laid by steam vessels. When the sea
bottom was a couple of miles down the weight of cable hanging from
the ship made it likely to snap if the vessel pitched too violently. So no
less a paragon of stability than Brunel's *Great Eastern*, whitewashed
against the heat of the Indian Ocean, carried the British–Indian burden
of cable, coiled like a mythical dragon all over her decks – including
more than 1,000 miles of it in the second-class saloon – to be uncoiled
at a rate of 6 knots. It was copper cable, wrapped in hemp, and the
dreaded *teredo navalis*, which had devoured an earlier cable laid in 1859,
was discouraged by the pitch in which the cable had been dipped. One
drawback to this otherwise sensible precaution was that the pitch was
inclined to melt in the Indian Ocean heat and make the coils stick
together.

Those involved in the operation, such as the engineer J. C. Parkinson,

29 *New Crowns for Old*: Benjamin Disraeli is offering Queen Victoria the imperial crown of India to add to her other titles

"NEW CROWNS FOR OLD ONES!"

lived in the utmost comfort. At Aden the public was allowed on board, members of the Parsee community prominent among the curious. The whitewash soon vanished beneath a coating of coal dust; 'you cannot be on her decks five minutes without having the face and hands of a coal-heaver,' grumbled Parkinson. The *Great Eastern* continued as far as Perim before handing over to her sister cable ship *Hibernia*. There was no room for such a monster among the coral reefs of the Red Sea, however well charted. But the *Great Eastern* had done well, wrote the patriotic Parkinson, in carrying out Brunel's original goal of bringing east and west closer together, albeit by electricity.

> They have wakened the timeless Things; they have killed their
>   father Time;
>   Joining hands in the gloom, a league from the last of the sun.
> Hush! Men talk to-day o'er the waste of the ultimate slime,
>   And a new Word runs between: whispering, 'Let us be one!'

At four shillings a word it would have cost Kipling £9 8s. to send this to England.[23]

Within a few months of the inauguration of the canal foreign warships

– French, Austrian, Prussian, Dutch, Spanish – were calling at Aden, asking for coal, determined to ensure that the Red Sea remained an international waterway. The British in Aden, in India and in London looked askance at such assumptions and from a simple way station Aden rapidly developed into a linchpin of British naval imperialism. In the same year that Disraeli bought the Khedive's canal shares for Britain he acquiesced in the Queen's desire to add 'Empress of India' to her already impressive list of titles: the Tsar was an Emperor – why not, therefore, the Queen, as a gesture to offset the advance of the Russian empire in Central Asia? In 1876 Aden received the ultimate accolade as well as its indisputable incorporation into the Indian Empire when Lord Lytton, proceeding that year to India to take up his appointment as first viceroy, landed at Aden from HMS *Orontes* as the first point in his new dominions, creating a precedent followed by every later viceroy.

Like most visitors, no viceroy stayed for long in Aden. After receiving eminent members of the community in ceremony suited to the status of the new Empress' envoy, Lord Lytton steamed out of Crater Bay into the Indian Ocean to the strains of 'Rule Britannia' and the honking of steamer hooters. A few days later he arrived in Bombay for an even more melodramatic demonstration of loyalty from this diamond in the imperial crown. With the opening of the canal, Bombay had reaped a just reward for its long patronage of steam communications with home. It thrived now not only on communications but also on trade, principally cotton. Increased shipping led to the expansion of its superb harbour, surely one of the most impressive on the Indian Ocean. After 1911 Bombay's pride would be symbolised by the great Gateway of India rising from the shore out of the mist, built to commemorate the coronation of King George V and Queen Mary. A state of perfection had indeed been achieved: no more than two to three weeks after leaving home shores newcomers to India could disembark to spend their first night on imperial soil at the Taj Mahal Hotel, turreted and domed on the Apollo Bunder, reclaimed from the Indian Ocean.

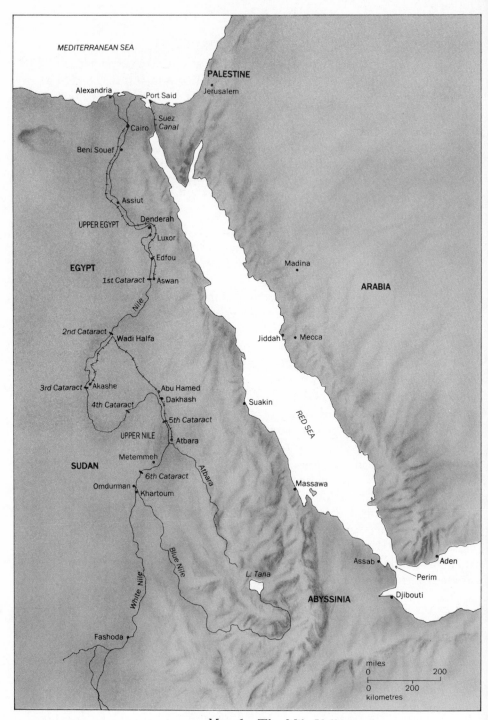

Map 6 The Nile Valley

9

The Capricious Stream

The improvement of communications with India brought an appreciation not only of the strategic importance of the lands between Europe and India but also of the cultural significance of the relatively little-known crossroads of the Middle East. While much of the Levant, Mesopotamia and Persia – to stick to the names of the period – had little to offer the traveller in the way of comfort, Egypt – largely thanks to Muhammad Ali's encouragement of the European entrepreneur – had acquired certain luxuries to entice the leisured.

Europe had been fascinated by Egypt long before anyone mentioned Suez Canals or Overland Routes but they, and steam, brought Egypt and its curiosities considerably closer. 'The capricious stream' was the term used by William Russell[1] to describe not the Nile but those who were now flocking for pleasure to steam up and down its rich silt-laden waters. For those en route to India or returning home, Keats had invented the excuse for a break in the journey:

> Nurse of swart nations since the world began,
> Art thou so fruitful? or dost thou beguile
> Those men to honour thee, who, worn with toil,
> Rest for a space 'twixt Cairo and Decan?[2]

Visiting the sights of Egypt by boat was no novelty; ever since Napoleon's expedition had revealed the splendours of ancient Egypt for the first time on such an impressive scale, Europeans had been sailing up and down the Nile on board elegant dahabiahs or feluccas, visiting Luxor and Karnak, Edfou, Denderah and Aswan. They were drawn partly by greed for the antiquities described by Napoleon's team of savants from the Institut d'Egypte but also by a taste for the safely exotic, enticed by Napoleon's superb publicist, the artist Dominique Vivant Denon. 'There, where the deities of the earlier world keep their colossal state in the silence of the Desert,' intoned Major Charles Head, a staunch advocate of the Overland Route, in 1833, '... it would be impossible to sojourn without pleasure, or to depart without instruction.'[3]

Following Napoleon's expedition, the French in particular developed close cultural as well as commercial and political ties with Egypt, demonstrated (to British discomfiture) by the decipherment of the Rosetta Stone by Henri Champollion in 1828. In 1857 Auguste Mariette established the Antiquities Service. Writers came and rhapsodised, such as Gérard de Nerval in 1843, Flaubert and Maxime du Camps in 1849; artists such as Horace Vernet, Antoine Dauzats and Prosper Marilhat painted an exotic, lascivious Orient reclining restfully on couches and cushions as they themselves had reclined rather less restfully on their Nile boats. In 1869 several boatloads of cultured French gentlemen, many of them members of learned societies, steamed up the Nile, viewing the wonders of ancient Egypt before being hustled to the modern wonder of the Suez Canal. On board the little *Behera* paddle-steamer were Eugène Fromentin, pen rather than brush in hand, Jean Léon Gérôme the painter, the sculptor Albert Guillaume, half a dozen journalists, Egyptologists and scientists. 'Le long panache de nos fumées, rabattues par le vent de Ouest, court sur cette immensité, mobile et plate, et y fait des ombres,' mused Fromentin.[4]

Meanwhile the development of the Overland Route began to attract the British. The actual overland part to India through Egypt was a mere 250 miles, most of it over peculiarly dreary desert. But the associations, the hypnotic power of those pyramids, the grandeur of the Nile – no other part of the route contained such mystery, and harmless mystery at that. Poets made play with it. Shelley (who, like Keats, never went near the Nile) dilated on the sources of the great river:

> Month after month the gathered rains descend
> Drenching yon secret Æthiopian dells . . . [5]

Leigh Hunt, also writing in London, was more vivid:

> It flows through old hush'd Egypt and its sands,
>   Like some grave mighty thought threading a dream,
>   And times and things, as in that vision seen
> Keeping along it their eternal stands,—
> Caves, pillars, pyramids, the shepherd bands
>   That roamed through the young world, the glory extreme
>   Of high Sesostris, and that southern beam,
> The laughing queen that caught the world's great hands.[6]

Stirring his own countrymen, Victor Hugo extolled Egypt in his *Le feu du ciel*:

L'Egypte – elle étalait, toute blonde d'épis,
Ses champs, bariolés comme un riche tapis,
Plaines que des plaines prolongent;
L'eau vaste et froide au Nord, au Sud le sable ardent
Se disputent l'Egypte; elle rit cependent
Entre ces deux mers qui la rongent.[*7]

The greater security in Egypt also attracted artists in search for topographic variety, a speciality of such British artists as David Roberts, Thomas Allom or the indefatigable William Bartlett, who died in 1854 on his way home from his fifth trip to the Near East. During it he must have produced well over a thousand drawings, which were engraved and published in a dozen or more books, such as his *Gleanings on the Overland Route*.[8] Some sketches made their way to the celebrated dioramas, collections of enlarged views described by one enthusiastic promoter as 'the embodiment of the poetry of oriental travel' – admission one shilling. Others were used to illustrate a kind of Overland Route board game, played between Southampton and Calcutta (see illustration page 41).

For British as well as French, archaeology began to have a great fascination. The portals of the Louvre and the British Museum were crowded with visitors gasping at the huge stones brought home from the Near and Middle East. In 1833 the French accepted Muhammad Ali's gift of an obelisk and in 1836 a special barge was sent up the Nile with a removable stern to collect it; the obelisk was rolled into the hold, the stern replaced and the barge towed down the Nile, across the Mediterranean and up to Rouen by *Le Sphinx*, a small naval steam packet built for the French in Liverpool. *Le Sphinx* had earlier been used in the 1830 French expedition against Algeria, steaming from Toulon to Algiers in five days. The obelisk was finally raised with great aplomb in the Place de la Concorde.

The British were rather more disdainful about a similar gift. Cleopatra's Needle had lain prostrate for many centuries in the Alexandrian dust until Muhammad Ali had the inspiration to offer it to the British to commemorate the coronation of George IV in 1820. Henry Salt, British consul-general at the time and an expert stone remover, was asked by the British government whether it was worth the expense of building a vessel just to take it back to England. Salt said firmly, no. 'I

* Egypt stretched forth, golden with corn,/her fields many coloured like a rich carpet, plain extending upon plain;/ to the north infinite cold waters, to the south the scorching sands/fight over Egypt; meanwhile she laughs,/caught between these two devouring seas.

wish they would offer the Trafalgar Square Pillar to the Egyptians,'
wrote Thackeray in 1844, 'and that both of the huge ugly monsters
were lying in the dirt there.'[9] But eventually a philanthropic spirit
emerged – Erasmus Wilson, a wealthy surgeon with a passionate interest
in Egyptology and antiquities, who in 1877 offered £10,000 for the
transportation of the obelisk. A special cylindrical vessel, *Cleopatra*, was
built round the obelisk and towed to England by the tug *Olga* in
September, a tempestuous time of year. In a storm in the Bay of Biscay
Cleopatra broke away from her tow and Cleopatra's needle was eventually brought up the Thames by the steam yacht *Eothen*, to be erected at
the Adelphi steps on London's Embankment above a cache of contemporary treasures: a Bible, toys, cigars, a razor, the dress and toiletries of
a fashionable woman, photographs of the most beautiful women of
Victorian England and a complete set of current English coinage. A
companion obelisk went to New York to be set up in Central Park.

   Despite pious hopes that steam would bring the benefits of Christian
civilisation to the unenlightened millions of the east, it was initially
better at bringing unenlightened Christians to gaze at the eastern

30 Proposals for transporting Cleopatra's Needle from Alexandria to
    London. The obelisk was nearly lost in a Bay of Biscay storm.

marvels. As early as 1828 Dr Madden met on top of a pyramid an English engineer equipped with 'a small pie, a piece of Cheshire cheese, and a bottle of English porter ... This, I thought, is the march of intellect indeed; a few years more and steam boats will "bridge" the Mediterranean; and our little Misses will pass the holidays at Memphis and eat sugar plums on top of the Pyramids.'[10] Madden was right, more or less. P.&O. realised the potential of augmenting its income from government mail contracts with that of tourists to Egypt and the Holy Land and had the good sense to employ some excellent publicists, notably Thackeray. 'A delightful excursion ... so easy, so charming, and I think profitable,' rhapsodised Mr Titmarsh in hindsight, although he was not always enchanted at the time, despite the free champagne on Sundays while on board after divine service; 'I can't but recommend all persons who have time and means to make a similar journey.' Thackeray was an experienced hack but he leaves the reader feeling faintly uncomfortable: is he being ridiculed? or is P.&O.? Or Thackeray's companions, or the whole world of those who, captivated by Regent Street displays of dioramas and panoramas, Bloomsbury's pyramids or Leicester Square's well-endowed Egyptian ladies supporting portals and palaces, vacated their armchairs to be borne there in person by P.&O.?

Royalty of course did not need to depend on P.&O. They had their steam yachts, most of them built in Scottish or New England yards that had specialised in the iron clipper or coastal paddle-steamer, treasuring a tradition of fine craftsmanship. Queen Victoria, representative of a young generation, sailed north aboard the old royal sailing yacht, *Royal George*, in 1842 and wrote in her diary that 'we heard, to our great distress, that we had only gone 58 miles since eight o'clock last night. How annoying and provoking this is!'[11] She hired a paddle-steamer for the return voyage and the same year the keel of her first steam yacht, *Victoria & Albert* was laid. A second-generation *Victoria & Albert* was built in 1855, and used by the Prince and Princess of Wales for their trip to Egypt in the spring of 1869. The interior was a celebration of Victorian Gothic, modified by Prince Albert's choice of rosebud chintz for the soft furnishings from canopied beds to the humble stool. Up the Nile they steamed, the Prince and Princess in fact more tranquilly in a dahabiah, the *hoi polloi* more noisily in the royal steamer or, humblest of all, the kitchen steamer. 'The worst of a steam boat, in one respect,' commented Russell who was with them, 'is that it always enables one to go on – and on he goes accordingly; whereas in a sailing vessel, odious as delays may be, there is much involuntary sight-seeing to be done when the wind is foul.'[12] Other royalty also saw the steam yacht as the ideal vehicle for communicating with far-flung territories in reasonable comfort. One of the most eccentric yachts was built at Fairfield in Scotland for Tsar Alexander II in 1880, and was named *Livadia* after a Crimean town where the Tsar had a palace. It was designed by Vice-Admiral Popov of the Russian navy, an enthusiast for circular ironclad batteries, who thought the design could be adapted for a steam yacht. The idea was that the circular shape would make it steadier and she was built with three funnels abreast. She came complete with rose garden, illuminated fountains and wine racks for 10,000 bottles. But alas for *Livadia*: the Tsar was assassinated before stepping on board and she was relegated to the ultimate disgrace of being a coal hulk.

Thus the hallmark of stateliness was set by Europe's monarchs. Those who did not display their grandest steam yachts at the opening of the Suez Canal made quite sure they both had them and displayed them thereafter. The rulers of Egypt had been quick to set an example; a private paddle yacht on the Nile not only would facilitate the movement of their entourage, it would also enable them to display their might and glory as rulers to the population of Egypt. This was a particularly important consideration given the reluctance of their sovereign lord, the Ottoman Sultan, to give them the status they hoped for. Muhammad Ali, captivated by the showier aspects of steam, led the way with his little steam yacht the *Nile*, designed as a potential fighting vessel but used to bring troops home from Syria to Egypt after the Egyptian invasion had come to an ignominious end. In the 1850s Muhammad Said Pasha had a flotilla of steamers, led by his own *Turquoise* of which de Lesseps wrote: 'it is quite beyond me to describe the luxurious character of the fittings, the painting and the furnishing of this vessel. With its doors in oak and citron wood, its locks and fastenings in solid silver, its medallions representing rivers and animals painted by distinguished artists, its staircases with silver balustrades, its divans lined with cloth of gold, its dining room 40 feet long and its bedrooms like those of a palace.'[13] His own quarters consisted of a 40-foot long saloon, with a large divan decorated with handsome Lyons silk brocaded in gold, a bedroom, a dressing-room and a bathroom in white marble. 'How lucky we are!' he exclaimed, 'to be making such a journey in so much comfort . . . Champagne flows as though it filled the Nile.'

When it came to Ismail, never one to curtail his views of the magnificence appropriate to Egypt's ruler, the Khedival household needed a flotilla of steamers whenever he took to the water. According to Ellen Chennells who was employed as governess for the Khedive's children in the 1870s, so large a retinue accompanied the Khedive on one winter's voyage that six large steamers and seven dahabiahs were required and Miss Chennells had to spend the night on board one of the dahabiahs and the day on board the steamer.[14] A very trying arrangement, she decided.

With such gleaming examples before them it is hardly surprising that the kings of industry, especially American and British, made sure they also demonstrated their power and glory, steaming up the Thames or the Bosphorus for a bit of culture, anchoring off Cowes or Kiel for the yachting season, basking off Cannes or doing a Cleopatra up the Nile. Understandably, Russell's ever-swelling 'noisy, odd, capricious stream' of humbler tourists also expected to take to the water with speed and comfort. Between them Waghorn, P.&O. and Mr Titmarsh had drawn the crowds.

Among the crowds, complaining about them but also attracting them, was Lady Duff Gordon. Lucie Duff Gordon lived in Egypt for seven years, battling with tuberculosis and setting a fashion for winter sojourns on the Upper Nile copied by the Prince of Wales on a second visit in 1872 and subsequently many others, and posthumously inspiring John Cook (son of Thomas) to build a hospital at Luxor for wintering invalids. 'The English milord, extinct on the Continent, has revived in Egypt and is greatly reverenced and usually liked,' wrote Lucie to her husband.[15] She herself found Cairo too damp and cold in the winter and steamed upriver on the government steamer to Luxor. Not the most comfortable of journeys; she had been promised the boat all to herself but the availability of such steamers was subject to the Pasha's whim, he had commandeered the rest of the fleet and Lucie was therefore joined by an assortment of benighted passengers. In addition there were quantities of fleas but, thankfully, no rats or cockroaches. Moreover the Pasha had emptied all the bunkering spots of their coal so that at Beni Souef not far from Cairo 'we kicked our heels on the bank all day, with the prospect of doing so for a week.'

In Luxor she lived in 'rickety rooms, constructed of very frail materials' built into a corner of the temple. It has since been cleared away but one can still savour Lucie's view by climbing up into the temple gateway. The house was painted by Edward Lear who was one of her many, sometimes too many, visitors. In a good winter season there could be over a hundred boats tied up at Luxor and ill-equipped tourists who had evidently not read their guidebooks would ask to borrow her saddle, camp-stools and umbrellas. 'This year I'll bolt the doors when I see a steamer coming,' she wrote. But she had partly herself to blame, for to finance her extensive residence abroad she published her letters and thus attracted an admiring throng of well-wishers. The steamer business was in full swing, and so were P.&O.'s timetables either side of the Overland Route. So nothing could be easier than breaking the journey with a few weeks' Pharaonic exploration. Tourists were advised to take candles for tombs, a fine sieve for sifting out those shards, and some small excavating tools. Also, if you have time to spare, asked Sir Gardiner Wilkinson, author of *Manners and Customs of the Ancient Egyptians*, in the guidebook he wrote for the publisher John Murray, be so kind as to copy the astronomical ceilings in the royal tombs of Thebes.[16]

Lucie finally lost the battle with her tuberculosis, and died most poignantly in February 1869. Later that year the Suez Canal was opened. Amongst de Lesseps' advance party for the inauguration was the elderly Thomas Cook, who had chartered a special steamer to take a group of passengers, first-class only, to the inauguration, a twenty-day trip costing 50 guineas for all travel and accommodation on board. Thomas Cook's first excursion had been by train from Leicester to Loughborough for a shilling a head in July 1841, a trip organised for the Leicester Temperance Society. Cook then specialised in outings for temperance societies. His great moment had come in 1851, the year of the Great Exhibition, to which he arranged numerous outings, the main emphasis being on their cheapness.

Thirty-two ladies and gentlemen took up the inauguration offer and travelled up and down the Nile as well as through the canal for over three weeks under the auspices of Mr Cook, who had already taken the continent and the Holy Land under his wing, and with the tender gastronomic attentions of Mr Eftzeinberger of the Hotel Victoria in Venice. They even had the bonus of following 'in full cry' the Prince and Princess of Wales in their little flotilla, the Prince 'in the abandon of shooting jacket, knickerbockers and felt hat.' Next year Cook offered the Nile and the Holy Land together, a popular combination that cost 155 guineas excluding wine but including twenty days on a Nile steamer. This time there were sixty English and Americans including twenty ladies. 'All honour to their bravery and endurance,' extolled the company brochure, *The Excursionist*, while everything possible was done to ensure that bravery and endurance were not needed.[17]

Under the driving personality of Thomas Cook's son, John, the company from its office in the grounds of Shepheard's Hotel briefly monopolised steam navigation on the Nile. They set up a regular steamboat service from 1873, became the sole agents for the government postal service between Assiut and Aswan in 1876, and developed a season of regular winter tours up and down the Nile. A range of British-made steamboats – barges, ferries, passenger paddle-steamers (some side-, some stern-wheelers) – were shipped out to Egypt and assembled and maintained at Cook's shipyard at Boulaq on the banks of the Nile. Their design was usually based on those already in service for many years on Indian rivers, combining high horsepower with shallow draught. One such vessel could accommodate 800 people in two tiers of cabins, surrounded by verandahs and covered with awnings. Standards of luxury varied according to the purses of passengers and how far they wished or could afford to imitate the wealthy on their princely pleasure yachts; Thomas Cook's own humble background led to the company making sure its Nile cruises were available to those of modest income as well as to would-be Pierpont Morgans.

Cairo hotels also flourished, nine-tenths of their clientele American and English, with a sprinkling of Belgians and French, wrote Amelia Edwards in 1877. 'Here are invalids in search of health; artists in search of subjects; sportsmen keen on crocodiles, statesmen out for a holiday, special correspondents alert for a gossip; collectors on the scent of papyri and mummies . . . and the usual surplus of idlers who travel for the mere love of travel.'[18] Among these hotels was Shepheard's, 'excellent cuisine and highly Anglicised,' wrote Théophile Gautier.[19] Amelia Edwards came to get out of the rain, fell in love with the Nile and quoted a Frenchman named J. J. Ampère who declared that 'un voyage en Egypte, c'est une partie d'ânes et une promenade en bateau entremelées de ruines.'[20] It should be taken slowly; even with the assistance of steam the tourist's pace matched that of the river, a tempo made leisurely by the grand expectations of the guidebooks of the period: hieroglyphs to be learned, ruins to be excavated, the health care and the meal times, the sketch pad and the journal.

Most tourists came for pleasure, but joining them in the 1880s and 1890s came those with a far from capricious aim: to take control of the Upper Nile. With the opening of the Suez Canal European rivalries in the Red Sea appeared, in British eyes, to threaten communications with India. By the 1880s these rivalries, stimulated by the new imperial aspirations of France, Italy and Germany as well as of Britain, extended to the wider sphere of the Indian Ocean and its shores, regarded by the British as the gateway to their prized possession. As Africa became part of the imperial struggle so control of that great waterway leading to the heart of the continent, the Nile, became its focus.

European involvement in Egyptian affairs grew during the Khedive Ismail's lifetime, partly due to debts incurred during the construction of the Suez Canal, partly to Ismail's extravagent expenditure on more dubious development projects, incurring huge debts to European bankers who then turned to their respective governments – French and British – to bail them out. In 1876 this had given Disraeli, then British Prime Minister, the opportunity to buy the Khedive's shares in the canal. In 1879 both French and British governments assumed financial control of Egypt and insisted on Ismail's replacement by his son Tewfiq, a situation so humiliating to the Egyptians that three years later a nationalist revolt broke out under the leadership of Colonel Ahmad Arabi. The revolt was aimed at the Europeans who had stepped in to administer Egypt and prevent the Khedive accumulating further debts. The British took action without the French, dispatching an army to Egypt, bombarding Alexandria and defeating Arabi at the battle of Tal al-Kabir. Among the vessels taking part in the bombardment of Alexandria were eight ironclad warships, the first time the British had used them in action; they included the 6,000-ton *Invincible*, clad with 8-inch armour, the 11,400-ton *Inflexible* and *Temeraire*. Arabi was exiled and the British reluctantly assumed control of Egypt, appointing Sir Evelyn Baring, later Lord Cromer, as British agent and consul-general effectively to rule the country.

Control of Egypt involved the British in the regions of the Upper Nile, thanks to Egyptian imperial adventures inspired by European expansionism. Along with Egypt the British acquired a commitment upriver to Sudan where a powerful revolt against Egyptian rule was being led by a Muslim fanatic known as the Mahdi, his followers as Dervishes. The Egyptian government first tried to suppress the revolt in 1883 with an expedition under a British mercenary, General Hicks. This had been annihilated by the Mahdi's troops and left the British with the problem of extricating remaining Egyptian garrisons before they met the same fate. In the eyes of the British public a rebellious Sudan constituted a threat to the Suez Canal and communications with India through the Red Sea. Moreover control of the Nile was regarded as essential to the control of Egypt. Sir Samuel Baker wrote to *The Times* in October 1888 that any civilised power could divert the river and cause 'the utter ruin and complete destruction of Egypt proper.'[21]

The one man who seemed capable of executing the almost impossible task of saving the garrisons was Charles Gordon. Gordon was intensely disliked by Prime Minister Gladstone, nicknamed the Little Englander because of his opposition to such imperial adventures. But Gordon was

31 British ironclads bombarding Alexandria to quell nationalist riots, 1882.
This led eventually to the British occupation of Egypt.

extremely popular with both Queen Victoria and the British public. He himself declared that 'if the whole of the Eastern Sudan is surrendered to the Mahdi, the Arab tribes on both sides of the Red Sea will take fire. In self-defence the Turks are bound to do something to cope with so formidable a danger, for it is possible that if nothing is done the whole of the Eastern Question may be reopened with the triumph of the Mahdi.'[22]

The story of Gordon's dispatch to Khartoum in 1884, his haphazard communications with the outside world, Lord Wolseley's failure to rescue him in 1885 and the successful defeat of the Sudan rebellion by Kitchener in 1896–8 is one of the great emotive sagas in British imperial history, of interest here because of the determination of certain British leaders that control of the Nile, by locomotive and steamboat, including its remote upper reaches, was essential to the security of Egypt and India. Control was to be exercised once again by steam communications. River communications on the Nile, fragile and erratic, using small paddle-steamers with shallow draught to cope with the low-water season, were fairly well established at the time of the Mahdi's revolt. There were even some rail communications from Cairo to Assiut and more planned above Wadi Halfa. Both trains and boats were taxed to their utmost, however, by the demands made on them by successive military commanders. Both ultimately demonstrated their strategic flexibility in war.

John Cook was commissioned to provide boats to convey Wolseley's expedition from Alexandria to Wadi Halfa. He combined relentless energy with considerable organising skills and did his best; it was after all a profitable contract to transport 6,000 men, 6–8,000 tons of stores and 400 Canadian whale boats and their crews. Wolseley had come across the Canadian whaler in his Red River expedition to Canada in 1870 and ordered a fleet of them, manned by Canadian *voyageurs* for his Sudan expedition. They were sturdy but heavy boats and all had to be carried over the Nile cataracts on the way to Khartoum. But the odds were against both Wolseley and Cook; a flock of tourists is more amenable than are battalions of soldiers, let alone their officers, and John Cook was later accused of making an undue profit. Moreover Cook's own boats might be fine for leisurely tourists but were not designed for military campaigns; Lord Charles Beresford described one of them as a cross with a kangaroo: if anybody touched the helm or walked from port to starboard the boat listed violently, knocking Beresford off the locker on which he was trying to sleep.[23] Cook was also blamed by some for the failure of coal supplies, which may well have helped bring about Gordon's fate at the hands of the Mahdi. Cook retorted that the military authorities had expected him to transport double the quantities for which he had contracted.

At first there had been talk of using and extending existing railways. One new railway was initiated – for the benefit of Indian troops landed on the Red Sea coast at Suakin; an armoured train was brought in to run on it but its single gun could be fired only straight down the line or at a slight angle to it. Both the Suakin line and the extension to the Nile line were beset with problems; the latter included time-consuming cuttings. Stores piled up at Assiut, rolling stock at Wadi Halfa consisted of four broken-down engines and soldiers had to push the only working engine round a sharp curve in the line. 'Engines on wheels and off wheels, tanks and tenders, bolts and boilers lay around while the walls and chimneys of buildings that were to have formed the terminus and steam house of the railway stood unfinished in the desert,' according to one of Wolseley's officers, Sir William Butler.[24]

Meanwhile Wolseley borrowed the Khedive's yacht *Ferooz* and steamed impatiently upriver, depressed by the monotonous landscape. He also ordered two stern-wheelers with particularly shallow draught from a Yarrow firm, based on what he remembered of American river steamers on the Mississippi during the Civil War. But the problems of Nile navigation above Wadi Halfa were considerably greater than those on the Mississippi. The river was inadequately surveyed and the timing of the annual flood open to endless debate, yet a high water level was essential if the boats were to get through the four formidable cataracts between Wadi Halfa's Second Cataract and Khartoum. As the Nile fell the coal ran out and the steamers had to be pulled over the Second Cataract wrapped about with protective mats. This clearly demonstrated the hopelessness of trying to transport an entire army by river.

Further on, the rat-infested steamer *Bordein* together with the little *Talahawiah*, luckily well plated given the hostility on either bank, struggled up the Nile, their fires stoked with wood collected from abandoned houses along the riverside, painfully dragging themselves over the final Sixth Cataract, even spending one night tied up in the middle of it. The expedition, at this stage led by Sir Charles Wilson, finally came within sight of Khartoum on the morning of January 28th, 1885. They saw immediately that there was no flag flying on top of the Governor's palace. Khartoum was in the hands of the Mahdi and Gordon was dead.

So demoralised were Wilson and his steamer crews that they managed to wreck both steamers on their retreat back down the river. They had to be rescued by Beresford, who displayed the ingenuity so characteristic of early steam handlers in ensuring his little *Safieh*, 'a penny steamer in a packing case', survived Arab batteries, bullet holes in the boiler, and potential treachery from the Sudanese crew (Beresford kept the local pilot handcuffed near the helmsman whom he was supposed to be guiding) to get near enough for Wilson to make a desperate escape.

One is struck by the extraordinary endurance of those little steamers. They were like matchboxes, packed around with improvised plating or padding, their engines under tremendous pressure, hot as hell, their only safety lying in the inaccuracy of the enemy's gunfire. Their endurance was matched by the courage of those on board who put their trust in them. Not surprisingly the steamers were in poor shape when they finally returned to Cairo with the news of their defeat and Gordon's death; certainly they were no use for first-class tourism. John Cook vowed he would have nothing more to do with government contracts, abandoned the Nile mail contract and had to rebuild his company's entire fleet. The failure of Wolseley's expedition was not the end of the story, but immediate revenge was out of the question; no sooner had

Wolseley returned to Cairo than British attention was diverted to India and Central Asia. The Mahdi died in June 1885 and was succeeded by the Khalifa Abdullah, but Cromer in Cairo was fully taken up with reorganising the administration of Egypt.

Almost ten years later, in 1895, general elections in Britain returned a Conservative government under that staunch imperialist Lord Salisbury. 'Obeying the call of the Nile,' as his daughter Lady Gwendolyn Cecil put it, 'the necessity of safeguarding the Nile from the intrusion of other white powers [became] a separate and dominating factor in his policy.'[25] Competition for new colonies was now undisguised and looked like being played out over the headwaters of the Nile. French intrigues were already rumoured in the region and Egyptian troops under British officers in fact re-entered the Sudan with the tacit aim of relieving Dervish pressure on the Italians in Abyssinia. Overtly the British government reckoned the time had come for the Khalifah to be taught a lesson.

The teacher this time was Herbert Kitchener. There was no rush to put down the revolt in the Sudan; Kitchener, who was now sirdar, effectively commander-in-chief of the Egyptian army, took his time. Once again the Nile was the main channel for communication and invasion but this time land was used as effectively as water. The river was better known now; Kitchener had a flotilla of gunboats organised and at least three armed steamers were used to patrol the river, sent out from Britain in sections, transported by rail to Akashe, 100 miles south of the Second Cataract and assembled by qualified men. The gunboats were sturdy vessels. With a draught of only 39 inches they could nevertheless steam at 12 knots, their decks protected by steel plates and on board every modern improvement – such as ammunition hoists, telegraphs, searchlights and steam winches. They were designed by a Mr Thubron of the Nile Engine Works in Cairo, built in eight weeks in London and in a subsequent journey of 4,000 miles they were transhipped seven times without a single important piece being lost. 'Train after train arrived with its load of steel and iron, or with the cumbrous sections of the hull, and a warship in pieces – engines, armaments, fittings and stores – soon lay stacked by the river,' wrote an ardent young journalist on the expedition, Winston Churchill, in his *River War*.[26]

The train and the railway on which it ran were even more crucial to Kitchener's success. 'In a tale of war the reader's mind is filled with the fighting ... The eye is fixed on the fighting brigades as they move amid the smoke; on the swarming figures of the enemy; on the General, serene and determined, mounted in the middle of his Staff. The long trailing line of communications is unnoticed. The fierce glory that plays on red, triumphant bayonets dazzles the observer; nor does he care to look behind to where, along a thousand miles of rail, road and river, the convoys are crawling to the front in uninterrupted succession. Victory is the beautiful, bright-coloured flower. Transport is the stem without which it could never have blossomed.' So wrote the impassioned Churchill.[27] 'Fighting the Dervishes was primarily a matter of transport. The Khalifa was conquered on the railway.'

The American Civil War in particular had demonstrated how potent a weapon a railway could be. From the earliest days of European railways it was recognised that while trains might not always move troops fast, they at least arrived in good health. In the American Civil War the Confederate army, outnumbered by the Unionists, could never have put up the fight it did without using railways to their maximum. A railway line offered a remarkable degree of flexibility; provided the contractor did his job properly, provided also that labour was plentiful, it is astonishing how quickly a strategic line could be laid and was laid, often over far more difficult terrain than the northern Sudan. Until the end of World War I almost all the railways in the Middle East and Central Asia were laid with this military role uppermost in the minds of their planners, although not all with the speed of the Sudan railway.

To avoid cataracts, to make supply routes flexible and to circumvent the Sudanese, Kitchener initially constructed the railway another 100 miles below Wadi Halfa. Having completed that as far as Akashe, he decided to build a direct 232-mile line across the desert to Atbara. It was built as far as Abu Hamad in 1897 and continued to Atbara the following summer. Water and money were the usual problems. Much of the line was being built at the hottest time of year. It had to be built before winter. It had also to keep to its budget. Railways had as bad a habit of exceeding estimates as major construction projects today. If one were working for Kitchener, however, one's estimates did not go awry. The lessons of that 12-mile line in Abyssinia had been well learned. According to Churchill the speed of progress was mainly due to a young Canadian, Lieutenant Edouard Girouard, to whom all the logistics of building the line were entrusted. Girouard had trained on the Canadian-Pacific railway and later became director-general of Egyptian railways, then of Sudan railways and subsequently governor-general of Nigeria. Churchill's list of his preoccupations are worth quoting as an indication of what was involved in building a railway line. How much carrying capacity was required? How much rolling stock? How many engines? What spare parts? How much oil? How many lathes? How many cutters? How many trolleys? How much water? How much coal? How many miles of rails, how many thousand sleepers? Where could they be procured at such short notice? What tools would be required? How much skilled labour was wanted? How were the workmen to be fed and watered? How Lieutenant Girouard must have sweated and swotted in his hut in Wadi Halfa.

It is scarcely within the power of words to describe the savage desolation of the regions into which the line and its constructors plunged. A smooth ocean of bright-coloured sand spread far and wide to distant horizons. The tropical sun beat with senseless perseverance upon the level surface ... Alone in this vast expanse stood Railhead – a canvas town of 2,500 inhabitants, complete with station, stores, post-office, telegraph office, and canteen, and only connected with the living world of men and ideas by two parallel iron streaks, a three-foot six inch gauge, growing dim and narrower in a long perspective until they were twisted and blurred by the mirage and vanished in the indefinite distance.[28]

Cromer wanted the line to be metre gauge to fit in with existing lines in Egypt but Kitchener, knowing that the most readily available rolling

32   Arrival at the railhead of the narrow gauge railway built to carry
Kitchener's expedition across the Nubian desert, 1898

stock and locomotives were in the Cape, insisted on 3ft. 6in. as being the Cape gauge. Labour was provided by a hastily recruited railway battalion whose only qualification, according to Churchill, was 'capacity and willingness to work' – Dervish prisoners, Egyptians, Dinkas, Shilluks and a hundred civilian Sudanese.

The first spadeful of sand was turned on January 1st, 1897; track laying began on May 8th. Sleepers were laid, railway spiked to sleeper, plate-layers spiking and ballasting, the great 80-ton locomotive edging its way south with the supply train bringing 'the letters, jam, whisky, soda-water and cigarettes which enable the Briton to conquer the world without discomfort.' One evening Kitchener's own whisky was mixed with water found with remarkable perception or luck by engineers digging through a rock structure at 'Station 4' in the hopes of finding water suitable for both drinking and the engines. Kitchener did not think much of the flavour but was delighted with the find, which confirmed the feasibility of the desert route. Abu Hamad was reached by November 21st, another stretch to Dakhash by December.*

It was then decided to extend the railway to Atbara, establishing the southern terminus at the great confluence of the Nile with the Atbara river, about 200 miles north of Khartoum, thus sealing the doom of the Dervishes. Gunboats ensured the safety of the railway while it was being built and provided reconnaissance. They also accompanied the final drive on Omdurman. 'The gun boat arrived on the scene and began suddenly to blaze and flame from the Maxim guns, quick-firing guns and rifles . . . The terrible machine, floating gracefully on the waters – a beautiful white devil – wreathes itself in smoke,' wrote Churchill.[29] Thanks to the power of steam on rail and river and Kitchener's effective use of it the Khalifah's forces were finally defeated and Gordon revenged at the battle of Omdurman, September 2nd, 1898.

The defeat of the Khalifah was never viewed by the British as the ultimate aim of Kitchener's expedition or the railway. Occupation of the Upper Nile was the goal. The French, ill reconciled to the British hold on Egypt, were known to have their eye on the all-important headwaters of the Nile, hundreds of miles to the south, as one means

---

* Churchill traced the journey of a box of biscuits from Cairo to the front: to Nagh Hamadi (340 miles by rail); from there to Aswan (205 miles) by boat; from there to Shellal (6 miles) by rail; from there to Halfa (226 miles) by boat; from there to Dakhesh railhead (248 miles) by military railway; from there to Shereik (45 miles) by boat; from Shereik to Bashtinab (13 miles) by camel; from there to Omsheyo (25 miles) by boat; from there to Geneitti (11 miles) by camel; finally from there to Berber (22 miles) by boat. Not much biscuit by the end of the journey.

33   *Off to Fashoda, fighting the sud* (weed-clogged stretches of the White Nile):
     Kitchener aboard the steamer *Dal*, leading the White Nile flotilla

of challenge. 'Once masters of the upper and middle basins of the Nile
they could at their pleasure fertilise or sterilise the countries of the
lower Nile by building a few barrages,' wrote the French colonialist
Pierre Monteil.[30] Germans, Italians and Belgians were also in the offing,
their imperial ambitions carried along Africa's great rivers aboard little
armoured river steamers. A month after the fall of Omdurman
Kitchener was once more heading upriver on board the steamer *Dal*
accompanied by four gunboats and several hundred troops to snuff out
any sign of French occupation. Sure enough a French party under the
redoubtable Colonel Marchand had indeed undertaken a 1,500-mile
crossing of central Africa with the help of some tiny but most efficient
river steamers and had pitched their tents near a small riverside
settlement notorious for malaria named Fashoda, some 350 miles south
of Khartoum. Two months later Kitchener came round the downriver
bend.

While the French and British governments in Europe were preparing
to go to war over their rival claims to the Nile, Queen Victoria telling
Salisbury she could hardly bring herself to consent to 'a war for so
miserable and small an object,'[31] on the waters of the great river a most
gentlemanly drama was enacted with even Kitchener behaving with

exemplary good manners. Marchand called to congratulate Kitchener on his victory over the Khalifah; Kitchener congratulated Marchand on his epic journey. They had lunch together and Kitchener called on Marchand in the afternoon. Marchand gave him some fresh vegetables for supper which perhaps accounts for the *Pall Mall Gazette*'s incensed attack on French pretensions as 'a French picnic that was outstaying its welcome.'[32] Diplomatic telegrams flashed between Paris and London; the British and French press attacked each other's imperialist bullying. In the end the French were obliged to recognise British control of most of the Nile; expeditions to sustain Marchand's claim would have faced an impossible task in reaching him. The French flag was lowered, British and French had breakfast together (croissant or bacon and egg?) and the French quietly steamed upriver, eventually to trek through Abyssinia to Djibouti on the Red Sea coast. Kitchener and his political masters could at least feel that British control of that particular gateway to India was assured.

10

Through Caspian and Caucasus

Long before the British on board their little steamers made their bid to secure the headwaters of the Nile, thereby adding to the security of their Red Sea route to India, the advance of technology had begun to bring significant political and economic changes on land. In the realm of communications these affected particularly those areas where Europe meets Asia, of great concern to the Russians anxious to expand into Central Asia. Many Russians regarded this somewhat amorphous area between the Black Sea and the western Chinese border as rightfully theirs, an empire potentially as vital to the Russian economy as India to the British. This theme, promoted in often bellicose articles and speeches, aroused consternation among the British in India, who with some justification saw the Russian advance in Central Asia largely as an advance on India.

As steam technology progressed, other gateways to India and the east appeared. Not only steamships but now also steam locomotives and the tracks they ran on were seen as posing a possible threat to national or imperial security. By the early 1880s Russian and British governments were watching triumphantly or apprehensively as through dripping forests of rhododendron, past torrents of erosive water pouring under the track, past clearings in the forest which the creepers were already engulfing, an engine laboriously pulled its load up into the Caucasus from the eastern shore of the Black Sea and more easily down to the Caspian shore. By the late 1880s, about 800 miles to the east on the other side of the Caspian Sea, another engine slowly pulled its train through the scorched windswept dunes on the edge of the Karakum desert, dunes that were inclined in a sandstorm to pile up on the track itself. The driver kept a wary eye out for camels asleep on the line. And at the same time about a thousand miles south-east of that track yet another engine toiled, through and over the gorges of the Bolan Pass of Baluchistan, which in a rainstorm can fill in a matter of minutes and wash away the track. This driver kept his eye out for gun-toting Baluchis and Pathans, inclined to take pot shots at his train. These were the railways of the Great Game, eyed anxiously by both players.

In 1884, inside one of the carriages of the first train, on the Transcaucasian line between Batum on the Black Sea and Baku on the Caspian was journalist Charles Marvin, erstwhile correspondent of *The Morning Post*, who belonged to, indeed fed, a growing body of Russo-phobe opinion in Britain and India. He had had a complicated journey to the Caucasus, steam propelled on land and sea (for £35 first class from London to Batum), and was now heading for the oil town of Baku on the western shore of the Caspian. The object of his journey was to demonstrate to his countrymen how the strong hold that Russia now had on the Caspian and the surrounding territory, particularly to the east, had one main objective: India.[1] Marvin was a contentious writer whose Russophobia sold well. Exaggerated misunderstanding existed on both sides of the substantial geographical barriers separating India and Central Asia, and Russian propaganda, much of it translated into English by intelligence officers in Calcutta, did little to appease the panic aroused by Marvin's polemic.

British concern about the security of sea approaches to India was paralleled by concern about land approaches. Russia was seen as steaming ever closer to the mountain and desert barriers that isolate India from the rest of Asia. Russia was equally anxious about the security of her new Asian empire, approached by land through the Caucasus and by sea across the Caspian and acquired as part of that search for stable frontiers noted in the Crimea. She was not averse to using this search deliberately to stimulate fear in British India – not difficult – and distract attention from other activities in the European arena. Similar moves by the British in India to consolidate their northern frontiers had the same effect on the Russians. Military mobility was essential to these far-flung empires. British mobility was to a large extent dependent on its navy; Russian mobility was to depend on its railways.

Even in the 1880s these were few and far between, especially once one stepped outside the confines of European Russia. Travel in Russia was certainly no pleasure trip – vast, empty, featureless spaces, frozen over through a long winter, then a sea of mud, or a dust haze; bone-rattling tarantasses the principal vehicles, ill-equipped posthouses the only source of sustenance. The springless tarantass was like a ram-shackle wooden boat, resting on long wooden poles, themselves resting on wooden axles of wooden wheels. But when foreigners complained about the poor state of Russian travel it was pointed out that Russia had

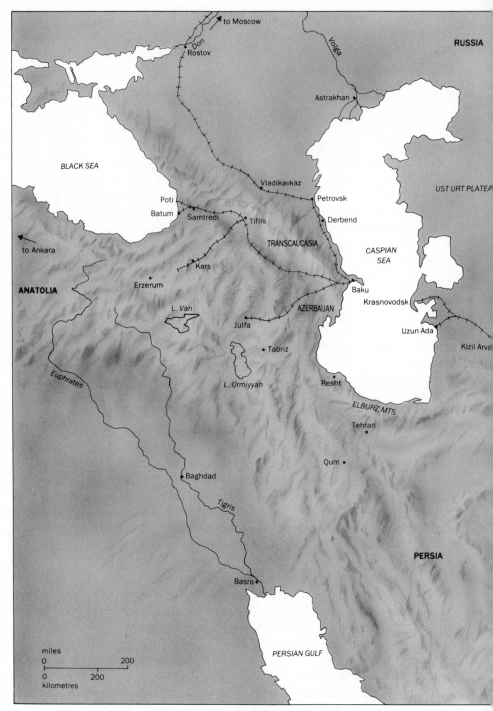

Map 7   The Transcaucasian and Transcaspian Railways

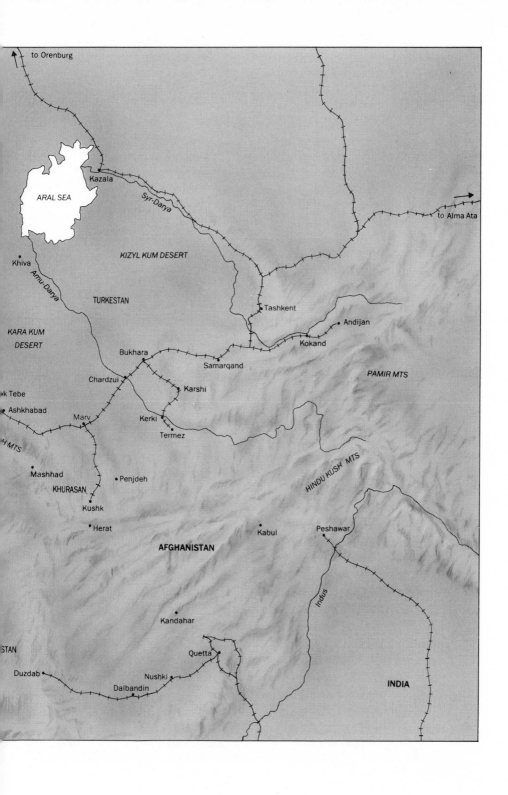

no natural barriers to invasion, therefore why speed up the passage of invaders? A proposal in 1835 to introduce railways to Russia was met by a characteristic 'nyet' from the Minister of Finance; such a network was unnecessary, costly and a danger to public morals. Railways, he declared, knowing the Tsar agreed, 'encouraged frequent purposeless travel, thus fostering the restless spirit of our age.'[2] Modern Soviet governments evidently agree with Tsars, if the problems of modern travel in the Soviet Union today are anything to go by.

The traditional way to move round Russia was by a vast network of waterways, some 50,000 miles in all, reaching from the Neva in the north to the estuaries of the Don and Dniepr in the Black Sea and the Volga in the Caspian. From May to October processions of barges, each 100 feet long and over 20 feet wide and laden with grain, trailed north and south over their placid waters. Sometimes they were pulled by horses, sometimes more cheaply by women whose husbands were no doubt singing those throaty, lugubrious boat songs to urge their women on. Along the major rivers were the market towns of the Russian interior whose annual fairs drew merchants from every corner of the empire.

When it came to imperial expansion and imperial defence the Volga was the most significant of these waterways. Rivers are to Russians what the sea is to the British or western prairies to Americans. They arouse profound emotion, a sort of soulful fatalism in keeping with their grandeur. They are so immense, so long, so wide. And the greatest of them all is the Volga. It rises in the north between Moscow and Leningrad (here referred to as St Petersburg), was linked by a series of canals with the Baltic by 1709 and debouches nearly 2,500 miles later, having flowed past the quays of Astrakhan, oozed through several miles of malarial swamps, and slithered over mud banks into the Caspian Sea. To this day it remains a principal channel between the European and Asian Soviet Union. Passage is not easy: the river freezes over between November and May, rises dangerously with flood water as soon as the ice melts and changes course when the floods bring down with them tons of sand, creating new shallows and rendering the channels of the delta yet more hazardous. Descriptions of the great river depend on the personality of the traveller, some fascinated by the varied communities along its banks, some dismayed by the vastness, the emptiness, the barbarism of the lands through which it flows. 'Je ne sais rien de plus triste et de plus uniforme que l'aspect du Volga,' wrote Alexandre Dumas the elder. 'Pas une île qui rompe la monotone de cet immense cours d'eau; pas une barque qui l'anime; c'est la solitude sous la sombre domination de son roi légitime, le silence.'³

Parties of European merchants, Marco Polo in mind, had tried since the sixteenth century to find a satisfactory approach to Indian spices via the Caspian and Persia but the principal drawbacks were always the climate and the violence along the route. The most diligent of these was Anthony Jenkinson who descended the Volga in 1591, crossed the north-west corner of the Caspian to Derbend and made his way through Azerbaijan to the Shah at Qazvin. He was followed within the next few years by several other British merchants but clearly there were easier ways to obtain oriental spices or to reach India, by then via the Cape. In the eighteenth century Jonas Hanway also investigated the route but was discouraged by the prevailing anarchy of northern Persia. Russian merchants tried to set up a regular shipping service down the Volga in the 1660s but Caspian pirates swooped on their barges. Nevertheless it was by water that Russian expansion southwards and eastwards began in the eighteenth century, under the energetic auspices of Peter the Great. Eyeing the legendary riches of India, to replenish his treasury and finance his modernisation of Russia, Peter sailed down the Volga in 1713 and out into the Caspian, where he informed his generals that they were only twelve days by camel from the Afghan frontier town of Balkh. And Balkh, no one needed reminding, even then, was only a few hundred miles from north-west India, on the route by which every invader had invaded the subcontinent. Despite the annihilation of the subsequent military expedition sent beyond the Caspian, by Turkomans in the service of the Khan of Khiva, Peter's remark was quoted by most British writers on Russian expansion in the nineteenth century, includ-ing the prolific Marvin, for by the 1880s this vast shallow sea had become a Russian lake.⁴ Together with the Volga it has been at the heart of Russian expansion, Russian trade and Russian communications ever since.

Steam was gradually introduced on Russian rivers beginning in the 1820s. Marine steam made slow headway on the Neva and the inshore waters of the Baltic but on the rivers serf power was cheaper than steam engines, partly because the technology and the fuel were imported. Robert Fulton built the first steamboat on the Neva but died before he could ensure a proper use for it; a Scottish engineer in St Petersburg, Charles Baird, built another small steamer in 1815 but too small to have much practical application; and a Frenchman Pierre Bazaine had a project for steam tugs on the Volga in 1817 but again without any further development. In due course longstanding links with Sweden meant that most Russian steamboats were built there, supplied with British engines and crewed on the rivers and the Caspian by Swedes and Finns. But shortage of capital dogged any large-scale development; private enterprise had to wait on government patronage which would emerge in due course to encourage transport across the Caspian. By Marvin's day the scene had changed profoundly. The government now wanted to develop its eastern possessions as a source of raw materials and markets. Steam thus came to the aid of the imperial and commercial interests building up in Central Asia and on the Caspian.

This vast inland sea is not kind to sailing vessels. Its shores are mostly low-lying, marshy and lacking in good harbours, while along the western littoral the mountains of the Caucasus almost meet the sea in high rocky cliffs. More important, 'it has ever been famous for the violence and suddenness of its storms,' ruefully commented *The Times*'s correspondent, Valentine Chirol;[5] even in good weather it was notorious for its 'long roll'. Compared with the magnificent Volga steamers of the late nineteenth century those on the Caspian were workaday affairs, distinctly lacking in frills. But they chugged across from east to west in all weathers, a service between north and south being limited by the great winter freeze. They were called *shkoutes* – small side-wheelers crammed full of deck passengers and skippered by Scandinavians. Meals were to be avoided; cabbage boiled in oil and stew were typical fare. In storms the cabins easily flooded. Luckily voyages were mostly short.

By the 1880s many of such vessels were needed to handle the traffic; passengers were thankful to find deck space on anything. Marvin counted nineteen steamers of the semi-governmental Caucasian and Mercury Navigation Company, obliged to be convertible into troop transports; more troops could be transported on board the oil tankers of the Nobel brothers based in Baku on the western shore. There were also privately owned steamers. And there was the tiny Caspian flotilla of half a dozen gunboats with a flag officer known as the Admiral of the Caspian, set up originally to wipe out the nests of Turkoman pirates that used to lurk in the offshore islands of reeds. Initially the flotilla was based on Ashurada Island, so small that in storms the spray swept right across it. 'It is but the other day that the Caspian was a distant Asiatic Dead Sea,' wrote Marvin. 'It is now a busy European lake, included in the European frontier of Russian maps.' He felt (unjustifiably, considering the success of his books) that he was crying in the wilderness: 'I wished I could take one of the fleet of Caspian steamers, and proceeding direct via the Volga, the Neva and the Baltic to Westminster Bridge, turn on a steam roarer and roar a few facts into the ears of the chatterers.' In the aftermath of the Russian Revolution the British took Marvin's advice and made a number of determined efforts to gain control of the Caspian.

The Caspian and the rivers flowing into it have one major problem – winter. North of about 45 degrees latitude even the salty waters of the Caspian freeze over, piling up in impenetrable floes at the mouth of the Volga. As Russia moved eastward into Central Asia, seeking raw materials for its infant industries, its need to overcome the winter freeze became essential. Railways could do it. There are few countries in the world where the coming of the railways made such an impact as Russia, finally compensating for the lack of year-round outlets to the sea, countering ice, drought and mud. They made fuel available, they moved coal, oil and iron ore and led to the exploitation of cash crops such as cotton to feed new industries, thus at last creating new wealth to expand the industry. And, as other European powers had already discovered, they could shift armies. Russia's defeat in the Crimea was at least partly due to the immobility of her forces. Other European powers had already discovered that trains, at that stage of development, might not get troops to battle quicker than marching, but the men arrived in better shape.

In the 1830s, when railways were being built all over Britain and Europe, Russia remained one of the least industrialised countries of Europe, but in 1836 Nicholas I, who disliked innovation, was with difficulty persuaded to look at steam as a possible solution to his country's economic backwardness. An Austrian engineer, Franz Anton von Gerstner, built a delightful little line over the 26 miles between St Petersburg and the Tsar's summer palace out at Tsarskoe-Selo as a demonstration venture. Gerstner had built the first public railway on the continent – the Danube–Moldavia line. In 1834 he was invited to Russia to visit iron ore mines in the Urals, communications with which so appalled him that he offered to supervise the building of a railway from St Petersburg all the way to Kazan on the Volga, taking in Moscow and the major market town of Nijni Novgorod (Gorky) on the way. The Tsar was unenthusiastic so Gerstner contented himself with the Tsarskoe–Selo line, known as 'Gerstner's toy', ready for use in 1837.

Gerstner died in the United States while looking for new locomotives for the Tsar, and those for the line were provided by Timothy Hackworth and Robert Stephenson. Hackworth's sixteen-year-old son John took his father's locomotive to St Petersburg in winter, a journey full of hazards. John and the foreman from the Shildon works, George

Thompson, had to put the locomotive, a double-trunk engine mounted on six wheels and costing £1,884 2s. 9d., on a sledge for the last part of the journey 'in weather so severe that the spirit bottles broke with the frost and they had to run the gauntlet of a pack of wolves.'[6] When it came to testing the engine in St Petersburg, the cylinder cracked from the cold; poor Thompson had to make a midwinter dash to Moscow to have another one made at the ordnance factory. But the journey had a happy ending when priests consecrated the locomotive for its first official ride in October 1837 with special prayers and chanting choristers. 'Many people crossed themselves at the sight of these gigantic machines as if they had been demons' while the Tsar, seeing the delight with which both his family and his subjects trundled back and forth between city and countryside, finally succumbed to technology. In 1839 he agreed to send a mission to Europe and the United States to look into the state of railway engineering. It returned with one of America's foremost railway engineers, Major George Washington Whistler, who was appointed to supervise the construction of a line between St Petersburg and Moscow.

Whistler, father of the artist, was working at the time on the Boston–Albany stretch of the Western Railroad, now the New York Central. Joseph Harrison of Philadelphia and Thomas Winans of Baltimore (son of the locomotive builder Ross Winans, who refused to go) joined him in St Petersburg and set up a locomotive and rolling stock works in a disused armaments factory on the edge of the city at Alexandrovsky. Winans did well out of the contract and built himself a palatial house at Baltimore, named Alexandroffsky after their engineering works, as well as a country residence named *Crimea*. Whistler's was hardly an enviable task, but 'the difficulties which would have discouraged most men in such a country and among such a people at the outset of such an undertaking, vanished before his unequalled industry, knowledge and tact,' according to an American visitor in 1848.[7] Russia's railway builders had to be men of great stamina and dedication and the problems faced by Whistler remained fairly typical of much railway building in Russia. Virtually all materials had either to be imported or manufactured for the first time in a country lacking the most basic machinery. The American brought twenty assistants with him but they did not stay for long because 'they could not support the ennui attending a residence where there are no public meetings, nor discussion, nor newspapers, nor elections, nor lectures, not even a temperance excitement to alleviate the pains of exile.'

The bulk of the labour came from a Russian innovation – the railway battalion, levied from the military. As semi-skilled labour these railway battalions turn up repeatedly, in snow, sandstorm, malarial rain forest, trained to lay tracks as fast as an impatient military establishment demanded, particularly those strategic lines in the Caucasus and Central Asia. Manual labour was provided by an army of serfs, several thousand of whom are believed to have died in the process of building the line. Whistler with difficulty reconciled the Tsar to a 5-foot gauge, to this day the standard throughout the Soviet Union, but in many other battles he was defeated. The materials were defective, there were not enough funds, and those that there were disappeared too often into other pockets on the way to the railway. Coal for the engines had to be imported from Wales and had often lost much of its calorific value by the time it arrived. Whistler himself died worn out two years before the railway was completed in 1851.

That line was as far as Nicholas was prepared to go. When the Crimean War began in 1854 there were still only 650 miles of railway in Russia and communications between the north and the scene of war were abysmal. Movement of troops and supplies was dependent on the seasonal flow of rivers and the demands of Russia's armies had far outgrown the means of transporting them, dispersed as the troops were in Poland, the Baltic provinces and the Caucasus as well as in the

34 A locomotive imported in 1836 for Russia's first public railway, from St Petersburg to Tsarskoe Selo

Russia. 1836.

Crimea. Nicholas died in 1855, and his son Alexander II was more easily persuaded of the civil and military benefits of a network of railways. As soon as peace was signed, Alexander sent one of Russia's richest financiers, Baron Stieglitz, to Paris to discuss railway finance. Stieglitz organised a European consortium including Crédit Mobilier and its founders, the Péreire family, which undertook to build five major lines between the Black Sea and the Baltic to facilitate Russian grain exports. Slowly the railways took off.

Railway development soon matched imperial dreams, enabling Russia to defend her territorial gains. Armies as well as merchants needed good communications. Russia's defeat in the Crimean War left her feeling even more vulnerable in the Caucasus, the neck of the empire that formed the western edge of the Great Game board; her navy was virtually excluded from the Black Sea and attempts to push Turkey back from the eastern end of the sea had failed. To the Tsar and his government it was clear that something had to be done to improve their communications with so vital a territory. The Caucasus is a narrow, exquisitely beautiful and mountainous neck of land between the Black Sea and the Caspian. It includes the high Caucasus range, rising to over 5,600 metres, an effective barrier between Europe and Asia except where the mountains fall into the Caspian at Derbend, north of Baku. The northern slopes are immense inclined plains, 'rent by deep and narrow valleys and vertical clefts'; there are surprisingly rich pastures on top for herds of sheep but 'the valleys are frightful abysses, the steep sides of which are clothed with brambles, while the bottoms are filled with rapid torrents foaming over beds of rocks and stones.'[8] 'Where did Europe end and Asia begin?', wondered J. P. Baddeley on one of his travels in the region,[9] for the 'purely practical reason' that his insurance policy excluded Asia. If the boundary between the continents was taken as the watershed, 'it might depend, when crossing a razor-edged pass and losing my foothold, upon whether I slipped down one side or the other, who would get or keep the sum insured!' It is an area hostile to invasion and it was certainly viewed in that light by its inhabitants for much of the nineteenth century.

Descending south along the Georgian Military Highway, carved through the mountains by the Russians to improve their Caucasus defences, the traveller heading for Tiflis, the ancient capital of Georgia, is struck by the relatively rich, peaceful landscape of what later became known as Transcaucasia, repeatedly invaded and divided in times ancient as well as modern, most recently at the end of World War I. To ward off aggressive neighbours, the last Georgian king abdicated in

1798 in favour of the Russian Tsar, Paul I. Two years later the kingdom was incorporated into the Russian Empire and the umbilical cord binding the two countries was built over the next two decades, the magnificent military highway. The western half of modern Georgia – Abkhaz on the Black Sea coast – remained part of the Ottoman Empire for another eighty years.

With the highway nearly complete the Scotsman Sir Robert Ker Porter, artist at St Petersburg court, was travelling south along it in 1817 en route for an artistic tour of Persia. He was impressed, as were all travellers, by the achievement of the highway, as it disappears between the cliffs of the Dariel Gorge, then soars over the Kazbec Pass. 'It remains for time and enterprise to prove,' he wrote, 'whether the two seas of the Caspian and the Euxine may not bring India nearer home to us, and by different hands.'[10] However, as Ker Porter would have been the first grimly to acknowledge, the general state of communications in Russia and its expanding empire left much to be desired. Steam took a long time to increase mobility in Asia.

Fifty years after its submission no one travelled unarmed through the Caucasus and to this day it remains one of the wildest parts of Russia. Georgia itself, though one of the hubs of Russia's southern defences against the Ottoman Empire, remained largely inaccessible, the military highway virtually the only link with the north. Russian attempts to enforce their control of the Caucasus and Transcaucasia brought them up against the Turks in Circassia as sharply as at the Dardanelles. The Turkish cause was espoused by early Russophobes, particularly the idiosyncratic Scotsman David Urquhart. Posted to the British embassy in Constantinople in the 1830s, Urquhart triggered the *Vixen* incident of 1836, when the Russians seized that British vessel on a charge (probably justified) of carrying arms to Circassian rebels. The incident caused a tremendous uproar in Britain, not only among Urquhart's allies but within the government as well.

But the Russians were concerned at least as deeply with another later rebellion in the Caucasus, in even more inaccessible Daghestan, which was led for twenty years by the remarkable Shamil. The British failed to give Shamil the overt strategic backing he needed for victory. Such an alliance, according to railway enthusiast W. P. Andrew (who with Chesney had been advocating a Euphrates Valley railway), would have protected the shores of India and made 'the ridge of the Caucasus the advanced line of defence of our Empire in Hindostan.'[11]

The revolt of the Daghestanis reconfirmed the strategic importance of the Caucasus in the eyes of the Russian government. Only by subjugating the area could they make the most use of links with the Black Sea, Persia, Turkey and even India. The British were slower to see its importance and howled all the louder when they did. 'Fatuous and frothy politicians of both parties' might ridicule Marvin's predictions, but his books aroused an enthusiastic following.[12]

So in 1867 the Russians embarked on the first attempt to link by rail their new Asian dominions with Europe. Over the next forty years they developed a network of lines in and out of that strategic isthmus linking Europe and Asia, each new branch of which sent an ever more violent shiver down British spines. In the aftermath of the Russian Revolution German and Turkish activity on and around the lines demonstrated how justified some of the shivering actually was.

North of the mountains Vladikavkaz (Ordzhonikidze today) was by 1875 connected by rail with Rostov on the Don, already one of Russia's major industrial centres, linking up there with the lines built to transport southern grain to the north. But there was no question of running a line through the Caucasus range itself to Tiflis. The Black Sea looked a possible alternative; at least it was connected by steamboat with the ports of the Crimea and rivers Don and Dniepr, although their potential was hamstrung by the freeze imposed on Russian naval shipping by the treaty terms that ended the Crimean War. Along the Black Sea coast lie the old princedoms of Mingrelia and Imeretia, cut off from Georgia by the Little Caucasus, or Suram Range. Its major peaks rise to 4000 metres but the Suram Pass has been used for millennia as a caravan route between east and west. A railway line could be run from the Black Sea port of Poti, the only harbour on the eastern littoral actually in Russian hands, over the pass to Tiflis, a difficult line to build and certainly not commercially justifiable, but at least usable all the year round.

It was a brief moment of glory for the town of Poti at the mouth of the river Rion, 'a most disagreeable feverish place,' according to General Cunynghame who visited it with his son in 1872; 'the swamps which surround it throw out most dangerous fogs and agues and the houses are infested with noxious vermin.'[13] Poti is surrounded by the malarial reed beds of the river estuary which give way in the foothills of the Little Caucasus to impenetrable forests soaked by the warm heavy rains of the eastern Black Sea. Its useless harbour was to have been improved after the Crimean War by a lengthy and expensive mole, but like many such projects arguments over cost meant that it was never finished; the virtual blockade of the Black Sea by the Turkish fleet after the Crimean War killed what local backing there might have been.

Russian expansionists in St Petersburg nevertheless argued enthusiastically for the railway from Poti along the ancient caravan route. The military and strategic advantages, they reckoned, would more than compensate for its expense – about £16,000 a mile, £9 million in all. For comparison, at this period Americans were laying tracks for as little as £1,600 a mile, the idea being to prove them economically viable before strengthening them. The average cost of an English track – the most expensive – was about £31,000, French £14,000; Indian broad-gauge tracks cost about £17,000 a mile.[14]

Such argument eventually won the day. Engineers arrived from Britain and France, railway battalions from other parts of Russia. 'The sickness among the English employed on the railway works is indeed terrible,' wrote Cunynghame, as the ill-climatised men toiled through the Poti marshes. The rails were made in a factory belonging to a Welshman named John Hughes, who had set up business in the Donetz coal basin; Poti's unsatisfactory harbour could just about be made to serve for landing men and materials. The line was expensive partly because of the lie of the land but partly also because of Russia's adoption of the 5-foot gauge, something of an extravagance through the mountains compared with narrow gauge or even the standard gauge of 4 ft. 8½ in.

The original locomotives came by a circuitous sea, river and land journey from Britain along with their mostly Scottish chief erectors or *chefs menteurs* to assemble and drive them. 'Le chef menteur,' wrote one of them, Robert Weatherburn, in the *Railway Magazine*, 'was, like the wandering Jew, to be met with in the most unlikely places in Russia, erecting his engines with the aid of the village blacksmith and a handful of peasants.'[15] Most of Russia's early locomotives were imported from all over Europe but by mid-century locomotives were being made at the Kolomna works south-east of Moscow. In 1871 John Hughes had opened his ironworks producing rails for further railway extension, using machine tools supplied by James Nasmyth. The rolling stock was mostly Russian, the carriages designed along what was known as 'American' lines. In these 'open-plan' carriages ladies and gentlemen even had to sit together, according to shocked European comment. Double glazing and double doors ensured the delicious fug so characteristic of Russian trains. (Even today no one will ever allow a window to be opened.)

The line follows the right bank of the river Rion, climbs up into the Suram range, over the Suram Pass and down to Tiflis. There, for the time being, it came to a stop – 2 miles from the town in typical Russian fashion. It was finished about 1874. Three years later Russia and Turkey were embroiled in yet another war. This time it was Slav Christians in the Balkans whom the Russian government decided to rescue from the Turks, when they rebelled in 1875 against Ottoman rule. Russia declared war on Turkey in 1877. The war was fought mainly in the European arena but as before, in 1828 and 1854, Russia was also able to put military pressure on the Turks in the east, in Ottoman Circassia, while also invading eastern Anatolia to capture the great fortress of Kars. Disraeli, championing the Turks for the last time, summoned 8,000 troops from India, transporting them to Malta through the canal by P.&O. In retaliation Russia sent a mission from Tashkent to Kabul, to the horror of the Indian government, which soon after embarked on the Second Afghan War. To the gambits and gestures of the Great Game was added renewed discussion among British railway planners of a Mediterranean to India railway, while their Russian counterparts brooded over a line from Tiflis to Peshawar.

Meanwhile the transport of troops and materials within Russia was once again in chaos. In the Caucasus, cut off by a Turkish Black Sea blockade which separated Poti from communications with the river and rail networks in European Russia, the Russians' only military offensive was that into Anatolia; otherwise they stayed on the defensive despite a strong military presence stemming from the days of Shamil's revolt. An armistice was declared in January 1878 and confirmed in March. In the Treaty of Berlin signed that summer, Russia extended its Caucasian frontier well into Armenian Asia Minor. It also extended its grip on the coast, all the way to the nondescript little harbour of Batum. Russia now controlled the entire territory between the Caspian and Black Seas. Now was the time to exploit communications to the Caspian and bring it closer to Europe. Or closer to India, the British were beginning to murmur.

Commerce rather than politics provided the initial impetus for improved communications, however. Oil producers of Baku on the Caspian were mounting pressure on the government for year-round outlets for their oil in Europe. They agitated for extensions to be built from the old Poti–Tiflis line, one linking it with the Black Sea at Batum, a rather better harbour than that of Poti, and another from Tiflis to the oilfields of Baku on the Caspian. This was to become the Transcaucasian Railway, an even more remarkable feat of engineering than the Poti–Tiflis line. British Russian-watchers such as Charles Marvin viewed the line as 'purely strategic', a first stage on the way to northern India. The Russians for the moment preferred its commercial potential for on the other side of the Caspian they were opening up their access to the agricultural potential of Central Asia. Strategic potential there too, said British observers.

Baku lies in a small bay on the south side of the Apsheron Peninsula. Today it is one of the largest cities in the USSR; since the late nineteenth century it has also been one of the most turbulent. About the same time as the railway reached Tiflis from Poti, the Russian authorities had lifted a punitive tax that had kept Baku's longstanding oil industry firmly localised for many years, starting a boom led principally by the Nobel family. Emmanuel Nobel had come to St Petersburg as a torpedo engineer at the end of the eighteenth century. While his eldest son Alfred studied explosives in Sweden and developed nitro-glycerine, his two younger sons Robert and Ludwig made their fortunes in Baku. To Ludwig in particular Baku owed much of its late-nineteenth-century prosperity.

Oil exploitation methods at Baku were traditionally primitive and costly. Wells were dug by hand with diggers often overcome by gas fumes, the oil drawn to the surface by horses working pulleys, taken away in skin bags either on camels, as noted by Marco Polo, or on carts with 9-foot diameter wheels to negotiate the sand. Once production was freed from govern-ment restraints the Nobels imported American drillers and steam engines to assist their drilling, replacing bags with barrels and finally building a pipeline from wells to refinery using a steam pump to force the oil through the pipe. In 1877 Ludwig Nobel introduced his own sea tanker service, importing steam-powered bulk carriers made in Swedish shipyards, taken in parts down the Volga to be assembled in Astrakhan. The larger ones were used on the Baku–Astrakhan run, the smaller on the Volga run. Thanks to an efficient distribution service Nobel soon came to monopolise the export of Baku oil into Russia; in northern latitudes, however, American oil was still cheaper because of the deadening blight of winter on the Nobel transport system. For five months of the year his barges were immobilised by ice.

Nobel's rivals in Baku, the small independent producers, were the first to moot the idea of a railway through to the Black Sea, by which they could sell their oil in Europe unaffected by winter freezes. They raised funds by mortgaging their properties to Rothschilds, already involved in railway financing in France, and giving the financiers exclusive rights to their oil. Batum was chosen as the Black Sea outlet, its rail link completed in 1882.

Batum's occupation by the Russians had been dictated by military necessity, but petroleum now became its life blood. Within a few years

35   Ludwig Nobel,
principal developer and
exploiter of Baku oil in
the nineteenth century

the little town, of no particular significance to the Turks, had blossomed
as vigorously as the steaming forest behind it. Vessels of every nation,
including a variety of 'tank vessels' to carry the oil to Europe, crammed
into its tiny harbour. A tank steamer consisted of separate iron tanks
into which the oil was pumped from reservoir tanks at Batum or Baku.
By 1890 new 4,000-ton tankers were being built, mostly in Tyneside
shipyards; Armstrong Mitchell and Palmer were the leading tanker
builders. Nobel's tankers were mostly built in Sweden.

Such activity was due to one achievement – the construction of the
branch line to Samtredi so that oil could be exported from Baku to
Europe. George Curzon, who was there to catch the train in 1890,
compared it with an American frontier town: 'palatial buildings alternate
with hovels, and broad streets terminate in quagmires and dust heaps.'[16]
Malaria was rife, as in Poti – 'after one or two years' sojourn, [it]
commonly asserts itself in physical inertia or decline' – and most
residents 'look forward to an early flight, with lined pockets and a
resolute intention never to set foot in Baku again.' There were
compensations: despite the 'abominable smell of petrol,' commented
the French traveller Gabriel Bonvalot in 1889, 'the population goes in
for plenty of amusement, as is often the case with people who are
making, or who think they are going to make their fortune'.[17] It acquired
a cathedral (blessed by Alexander III in 1888) as well as churches,
esplanade, post office, consuls and patriarchs of all nationalities and

creeds, with a British community organizing cricket and football matches and a volunteer fire brigade.

Work on the extensions began in 1879, with French engineers from the École Polytechnique organizing Russian railway battalions. Russia's first railway battalion, learning from the use of army labour on other lines, had been formally established in the 1877–8 Russo–Turkish war. The line took over three years to complete, treading, as Marvin and his fellow Russophobes were careful to note, in the steps of Pliny along the ancient silk and spice route that begins in India and runs via Kabul, Balkh, the Amu-Darya or Oxus and the Caspian through Georgia and down the Rion River to the Black Sea. There was no question in Marvin's mind, as he steamed along the line in 1884, but that Russians, soldiers as well as merchants, would follow the same route. From Tiflis to Baku was technically straightforward; the challenge came between Tiflis and Batum. This stretch included a new line from Batum to Samtredi on the pre-war Poti–Tiflis line and a strengthening of the old line over the Suram Pass. A difficult section to build particularly in that heavy rainfall; only fifty days out of six months were fit for working, the rails were frequently washed away, the labourers, both railway battalions from the army and local peasants, were decimated by scurvy and malaria.

> The way is straight, the embankment narrow,
> Telegraph poles, rails, bridges,
> And everywhere on both sides are Russian bones –
> Vanechka, do you know how many?

So wrote the poet Nekrasov about the St Petersburg to Moscow line.[18] He might have said the same about the Transcaucasian Railway. But when it was finished in 1882, it was possible to steam all the year round from London to Baku. In summer this had been possible via the Volga; now, in winter, it was possible via the Black Sea and the Caucasus. The line was expensive to build and standards of maintenance, which was also expensive, were poor; foreign engineers were inclined to underestimate the heavy rainfall which undermined the uneven track, and trains were often derailed; passengers spotted them lying mournfully on their sides in the undergrowth beside the line. The importance of the line was exaggerated by both Russian and British imperialists, the ambitions of the one fuelling the fears of the other; the Caspian was still far from being linked all the year round with continental Russia. But the potential was plain for all to see.

'The Russian trains are constructed on the American principle,' wrote one of their admirers, Fred Burnaby on his way to Orenburg in December 1875.[19] Burnaby, a British officer with an insatiable appetite for adventurous travel, was 6ft. 4in. tall and weighed 15 stone, so he greatly appreciated the larger dimensions of Russian rolling stock. 'You can walk from one end of them to the other if you like, whilst two attendants in each carriage supply every want of the traveller. I must say that in this respect travelling in Russia is far better arranged than in England, and the refreshment rooms are unequalled by any in this country.' Despite all these advantages Burnaby had one reservation: 'the slowness of the pace which, when travelling through a vast country like Russia, is a matter of considerable importance.' Most modern travellers on Russian trains would probably agree; so did George Curzon: 'yes, he has a greater eye for comfort than speed has the Russian traveller.' Progress on the Transcaucasian line has always been leisurely – 15 miles an hour in Marvin's day – and timetables then were as irrelevant as they are today, complicated by the fact that clocks at railway stations are always kept to Moscow rather than local time. The average speed of a European train had risen by this time from the 15 m.p.h. of the Stephensons' *Locomotion* to around 60 m.p.h. Comforts included, as today, a steaming samovar in every carriage; all carriages except third class were heated, a tribute to the Russian winter but unusual enough in those days of unheated trains for European passengers to remark upon with pleasure. Charles Marvin found the rolling stock, mainly built in the north at Riga, ill designed to cope with the southern climate; the carriages leaked and he recommended that future passengers equip themselves with umbrellas. The problem was the difference in climate either side of the mountains – one humid, the other dry: 'there was not a door that would shut without terrific banging.'[20]

The crowded train left Batum once a day for Tiflis. For the first few miles the track hugs the coast, catching the full force of the weather but at least obviating expensive tunnels. 'This railway journey is the most striking and beautiful in Europe and must sooner or later become a favourite one with English tourists,' wrote Marvin. The track winds through the luxuriant rain-soaked forests of the Black Sea coast, rhododendrons, laurels, hazels hanging over the track, in summer forming a steaming greenhouse. 'What a tangle of trees we passed through,' exclaimed Bonvalot in 1889: 'an inextricable thicket, and in some of the densest parts we saw the wild boars feeding in perfect security.' 'We twist and turn about, go through many tunnels and cross the boiling, bubbling, noisy and impetuous river at least twenty times,' he marvelled.

At the foot of the mountains, soon after the junction with the old Poti line at Samtredi, the ordinary locomotive was unhooked and two Fairlie engines, already famous for their pulling power on steep track, replaced it. Trains on the Transcaucasus started out with 0-4-4 engines built by the Yorkshire Engine Company but in 1880 the railway began to acquire Fairlie locomotives, articulated double-boiler engines on which each boiler was supported by a motor bogie, designed to run through steep mountain terrain, often on narrow-gauge tracks. Some forty-five of them operated on the line until electrification in 1933, designed initially for wood fuel but later converted to oil. A 'chief erector' composed a special Fairlie drinking song:

> Ben Bogie is my name,
> Double Fairlies are my game;
> Good for any game tonight, boys,
> And always ready for a spree.[21]

Handbrakesmen were employed on each carriage or wagon.

Then began the climb into the cloud-topped Little Caucasus, 'through solemn gorges and magnificent glens', past precipitous villages and ruined forts. 'The station platforms are crowded with wild Georgian urchins' – George Curzon liked to indulge in the occasional purple passage – 'anxious to exchange for a few kopecks long strings of chestnuts or miniature bunches of grapes' while 'stately bearded figures . . . attend the arrival and departure of the trains with military regularity and survey the scene with stalwart composure.'[22] And so up to the Suram Pass, and the desolate little station of Poni, 3,000 feet above sea level, an extraordinary feat with gradients of 1:22¼ at its tightest; Marvin's train had to be hauled up by three engines, one of them a 60-ton Fairlie. Even the Fairlies could only pull a few loaded trucks over at a time: 'the operation is naturally slow, but the magnificence of the scenery repays the traveller for the delay.'

Nobel subsequently proposed building a pipeline parallel with the entire route but the government was afraid of losing vital rail revenues and he had to content himself with a small 40-mile stretch of pipeline over the Suram Pass. Nobel then suggested a tunnel and by 1890, when Curzon travelled on the line, had had his way. A tunnel had been built, larger than any European tunnel of the period, and 'opened, after the Russian fashion, with a religious service.' Curzon compared trains of oil cars with gigantic armour-plated caterpillars, each laden with a wealth compared with which that of the Golden Fleece was nothing. More rationally suspicious of the Russians than Marvin, Curzon nevertheless immediately saw the military significance of the tunnel. The construction of a pipeline was delayed until 1906 by the government's insistence that it be built of Russian materials. The Suram Pass stretch was also the first Russian line to be electrified.

From the watershed the train rolls gently down to Tiflis. For many the Georgian capital provided the last or the first taste of civilisation for a long time. It was a prosperous watering spot, popular with Russians following in the spirit of the romantic Lermontov, a Russian Byron who died in a duel in the Caucasus. Dashing officers and doe-eyed Georgian damsels frequented *thés dansants* in pillared ballrooms, bathed in hot sulphur springs or explored emporia stocked with the latest Parisian fashions. In the Hôtel de Londres Curzon studied 'the most wonderful rendezvous of varied personalities that is to be found in the East. Situated on the dividing line between Europe and Asia, and on the high road to the remote Orient, almost every pilgrim to or from those fascinating regions halts for a while within its hospitable walls.'

And from Tiflis – the countryside fast drying out, the hills arid, treeless, baking in summer – on down to Baku, that 'region of eternal fire' as Marvin so aptly called it, across the sandy salt marshes of the Apsheron Peninsula. The stations are almost the only sign of European life in the landscape, developing as prosperous little market centres. Station restaurants were good and there was usually a small bazaar on the platform where passengers could buy freshly picked fruit; Marvin was ecstatic about the water-melon which he bought for next to nothing. Even today a list of station halts that is pinned up in the corridor indicates how much shopping time passengers can expect at each stop. And still today the train as it nears Baku passes ancient derricks climbing up narrow gullies into the bare hills, salt flats densely planted with rigs which in the old days covered the ground with stinking pools of oil. The train steamed past the oilfields into Baku, coming to rest in a station whose design is remarkably reminiscent of the Red Fort in Delhi, 'one of the architectural glories of the town.'

Baku thrived on the railway even more than Batum, as the visitor can tell by the imperious offices along the streets of the business quarter that once thronged with the fashionably dressed wives of Europe's oil magnates; Nobel's initiative attracted other investors and much of the new capital in Baku was British, French, American and German; Valentine Chirol, visiting Baku in 1902, described it as a western rather than a Russian triumph.[23] By the 1880s it was 'a town of crude and as yet undigested wealth.' 'Dense clouds of smoke either hang like a pall overhead,' wrote Marvin when he arrived in 1884, 'or drift lazily with the breeze backwards and forwards.'

One might as well fear an earthquake swallowing up London, Marvin commented, as exhausting Baku of its oil. 'Russia could light all the world, lubricate all the world and paint all the world,' Ludwig Nobel boasted at a Moscow lecture in 1882. The two main oilfields were Bibi-Eilat to the south and Balakhany to the north. In the middle lay Black Town, so named because of the refineries which mushroomed there from the middle of the nineteenth century, and White Town, the residential quarter which sprang up after the lifting of prohibitions on foreign investment in 1872. 'A more noisome town than the Black Town it would be difficult to find,' wrote Marvin. By 1901 there were 1,900 wells producing 12 million tons of naphtha a year, converted in Black Town's refineries into kerosene – mainly for export – and 'residuals' used as fuel on steamboats and trains, including the Trans-caucasus trains by the 1890s. The Russians, and particularly the Nobels, were already experimenting with petroleum refuse (*astatki* or *mazoot*), previously burnt in huge pits or dumped out at sea, when in 1862 John Bidley in the United States patented an oil furnace for steamers. Two engineers in Russia – Aydon who was British and Shpavkosky who was Russian – then devised an apparatus to 'atomise' the refuse and blow it into the furnace in the form of spray. This enabled the boiler of a locomotive or a ship to be heated with the *astatki*. Early in 1869 Kamensky, the government engineer in charge of Baku port, was the first to use this in the Caspian area. As the idea of bulk oil carriers took off so did the fortunes of Britain's Tyneside shipbuilders, though Nobel's vessels were mostly built in Sweden and were able by the end of the century to carry 2–3,000 tons of oil. In 1890 a steam tanker, built by Armstrong Mitchell of Newcastle, carried George Curzon across the Black Sea to Batum.

The Russian authorities soon made it clear that they did not after all regard the Transcaucasian Railway as purely commercial. Within a year of its opening the government reimposed import taxes at Batum, thus depriving it of its status as an international free port; it remained the principal outlet for Baku oil but was no use to those European merchants who had hoped to base their trade with northern Persia there. The Russians regarded northern Persia as their own exclusive sphere of influence. It was principally the British who were affected and who interpreted the tax as yet another move in the Great Game.

As the Russian hold on Central Asia widened, a year-round rail link between European Russia and the eastern shore of the Caspian became essential to ensure the strategic mobility so vital to imperial ambitions. A line directly through the Caucasus to Tiflis was investigated – over those terrifying gorges, every bend a potential ambush by the still rebellious inhabitants. Tunnels, bridges and not least weather would have made it one of the most expensive railways in the world – £30,000 a mile – and structurally almost impossible with the wide 5-foot Russian gauge. The alternative was to extend the existing line terminating at Vladikavkaz to the little deepwater port of Petrovsk on the Caspian (now Makach-kala, after a revolutionary martyr). Such a line would also link up the newly discovered north Caucasian oilfields at Grozny and elsewhere.

Petrovsk is just south of the freeze line; vessels could use it all the year round and it was later to be linked with Baku by a storm-splashed track squeezed in between mountain and sea. Once a week the 'Petroleum Express' ran from Moscow to Rostov, Petrovsk and Baku in sixty-two hours, much the same time as today. In itself relatively insignificant, those last few miles between Petrovsk and Vladikavkaz served, like the Georgian Military Highway, as an umbilical cord to bind Russia's new Central Asian possessions to the mother country. The consolidation and defence of these possessions had become of overriding importance.

Not for Trafficking Alone

The Caucasus forms the watershed, as Baddeley's insurance problems demonstrated, between the Eastern Question of Europe and the Great Game of Asia. The Great Game was actively played over the mountains and deserts of a wide area – Persia, Afghanistan, Central Asia to the north, and north-west India to the south. It is not ideal terrain for communications, as both Russians and British found as they edged closer to each other in the 1880s and 1890s.

In 1888 a *shkoute* steamed east across the Caspian to the port of Uzun Ada, to connect with the newly opened Transcaspian Railway, linking European Russia via the Caspian with Russia's new Central Asian possessions. The most superior person on board was George Nathaniel Curzon, a young Member of Parliament already making his mark in government circles, who had been asked by *The Times* to visit the new Transcaspian Railway on its behalf. Trains were steaming for the first time that year between the Caspian and Samarqand.[1] 'We travel not for trafficking alone,' sang James Elroy Flecker's merchant in *The Golden Journey to Samarkand* in 1913, 'by hotter winds our fiery hearts are fanned,' and this certainly applied to Curzon. Politically and intellectually he dominated the Great Game for over twenty years, fixing its rules in the minds of his countrymen so that later generations remained imbued with its principles. As far as the railway was concerned he was one of many pointing emphatically at its strategic implications. Both British and Russian players of the Great Game knew that the seemingly insuperable physical obstacles of the region had frequently been crossed over preceding millennia by invading armies, several players on either side recently crossing the mountains to prove the point. The railway was merely the latest means to yet another such invasion.

While the British in India fumed at this steaming threat to Indian security and were already building their own in response, the Russians were now the ones to proclaim the civilising powers of steam and its benefits to the darkened millions of the east. If 'civilising' is at least partly equated with economic prosperity, then the Russians came rather nearer to fulfilling their mission than those who had earlier extolled for similar reasons the Overland Route to India. The American Civil War cut off Russian supplies of raw cotton but the fertile valleys of Ferghana were seen as offering an alternative source of supply for the country's budding textile industry.

Steam on land in Asia, therefore, acquired an economic significance along with a political and strategic force at least as powerful as its civilising mission. The British on the other hand never accepted that Russia's Central Asian railways were built primarily for commerce. There was some justification in this in so far as the Transcaspian Railway and its branches were built under the auspices of the Minister of War, Count Dmitri Miliutin, designed, laid and administered by soldiers – engineers, stationmasters, even white-aproned porters, while the Russians themselves, both those in St Petersburg and those on the spot, often justified their railway expenditure in the imperialist jargon of the day. An American engineer named Berry had offered to build the line at his own expense and operate it for an annual fee but was turned down by the Russian government. Indeed until the line was complete there were very few Russians other than the military in Central Asia, although its completion was the signal for all sorts of Russian entrepreneurs to steam into the region to exploit its considerable natural resources.

'I endeavour to [place before my readers] the present situation of affairs as modified, if not revolutionised, by the construction of the Transcaspian Railway,' Curzon wrote in his account of the railway, *Russia in Central Asia*,[2] advising his readers to travel to Central Asia as soon as possible. He himself was ambitious, meticulous and possessed of an overwhelming curiosity in particular about Asia, personally travelling on the routes eyed with such suspicion by his countrymen and with such optimism by the Russians. No sooner had he finished a detailed and witty account of his journey to Central Asia than he was off again in 1890 for Persia, steaming there via the Caucasus and Caspian. Few statesmen had such a thorough geographical knowledge of the board of the Great Game, and of the linkages that steam had made – and might in the future make – across it.

Central Asia is a vague and evocative world where ancient caravan tracks between east and west are hemmed in by some of the most impenetrable deserts and mountains in the world. More particularly it refers here to the area between the Caspian Sea on the west and the Pamirs on the east, bordered by Persia and Afghanistan to the south and by the Kazakh steppes to the north. Its geography is dominated by two rivers, both emptying into the Aral Sea: the Syr-Darya or Jaxartes to the north, which rises in the Tien Shan mountains, and the much more important Amu-Darya or Oxus to the south, rising in the Pamirs. This magnificent river, sometimes a mud-filled flood, at other times a wasted expanse of shallows, is known locally as the mother of two daughters, the Kizilkum and Karakum deserts, the Karakum by far the more hostile of these two offspring. 'How this eternal sadness of the plain, from which every trace of life is banished, wearies the traveller,' sighed the Hungarian traveller Arminius Vámbéry, an avid Anglophile after his Central Asian travels, crossing it in 1863.[3] It is eroded by wind, water and extreme temperatures and wreaked a terrible vengeance on anyone who took its dangers too lightly, a sea of troubled waves, billow succeeding billow in melancholy succession.

This is the grandest arena of those traversed by steam. Its forbidding features are relieved by large and fertile oases, many of which were to be linked by the railway, strung along riverbeds occasionally fed by melting snows from the mountain ranges of south-east and east, by far the grandest of which was Bukhara. Famous for its exuberant richness, Bukhara had a longstanding reputation with Europeans for the Muslim fanaticism of its inhabitants and the intermittent cruelty of its rulers. For the British this was established with the tragedy of Stoddart and Conolly who died there in 1842, executed as spies by the Amir of Bukhara. Vámbéry, later a leading polemicist against Russian expansion in Central Asia, was more fortunate in 1863, despite being disguised with foolhardy courage as a wandering dervish. Even in the late 1880s, when finally exposed to regular foreign visitors by the arrival of the train, its 100,000 Tajik inhabitants often showed a fanatical hostility to foreigners. Meanwhile the vastness of the distances covered, the extremes of climate, the vision of those fiery 'devil's carriages' sending showers of sparks over the desolate land encouraged a dangerous excess of hyperbole among imperialists of the latter half of the nineteenth century, both Russian and British, as strong an emotion as the Tajik fanaticism.

Alexander's travels were perhaps the most exhaustive of all invading generals, ranging swiftly over its forbidding geography although, as Curzon pointed out, 'in these parts anything old, and misty, and uncertain is set down with unfaltering confidence to the Macedonian conqueror'. From the west Alexander established those contacts with the east which in following centuries developed into the prosperous trade of the silk route. Chinese Han emperors wanted western lead, glass and vines. The Graeco-Roman world wanted silk, cotton, tea and spices. Indian princes wanted precious stones from the Urals. And everyone wanted the famous Ferghana horses so beloved by the Son of Heaven, Wu Ti, herded south, east and west.

In later centuries the wily ways and long travels of the horse merchants often proved a convenient disguise for foreign agents. But Alexander was followed by other invaders as much as by traders, always along the same axis – Chinese, Huns, Persians, Parthians, Arabs, Turks, Mongols. Later came Marco Polo, a typical beneficiary of the Mongol empire of the thirteenth to fourteenth centuries during which a man could travel safely from one end to another of the Mongol domain, from the Dniestr River to the Pacific. The route was disrupted from the mid-fourteenth century by the Black Death followed by Timur Lang and later the Ottoman Turks and never regained its security.

From mid-fifteenth century east–west trade routes shifted to the ocean and by the nineteenth century Central Asia had split into a number of independent khanates, most of them suffering from chronic unrest, in particular Bukhara and Khiva but also among the semi-nomadic Turkomans along the Persian border. This interfered with the overriding Russian desire for a safe well-demarcated southern border. It also upset plans to develop trade with potentially safe markets, free from European competition. Peace would facilitate irrigation of agricultural produce; local raw materials could be used to feed new Russian industries, especially cotton. 'The fertility of the soil as soon as it is given any water is incredible,' commented Count Pahlen, visiting the area in 1908 as leader of a commission of inquiry into allegations of corruption in the administration of Central Asia.[4]

A lengthy cast of military and scientific explorers had partially prepared the ground for Russia's railway surveyors when they disembarked at the small Caspian quay of Uzun Ada in 1885. The explorers were remarkable for their stamina and enterprise, pursuing their tasks slowly and laboriously, often in disguise and always well armed. Many were sped on their way by the Imperial Geographical Society, in many respects as avid a participator in the Great Game as the British Royal Geographical Society. Among them were Russians such as Valikhanov, described as a man of good education, the son of a Kirghiz sultan who travelled disguised as a merchant, botanists such as Karelin and Schrenk, the first governor-general of Transcaspia, and coleopterists such as General Kumarov who was out collecting his beetles the day before leading the attack on Marv. Several Frenchmen, including Gabriel Bonvalot and Xavier Hommaire de Hell, were among them; American journalists James MacGahan and William Curtis and MacGahan's diplomatic companion Eugene Schuyler; British soldiers, often solitary travellers on semi-secret missions, such as Alexander Burnes and James Abbott, Charles Stoddart and Arthur Conolly murdered in Bukhara, even the intrepid Dr Wolff, previously encountered in Wahhabi Arabia. British agents among the khanates had a reputation for being 'wild, addicted to keeping fierce dogs and native harems and in general as being as uncivilised as the tribes they worked with'.[5] James MacGahan, correspondent of *The New York Herald*, and Eugene Schuyler of the US legation in St Petersburg, travelled together to Central Asia in 1874. MacGahan left Schuyler to make a wild dash across the desert to find the Russian campaign against Khiva, brilliantly described in his *Campaigning on the Oxus*. Many of the Russian accounts, originally published under the auspices of the staunchly Imperial Russian Geographical Society, were translated by worried British observers in Calcutta.

With the subjugation and final annexation of the Caucasus complete by 1864, Russia for the next twenty years endeavoured to establish a southern border in Central Asia that would leave the settled steppes of Kazakhstan free of marauding Tartars. The same desire for secure frontiers also impelled the British northwards through India. Movement of troops in Central Asia was extremely difficult; there was often very little water and no local source of provisions. Camel trains were an essential accompaniment, but also needed water. Thousands of the beasts died in the course of the Russian campaigns: 'the camel, however useful for peaceful caravan purposes, has been tried [for the transport of armies] and found utterly wanting,' wrote the builder of the Transcaspian Railway, General Annenkov.[6] Even peaceful travel had to contend with the Central Asian climate, potentially as great a deterrent as any military campaign. 'Travelling in Central Asia,' wrote MacGahan in 1873,' is a never-ceasing, never-ending struggle against difficulties.'[7] MacGahan's 2,000-mile journey from the Volga had taken him across the Urals to Orenburg, generally regarded as the frontier town of Central Asia, over the endless plain, 'the monstrous treadmill', of the steppe to the banks of the Syr-Darya and the town of Kazala. A string of forts was spreading eastwards along the Syr-Darya, one of the most meandering of rivers, the forts linked erratically by two little steamboats brought from Sweden via Orenburg to the Aral Sea, an epic journey in itself. They were beset with problems, not least the changing course of the river, and shortages of fuel and engineers, and like the forts vulnerable to Tartar raids. The Russian military authorities had initially ordered two flat-bottomed stern-wheelers from the Hamilton works in Liverpool. These were brought some 600 miles from Orenburg by camel, and launched in 1862. They were flimsy, drew too much water, and the boilers were too far from the engines. Belgian shipyards provided the next pair, *Samarkand* and *Tashkent*, that spent as much time aground as afloat. The river was the problem rather than the boats, with daily as well as seasonal changes of flow: 'the most eccentric of rivers, as changeable as the moon without the regularity of that planet,' wrote MacGahan, 'a very vagabond river.'

Further campaigns were designed to stop the Tartar raids and impose or encourage stable government but on the whole the government, thousands of miles away in St Petersburg, was cautious about intervening in the khanates' internal affairs. Those on the spot often thought differently and acquired a certain freedom of action because of distance. The khanate of Khokand was defeated and subjugated in 1863. Demand for raw cotton to replace supplies lost in the American Civil War, combined with movements of the British in northern India, kept up the pressure for action in Central Asia. Miliutin gave his blessing to territorial expansion when he wrote that 'by ruling in Khokand, we can constantly threaten Britain's East-Indian possessions,'[8] and those in authority in Central Asia found distance from St Petersburg a useful ally when it came to freedom of action. Tashkent was captured in 1865 and annexed to Russian Turkestan with Samarqand the following year. Tashkent then became the capital of Russian Turkestan and the base for further expeditions. Some of the newly acquired territory had previously belonged to the khanate of Bukhara; continuous quarrels with the Amir, often involving his extensive slave trade, led to a Russian campaign against Bukhara and its defeat in 1868, leaving the Amir with a limited autonomy. A gruelling campaign was next conducted against Khiva, an oasis harbouring some 30,000 Persian slaves, marooned between the vast sands of the Kizilkum and Karakum. It became a Russian protectorate in 1873.

This brief summary of Russian expansion in Central Asia does not do justice to the arduousness of the campaigns, the logistical problems, the terrible loss of life among the defeated. Campaigning over the deserts and in the extreme temperatures of Central Asia demanded skilled leadership. Those who undertook the campaigns often acted independently of the authorities in St Petersburg – in the absence of railways, several weeks away from the scene of action – who were sometimes dismayed by the impact of the campaigns on their European policies but not entirely averse to the deed once it was done. Advances were made, wrote MacGahan, 'through the ambitions of military chiefs, who were only too glad to take advantage of the blunders and perversity of Central Asian despots to distinguish themselves, or win a decoration.'⁹ Campaigns were masterminded from Tashkent, some fifty to sixty days from the nearest railhead at Orenburg. 'Everything, even the most trifling articles, are obliged to be brought from the Orenburg line.' Communications, supplies, above all men were put to the severest of tests in the campaign against the main Turkoman stronghold of Geok Tebe in 1879.

The possibility of easing transport and communications problems with a railway had been discussed on and off since 1854. In 1873 Ferdinand de Lesseps and his Suez engineer colleague Lavalley came up with the idea of a Calais–Calcutta railway, not only linking Tashkent with Orenburg but continuing with a well-earned disregard for geography across the Pamirs and the Hindu Kush to meet the Indian railway network at Peshawar. They were unsuccessful, sadly for future generations of railway enthusiasts; the British government objected because it did not want the natural ramparts of the northern Indian frontiers to be breached and the Russian government, which should have been keen at least on political grounds, said it was too expensive. By 1880 some forty projects had been aired, most favouring the Orenburg–Syr–Darya–Tashkent route, a few sending the line due south

36 Steam barges on the Syr Darya, used for communications along a chain of riverain forts built by the Russian government in the mid-nineteenth century

from Orenburg over the grim Ust Urt plateau between the Caspian and Aral Seas and some favouring a thrust east from Krasnovodsk on the bleak shores of the eastern Caspian.

Meanwhile the fierce Tekke Turkomans, half settled around the nominally Persian Akhal and Marv oases, remained to harass the security-conscious Russians. A campaign against them in 1879 had been dependent on camels for transport and its failure was partly due to the death of over 8,000 camels out of a total of 12,000 beasts. In 1880, as part of a renewed campaign against the Turkomans, General Skobelov reluctantly accepted the suggestion of his transport commander, General Annenkov, that he should lay a small light railway from Mikhailovsk (later moved to Uzun Ada) on the Caspian some 70 miles south-east to Kizil Arvat. These light, easily laid tracks were named after their inventor, Paul Décauville, a Frenchman who had studied the 1 ft. 11½ in. gauge Ffestiniog railway in North Wales, which was built in 1832. He designed his 600mm gauge track originally for transporting French sugar beet (it is still used on Egyptian sugar cane fields today) and other agricultural produce during a glut in 1876. The tracks were swiftly seized upon by military authorities all over Europe and also by the British on India's North-West Frontier (where a small Mallet articulated locomotive, designed in two sections, was transported to the railhead by elephant). In due course they proved particularly useful in trench warfare in World War I.

General Annenkov, had first used Décauville tracks in the Balkans where he had been in charge of transport during the 1877–8 Russo–Turkish war. There he had learned the value of a well-supplied army not exhausted by days or weeks of marching to the front. Now he recalled depots of rails left in the Balkans at the end of the war. Why not use them in Transcaspia? Rumours of British railway development in north-west India provided added incentive. The rails were summoned but had a long journey; the Transcaucasian Railway was not yet laid and the Poti line only went as far as Tiflis. All materials had therefore to be transported from the Black Sea up the Don to Kalach, by land for 30 miles to Tsaritsin, down the Volga to Astrakhan and so across the Caspian to Mikhailovsk, south of Krasnovodsk, to the starting point of the line. Décauville and the Russian firm of Maltseff were asked to provide trucks and further rails for a 600mm gauge. Locomotion was to be provided initially by the tough local horses, and a thousand of them were bought for the task.

Surrounded by some 7,000 well-armed, well-victualled Russian troops, the principal Turkoman fortress, Geok Tebe, was now gruesomely subjugated by General Skobelov who declared, after his army had killed some 15,000 of the enemy in and around the fortress, that 'the duration of peace in Asia is in direct proportion to the slaughter you inflict on the enemy. The harder you hit them the longer they remain quiet.'[10] Russia's domination of Central Asia was now divided between the province of Turkestan in the north with its capital at Tashkent, and that of Transcaspia with its capital in Ashkhabad from 1882. Despite denials of interest, in February 1884 the Russian army this time bloodlessly occupied the small but significant oasis of Marv, or Merv, grandly termed 'Queen of the World', just 30 miles north of the newly demarcated Persian border. Russian merchants, Russian explorers and Russian officials now made their presence felt in the neighbouring Persian province of Khorasan, adjoining Herat, and a much-used route to India. It was the last straw for a vociferous and influential body of Russophobes in the British and Indian governments, smitten by a severe bout of 'Mervousness'.[11] News of a railway through these regions added fuel to their fire.

Annenkov's light military track had begun on the Caspian shore at Uzun Ada, a long strip of sand adjoining Mikhailovsk about as unattractive as its name, and ended 70 miles later at Kizil Arvat in mid-desert. Initially it appeared to have no strategic purpose once Geok Tebe had been captured although Annenkov, aware of British advances in north-west India, was fond of suggesting that it should be continued either to the Amu-Darya or via Marv to Herat and thence to Quetta in north-west India. 'The English claim they are the only ones to bring the fruits of civilisation to the benighted east,' he complained;[12] they failed to realise the enormous benefits bestowed by the Russians on the barbaric lands of the Tartar. As a leading enthusiast of transcontinental rail travel, Annenkov pointed out, to the horror of British Russophobes, that a line from Paris to the Indus, via the Caspian, Kizil Arvat, Herat and Kandahar – some 4,300 miles – was by far the shortest land route between Europe and India, with the great advantage that only 82 miles were over lifeless desert. Paris, he argued, could be nine days from the Indus. Then, in 1885, came the Penjdeh incident.

Penjdeh is a small oasis on the Murgab River in the modern Soviet republic of Turkmen. It sits astride the approach to Herat from Marv. The border here between Afghanistan and Bukhara had long been disputed. An Anglo-Russian boundary commission, the first of many similar bodies, had recently been set up and Russian troops (under the coleopterist Kumarov) and Afghan troops had been facing each other at Penjdeh for some months when fighting erupted in March 1885. The

Russians swiftly overran the Afghan defences and installed themselves
in the oasis. Reaction in Britain when the news broke was violent in the
extreme, leading to a general election and the fall of Gladstone's Liberal
government, which was already beset by Gordon's problems in Khartoum; British as well as Indian army reserves were mobilised and Lord
Salisbury as Prime Minister and Foreign Secretary began worrying
about the security of coal supplies. Threatened with war, the Russians
temporarily withdrew their troops. Under the settlement finally reached
three years later by the boundary commission, the Russians retained
Penjdeh in exchange for a strategic pass further west. War was not only
averted but the Russians would accept the inviolability of the frontier
for nearly a hundred years. They nevertheless experienced revived
insecurity about their own southern defences. One way to improve these
was to follow Annenkov's advice and extend the railway as close as
possible to the border areas.

From beginning to end the construction of the Transcaspian Railway
was a military affair, organised by the Ministry of War and built by railway
battalions of the army. General Annenkov, its staunchest advocate, was
once again in charge, dedicated to completing the line as far as Samarqand
as cheaply and swiftly as possible. From Uzun Ada and later from
Krasnovodsk a few miles to the north, finally as far as Tashkent, it ran for
1,150 miles. Excluding the stretch already built to Kizil Arvat, the line
took only three and a half years to build. Much of the route had already
been surveyed by the army and lay over relatively flat but waterless desert.
Railway battalions of Smolensk navvies were ferried to Uzun Ada by
steamer from Astrakhan; technical expertise was provided by military
sappers, often armed to ward off attack by locals distrustful of their
surveying methods; only the unskilled labour was civilian – Turkomans
and Persians working in surprising harmony given their previous relationship of slave-owner and slave, paid in silver imported from Hamburg and
minted in Bukhara into acceptable local currency. Curzon brusquely
dismissed the labourers as 'strong as oxen but incurably idle and very
cowardly' but work conditions were hardly agreeable. There was the same
rapid turnover in the workforce as in the western Caucasus; malaria and
dehydration in the summer and frost-bite in the winter contributed
nothing to healthy living despite the efforts of the German chief of the
medical staff, Dr Heyfelder. A special accommodation train was put
together, with stores, beds, canteen, infirmary, baths, smithy, even the
engineer's office included in the two-storey wagons, later used for third-
class passengers. Here the railway battalions lived during the construction, moving forward with the line.

Annenkov, well known for his passion for economy and 'a plausible balance sheet', knew the success of his line depended on the cheapness and speed with which it was built. He had a zest and verve reminiscent of the great American railway builders and indeed an influential member of his staff, Prince Khilkov, was described by *The Times*'s St Petersburg correspondent, George Dobson, as an Americanised Russian 'with a Yankee tuft on his chin and the real American accent in his speech.'[13] As in the United States the aim was to get the line open as cheaply as possible, then use the revenue to complete and improve it. The cost was estimated at about £7,700 a mile.

The resulting railway therefore was essentially rough and extremely uncomfortable, according to those invited for its inauguration, only slightly better than taking a camel. It was not a difficult line to build; when one reads of the problems Robert Stephenson met with in building the London to Birmingham line in 1838 (quicksand, blue clay, navvies having to be floated up tunnels to brick out water which threatened to jam them against the roof) it is not surprising that visitors on Russia's Transcaspian Railway described as relatively straight-forward its construction over the flat and empty spaces of Central Asia. It must have been an extraordinary sight in the middle of such proverbial desolation, recalling Churchill's description of the laying of Kitchener's Sudan railway ten years later – hundreds of soldiers stripped to the waist, baggy-trousered Persians and Turkomans throwing shovelfuls of sand, camels groaning and moaning as they bore unwelcome burdens, the noise and clank of rails, hammering, the whistle of the engines. 'In this burning whirlwind one encounters an activity which is quite bewildering when one has just emerged from the absolute of the desert,' wrote Gabriel Bonvalot emerging at Marv from the direction of Persia in 1889. 'No one can tell better than we how invaluable the new railway will be' – no need for water bottles, camels, guides, no fear of losing the way.[14]

The line was built to the usual Russian 5-foot gauge, using Russian-made steel rails to encourage local industry, with wooden sleepers – 2,000 for every mile, simply spiked down without chairs or bolts. Every bit of timber had been brought down the Volga and across the Caspian to the treeless waste; there were not enough steamers to carry the materials and sailing vessels had to be used as well. The line was laid upon a low earthwork or embankment raised by 20,000 local labourers; the actual rails were laid by the railway battalions. Stations were usually 15 miles apart and built of local mud-brick or stone from the nearby Kopet Dagh Mountains. They ranged from dingy wooden shanties half buried in the sand to such substantial structures as those of Ashkhabad, Marv, Chardzui, Bukhara and Samarqand. 'I should be sorry to accept the situation of station master at the well of Utch-Haji, even with the salary of a prime minister,' commented Bonvalot of one of these minor stations.

Sand, the fine, shifting desert sand that blows in streamers off the tops of dunes, was one of Annenkov's main problems, even more than the camels or sheep occasionally found browsing on the rails. Over a third of the line ('the sabulous line,' as it was nicknamed by George Dobson) runs through a wilderness of sand, swept hither and thither by powerful winds. Various methods of stabilisation were tried: spraying it with sea water near the Caspian; covering it with clay; planting it with desert shrubs, in particular the scrubby saxaul bush, 'that strange and interesting denizen of the wilderness', a species of juniper with wide-spreading roots to gather up moisture. Such measures kept the sand at bay, but once trains began running battalions of labourers had to be kept always at work clearing the line of its 'insidious and implacable enemy.'

Water was another problem. For the first hundred miles from the Caspian there was no sweet water at all. Supplies for both workers and trains were brought initially by camel, later by train, mainly from temperamental rivers. Efforts were made to establish desalination units on the Caspian but they were always breaking down. William Curtis of the *Chicago Record-Herald* reckoned there were over 1,000 water tanks on the line in 1910.[15] And then there was the question of fuel, although just as the line was laid the conversion of *astatki* into liquid fuel was being tried out on the other side of the Caspian. Saxaul was used for a while as an alternative to coal, with locomotives characterised by great spark-arresting chimneys as on American locomotives, but it was more valuable as a dune stabiliser and before long all locomotives were running on the more abundant liquid fuel. Locomotives and rolling stock came down the Volga, hauled over the frozen river by local peasants, and floated across the Caspian. 'And how accomplished, I blush to say,' wrote that loquacious chief erector, Robert Weatherburn, in the *Railway Magazine*, 'for the Russian character is strongly leavened by drink . . . It was done by Wodka, Natchai [tips] and brute force, the true stimulus of Russia, wielded and directed by Englishmen.'[16] Locomotives for the Transcaspian Railway were Russian-made, at the Kolomna works: 0–6–0 for freight, 2–4–0 for passengers. Diesel engines were introduced as early as the 1930s on the Transcaspian line because of the lack of water for steam engines.

Annenkov, 'His Energy', as he was known, was determined that the inauguration of the railway in May 1888 should coincide with the anniversary of Alexander III's coronation. The final four miles were laid only the day before the opening. He invited a number of guests as well as his own family, though the foreigners among the guests (rather too many of them French, Dobson reckoned) were subject to the usual Russian suspicions and until they arrived in Baku could never be quite sure they would reach the railway. 'Turkestan is a closed country,' wrote William Curtis. 'All foreigners are unwelcome,' as most foreign visitors to the Soviet Union will testify to this day. The inaugural run was described by George Dobson with a certain resignation. It had all the problems of a dress rehearsal – nothing running on time, sand in their wheels disabling many locomotives, uncomfortable carriages. Dobson and his fellow guests for the inauguration were put out by having to wait two days in Baku for a steamer across to Uzun Ada, especially after all Dobson had heard about the great traffic on the Caspian. He eventually crossed on the *Prince Bariatinsky*, engined (as

37 The terminus of the Décauville railway at Mikhailovsk on the Caspian: the Caspian terminus was later moved to Uzun Ada and finally to deep water at Krasnovodsk

38 Working train on the Transcaspian Railway, including 'double decker'
coaches used as dormitories for railway workers

were several other Caspian vessels) by John Penn of London, with a
Swedish captain. As for the train, there were no first-class carriages
and the old double-deckers of the accommodation train offered second-
class accommodation below, third-class above. Muslims destined for
Mashhad, a popular Shiah place of pilgrimage, were allotted special
carriages with timetables printed in Persian and portraits of the Shah
on the walls. Everyone had to disembark at one point where the line
had been washed away by a flash flood. 'It is one thing to describe the
Central Asian Railway,' Dobson moaned to readers of *The Times*, 'and
quite another to experience its many discomforts.'

By the 1880s the quickest route from Europe to the Caspian was by
train to Constantinople or Odessa, thence by boat to Batum and by rail
across to Baku; or by rail to Tsaritsin on the Volga and thence by boat to
Astrakhan. The quickest route through Europe was via Vienna. Curzon,
invited to travel on the line a month after its inauguration, had to secure
permits for onward travel in both St Petersburg and Moscow from five
different authorities, but at length succeeded.[17] Any fool can be uncomfortable, might have been his dictum on this journey as he armed himself
with a portable rubber bath, tinned meat, chocolate and flea powder. He

also included notebooks and camera to record his impressions of a region whose history had fascinated him since his Eton schooldays.

After crossing the Caspian on the *Prince Bariatinsky*, he finally reached the head of the line at Uzun Ada. Here the shallow harbour froze over in winter, making it impractical when links with unfrozen Baku and later Petrovsk were developed. The terminus of the line was then transferred a few miles north to Krasnovodsk, now a large industrial city, but then a huddle of miserable huts. Curzon found Uzun Ada little better, an uninspiring spot built of prefabricated houses brought over from Astrakhan. Having plodded through the sand from boat to train, he found the first 30 miles 'a funereal tale of destruction, both to man and beast' and the peaks of the Balkhan range of mountains a welcome relief, merging after a while into the splendid barrier of the Persian mountains, Kopet Dagh, overhanging the railway for nearly 300 miles. Soon the train was swallowed up in the doleful plain of the Karakum desert, relieved only occasionally by a cluster of Turkoman tents.

From time to time the train passed through an oasis. The day after leaving the Caspian it reached the mouldering ruins of Geok Tebe, the capture of which had so shocked British Russophobes, all the more so because of the extraordinary character of the captor, Skobelov. For the British he was notorious not only for his slaughter of the Turkomans but also for a remark made in 1877 in a memorandum on the invasion of India: 'it will be in the end our duty to organize masses of Asiatic cavalry and to hurl them into India as a vanguard, under the banner of blood and rapine, thereby reviving the times of Tamerlane.' It is hardly surprising the British were worried about the possibility of a Russian invasion of India.

Ashkhabad was already growing rapidly but drably, banking on the railway and its role as capital of Transcaspia. From Dushak, the next station, the Russian civil engineer, explorer and diplomat, Paul Lessar, had already surveyed a possible rail link with Herat. As a Russian commented to Charles Marvin, Central Asia had a way of drawing people ever onwards over its empty spaces. But in the meantime the train turned away from the mountains, crossed the Tejend river and once again entered the sands. Two days after leaving the Caspian the train reached Marv, 'a nascent and as yet very embryonic Russian town,' with some station buildings, two or three streets of irregular wooden houses and that was all. 'A small commonplace Russian town with a bad reputation for malaria,' commented William Curtis in 1911.[18] It had a brief moment of prosperity as Annenkov's headquarters during the building of the railway – shops, a club house, even a music hall echoing to the music of Offenbach and Strauss. Ancient Marv lies in ruins 10 miles away across the plain, always an anticlimax to British visitors expecting a grander cause of the Mervousness of British politicians.

Tortoise-like the train now approached the great Amu-Darya, goal of so many weary travellers in Central Asia, heralded by orchards and gardens that had so often caught the itinerant imagination. Even so island-bound a poet as Matthew Arnold was ensnared, in the tragedy of *Sohrab and Rustum* played out on the banks of the Oxus.

> . . . Then sands begin
> To hem his watery march, and dam his streams,
> And split his currents; that for many a league
> The shorn and parcell'd Oxus strains along
> Through beds of sand and matted rushy isles . . .[19]

So impressive was the sight of the river after days or weeks of wandering through the desert that the British, from Matthew Arnold onwards, came to give it a greater significance in terms of the Russian threat to India than it really deserved. Curzon endeavoured to put the river in perspective, in particular the 'much-vaunted Oxus flotilla, so dear to the imagination of Russian Jingoes,' as providing a possible line of advance on Afghanistan. It consisted of five paddle steamers built in Finland, two of them equipped with 500-horsepower engines that made slow headway against the river in flood although they could allegedly do 16 m.p.h. in smooth water. Each could carry 300 men and 20 officers upstream to Kerki, strategically the point from which a Russian advance on northern Afghanistan might be expected but difficult to reach because of the shifting course and current of the river. The source of the Amu-Darya was still an enigma in 1888 but one which Curzon himself tried to solve on his exploration of the Pamirs in 1894.

Bridging the Amu-Darya had been one of the few technical problems faced by Annenkov in his construction of the line. A bridge was constructed with great speed and Annenkov's usual economy, 'an inelegant structure, built entirely of wood which was brought all the way from Russia,' in four sections totalling over a mile in length. It took half an hour to cross with a man walking in front to ensure the correct speed. When Dobson arrived on the inaugural run the bridge had been cut in half to let a steamer through with an important general aboard and passengers were crossing the river in boats. Those sceptical of its durability were to be confounded; thanks to the pedestrian in front and to the lavish provision of fire stations in case a chance spark from the train should set fire to the wood it lasted until 1910, when the river was finally bridged by iron. No one, not even a chain-smoking Russian, was allowed to smoke while crossing the wooden bridge.

At Bukhara beyond the river the station had deliberately, at the request of the Amir, been built 10 miles from the old city. In the old days Bukhara had been the commercial centre of Central Asia but the Amir regarded the railway as 'foreign, subversive, anti-national, and even Satanic,' and the rival Russian town which developed in due course around the station, inevitably benefited from the better communications. This was the traveller's first glimpse of so fabled a city – in 1885 still an inferior wayside station that Dobson described as a 'chaos of wooden shanties, Armenian eating booths and bare brick walls'.

In fact the locals, far from being scared, were soon flocking in crowds to see the trains, cramming into the third-class carriages and waiting for hours for the train to start. For a while the Amir maintained his disdain but before long he was having a palace built between old and new towns, designed by a German architect and described in 1897 as 'the finest building this side of the Caspian.'[20] In 1898 he ordered his own private train to run on a newly completed branch line to the old city. The train also took the Amir to his villa at Livadia in the Crimea. During the Russo–Japanese War his relations with the Russians were benign enough for him to present the Tsar, a summer neighbour in Livadia, with a destroyer specially built at Kronstadt and named *Amir of Bokhara*. Curzon explored the old city at length and with delight, rejoicing at having seen it 'in what may be described as the twilight epoch of its glory.' Later visitors, he feared, might find electric light, window panes, Russian restaurants and Russian beer. 'Civilisation may ride in the Devil's Wagon, but the devil has a habit of exacting his toll,' he noted gloomily.

It is 150 miles from Bukhara to Samarqand by rail. The track follows the Zarafshan River, 'a veritable garden of Eden,' according to visitors, 'incomparably the most fertile part of Central Asia,' according to Curzon, thanks to the centuries-old network of irrigation channels meandering in and around orchards and fields. At Samarqand Curzon's train journey ended, the station a scene of great activity because still in the hands of the builders. Despite annexation by Russia in 1868 and the development of a sizeable Russian settlement, Samarqand had previously been isolated: a telegram from there to Bukhara had taken several days to go via Tashkent, Orenburg, Moscow and Baku while the post from St Petersburg took nearly a month. Now that Samarqand was

drawn into the imperial system the journey from St Petersburg could
be reduced to nine and a half days, provided the connections were
good. Curzon went on to Tashkent by road, an experience which
brought home the advantages of the railway. 'The luckless traveller
condemned to the amenities of a tarantass across the Golodnaya, or
Famished Steppe, hankers after the second-class carriages of General
Annenkoff as eagerly as did the Israelites in similar surroundings after
the flesh-pots of Egypt.'[21]

With his railway Annenkov had linked by an unbroken chain of steam
locomotion the capital of Peter the Great with the capital of Tamerlane.
The journey between the two was still long enough, however, to
maintain the administration's independence of St Petersburg. Annenkov
meanwhile boasted he could put 140,000 Russian soldiers into action
against India along his projected Herat line south of Marv. There were
only two breaks in the rail link with Central Asia – the 135 miles of
mountain between Vladikavkaz and Tiflis and the passage of the Caspian.
A line was already planned from Vladikavkaz to Petrovsk on the Caspian,
and Petrovsk, with deeper water than Astrakhan, had the great advantage
of remaining free of ice in winter. The completed line justified the switch
of terminus from Uzun Ada to the port of Krasnovodsk, which was deep
enough to take the same steamers as Petrovsk.

Meanwhile, in 1898, the Transcaspian Railway was continued to
Tashkent, the extension delayed only by the expense of building bridges
over the Zarafshan and Syr-Darya rivers on the way. There were few
running problems; 'camels are inclined to stray across the line but there
is not much danger from them,' a correspondent in the *Railway
Magazine* told his readers in 1903, 'as camel bones are soft and easy to
be crushed'. Tashkent was finally linked to Orenburg in 1906; Moscow
was only six and a half days away. Now, as Tsar Nicolas II had
expressed it a few years earlier to his sister, 'the strongest fleets in the
world can't prevent us from settling our scores with England precisely
at her most vulnerable point.'[22] Other lines followed: a branch line to
Kushk in 1889, only 60 miles from Herat, and another in 1899 to
Andijan about 50 miles from the Chinese border, where it was halted
by the towering wall of the Tien Shan mountains. In 1910 private
Russian capital negotiated with the government to build a railway from
Bukhara to Termez on the Afghan border via Karshi and Kerki, the
'wildest and weirdest place' connected hitherto with Russia only by the
unreliable paddle-steamers on the Amu-Darya; American engineers
supervised the building, which began in 1914 and was finished in July
1916 with the help of Austro-Hungarian prisoners of war.

39 Clearing sand blown on to the Transcaspian Railway, a hazard on the desert crossing until the dunes were stabilized with plantations of *saxaul* bushes

These extensions were primarily strategic, stimulated by moves in the Great Game. They also had an immediate commercial impact, providing rapid cheap transport for Central Asian cotton, the cultivation of which was improved by imports of American cotton seed, tools and farm machinery. Soon visitors were commenting on the bales of cotton stacked up on station platforms, the camel caravans loaded with goods from the interior. The year after the railway opened, the Caucasus and Mercury Steamship Company had to lay on five extra steamers to cope with the cotton harvest. With the collapse of the Russian army after the Revolution in 1917, ownership of that stock of cotton, used for munitions in World War I, became a major factor in Central Asian moves by Bolsheviks, Germans and British.

Meanwhile more tranquil travellers on the railway included a party of tourists organised in 1897 by Thomas Cook's, equipped with their guidebooks as well as their own linen for the train. They travelled in three special saloon carriages, half of each saloon furnished as a sitting-room upholstered in Morocco leather. There were bedrooms with writing tables and washrooms at least as comfortable as those available on a Cook's tour up the Nile. The food was commended although a diet of cabbage and sturgeon became a little monotonous. Caviare was always available but 'hardly appealed to the ladies.' Cautiously dressed and demurely behaved, they toured the bazaars of Bukhara, the mosques of Samarqand, the mouldering walls of ancient empires, noting Russian improvements with approving nods. There was dancing and feasting at Chardzui and a military band conducted by an Italian homesick for Rome. A longstanding tradition of musical performances on station platforms had been initiated by Gerstner at the terminus of the Tsarskoe–Selo line at Pavlosk and sustained in the early 1860s by Johann Strauss, who gave a series of concerts there. 'No one could doubt,' wrote one member of the party, Mr Woolrych Perowne, 'the moral good of Russian expansion.'[23]

Today's trains are diesel or electric but the atmosphere has changed little. Fred Burnaby heading eastwards for Orenburg on his way to Khiva in 1875 would still feel at home in spacious carriages reeking of distinctive Russian tobacco and in winter of the damp sheepskins worn by local passengers. Dobson would find his fellow passengers as reluctant to bury themselves in a newspaper or a book as he found them in 1888. There are still no dining cars and station fare has changed little; everyone piles out to buy fruit, buns, radishes and dried mulberries on the platform, but in the station restaurants the menu is as meagre as when Curzon passed through. Unfortunately neither Mr Perowne nor the ladies in his party would find caviare on offer today and there is no more music on the platform at Chardzui.

And to this day there is still no railway line in Afghanistan.

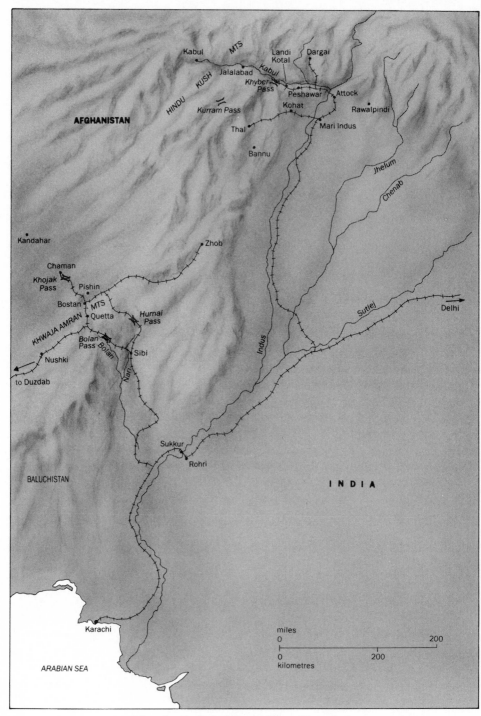

Map 8 India's North-West Frontier

Road Improvement Schemes

British strategists were as quick as the Russians to recognise the military potential of railways and as the Transcaspian chugged east and north through the wastes of Central Asia another railway line was struggling with the geography of north-west India and the approaches to Afghanistan, this time from the south-east. Today's Bolan Express runs over one of the most dramatic railway lines in the world, whose construction was one of the great achievements of railway engineers. It is named after the Bolan Pass through which it chugs – one of two gateways to India from Afghanistan, from Central Asia. The other is the Khyber Pass. A third, minor, pass is the Kurram, seldom a major invasion route but used by General Sir Frederick Roberts to enter Afghanistan during the Second Afghan War and much frequented today by Afghan guerrillas.

The mountains through which the Bolan Railway is laid rise sheer from the arid Kach plain, separating India from the highlands of Baluchistan and Afghanistan. 'A close defile,' wrote Arthur Conolly who rode through it in 1833.[1] 'At first there was but breadth for a dozen horsemen between the rocks which rose like walls on either side to a great height . . .' On the one hand 'it is a defile which a regiment of brave men could defend against an army,' but on the other 'many graves were here and there pointed out as those of murdered travellers.' Cliffs tower above the line; rocks precariously overhang it and alongside it the Bolan River hurtles south. On the shingle long caravans wind through the spring flowers towards the highlands. Stations crammed on ledges beside the line have lamp rooms, godowns and handsome brass bells struck by Baluchis in sequined waistcoats when it is time for the express to leave. There are long pauses for passengers to buy their chapattis and curry, fruit and flowers and to fill their earthenware pots with water, for in summer it is a parching scramble up from the plain. Tunnels have fortified entrances in castellated defiance of the local tribes who still from time to time swoop on lesser trains and hold the guard or passengers to ransom. The tunnels also have names – Mary Jane after the wife of the chief engineer, Cascade and Windy Corner. Catch sidings and brake warnings indicate the steepness of the ruling gradient, 1:23, with curves of 200-foot radius; the locomotives are now diesel but it still takes two of them to haul up the express. The train eventually emerges from the pass on to the plateau of Baluchistan dotted in spring and summer with the tents of Baluchi or Pathan herdsmen. A few minutes later it rumbles into the station at Quetta, the most significant military base in Pakistan ever since the British acquired it in 1876.

This is not a civilising railway. It runs through what is still an anarchic part of the subcontinent although conditions have improved since the traveller Henry Bellew wrote, in 1874, 'tyranny and insecurity, oppression and violence, reign everywhere all over the country.'[2] During its planning and construction no one held forth about the advantages it would bring to the darkened masses or rhapsodised about the radiant light of progress and burgeoning commerce as the assembled dignitaries greeted the first train to run through the Bolan Pass into Quetta in 1885. None of the railway lines of this chapter had any purpose other than strategic, even if the 'unenlightened hordes' did jump aboard with their baskets and bundles the moment they saw the trains as a quick way of getting to market.

Curzon opened his account of the Transcaspian Railway with a stern warning to his readers about Russian intentions, dedicating it to the ignoble terrors of Russophobes, Marvin no doubt in mind, and the complacency of Russophiles.[3] Russian intentions were not as bad as some made out, but India, and the British governing it, needed to be on guard. How seriously the Russian government considered invading India is a moot point but their generals in Central Asia, remote from the control and policies of St Petersburg, made such bellicose suggestions from time to time as wholly to justify panic in Calcutta, Simla, Delhi and London. On the whole it suited the government in St Petersburg, concerned with the shifting pattern of European alliances, that they should do so. Fears of a Russian threat to India had been stimulated since the 1830s by the long shadow of Russia falling over the decrepit Persian Empire as well as over Central Asia, twice aggravated by Persian attacks on Herat, in 1836 and 1856, allegedly encouraged by Russian agents. Russian activities in Afghanistan in the 1830s also stirred up a British reaction, which never truly simmered down thereafter. On the Indian side of the great Afghan divide nerves were as taut in the last thirty years of the nineteenth century as they were to the north of it, as the British watched the Russians steam eastwards and southwards across Asia. Turkestan, Afghanistan, Transcaspia and Persia were viewed as pieces on a chessboard upon which was being played a game of imperial dominion. Much of the board was militarily inaccessible; railways made the rest approachable.

As with the Russians in Central Asia, so for the government of India it was a question of stable frontiers. To some extent geography was in Britain's favour; forbidding mountain ranges and deserts ringed north-western India. The two principal gaps in the ring were the Khyber and the Bolan Passes. The Bolan Pass worried the British most of all. North of the pass the plain lay open to Kandahar in Afghanistan, to Herat, Mashhad or ultimately Marv. Even today, as one emerges from the mountains on to the plain, the impact of untrammelled space is as powerful as it was a hundred years ago. So are the apprehensions it arouses. Most invasions of India – by Greeks, Chinese, Arabs, Mongols, Persians – came through these mountain gates. One observer counted twenty-six invasions of India through these mountains since about 2000 BC, almost all of them ending in conquest.

Attempts to create a buffer state out of Afghanistan foundered on the chronic anarchy of such a tribal country. British frontier policy zig-zagged between an active 'forward' policy and one of 'masterly inactivity' (unmasterly, said Curzon, who was of the opposite persuasion). If this wild and exotic land were to fall into the hands of an enemy it could jeopardise the stability of all British India. So argued British strategists in India, who were dependent for information on a succession of agents scouting through outlying areas thinly disguised as horse dealers, and often no better trained in political or geographical reporting than in judging horseflesh. While Russian armies to the north, to secure their southern border, moved into lands claimed by the rulers of Afghanistan, British armies twice invaded Afghan territory from the south in response to real or imagined threats to India's northern border. Russia was always seen as the *éminence grise* behind the threats, and the Bolan Railway was built expressly to meet them.

Already in the 1830s the presence of Russian emissaries in Kabul stimulated the British to replace as a ruler of Afghanistan the able but independent-minded Dost Muhammad with the more pliable Shah Shuja, who could only be maintained with a British army of occupation. In 1842, in the First Afghan War, that army was destroyed by the Afghans themselves, who were then left to their own devices; they were brought closer to British India, however, by Britain's annexation of the Punjab in 1849, including the tribal areas of the north-west highlands. In due course Russia's advance through Central Asia in the 1860s and 1870s was viewed with as much alarm by the Amir of Afghanistan, Sher Ali, as by the British, but his repeated requests for British help were ignored. With a despairing gesture of defiance he therefore accepted a Russian mission to Kabul in 1878, a mission which the Russians saw as a means of distracting British attention from the war with Turkey 1877–8 in Europe. The move happened, however, not long after the arrival in India of a new viceroy, Lord Lytton, despatched by Benjamin Disraeli.

Lytton was a 'forward' man in his approach to the frontier problem. Disraeli, who liked him, described him as 'a man of ambition, imagination, some vanity and much will'. Lord Salisbury, Secretary of State for India, who did not like him, reckoned Disraeli did not 'realise sufficiently the gaudy and theatrical ambition which is the Viceroy's leading passion.'[4] Warming instantly to the rivalries of the Great Game, Lytton himself wrote that 'the Russians have always pushed forward their policy of encroachments as far as the apathy and want of firmness of other governments would allow it to go, but have always stopped and retired when it was met with decided resistance.'[5] That Lytton was determined to provide.

Lytton was not prepared to allow Sher Ali his defiance. To the dismay of several of his superiors in Britain Lytton insisted not only on sending a British military expedition to rebuke the Afghan ruler but also made the expulsion of the Russians a preconditon to reopening negotiations for assistance. The Russians were meanwhile launching their first attack on Geok Tebe. Disraeli in London was left little alternative but to back Lytton by declaring that India's North-West Frontier was a 'haphazard and not a scientific frontier,' a situation which should be rectified.[6] The Amir refused to answer Lytton's ultimatum and the expedition crossed into Afghanistan through the three main passes, seizing its goals of Kandahar, Jalalabad and the Khyber Pass to enforce the British ultimatum. Sir Frederick Roberts entered through the Kurram Pass, Sir Sam Browne through the Khyber and Sir Donald Stewart through the narrow dangerous defiles of the Bolan to Kandahar, all planning to rendezvous at Kabul. This was too much for Sher Ali. He fled north and died at Mazar-i Sharif, leaving the country in the hands of his son Yakub Ali who, at the Treaty of Gandamak, was obliged to accept the British mission. Lytton appeared vindicated. Five months later, however, the head of the subsequent mission to Kabul, Sir Louis Cavagnari, and his entire staff were slaughtered in Kabul by rebellious Afghan soldiers. Lytton was now in a real Asiatic tangle, the more inextricably so because Disraeli had been ousted by the liberal and pacific Gladstone.

British troops were still on the Afghan borders, however, Stewart still in Kandahar. Once again the British advanced on Kabul. Roberts camped triumphantly outside Kabul, defeating an Afghan force of some 60,000 and executing those accused of Cavagnari's murder and directed by the government in India to recognise Sher Ali's dissident nephew Abdur Rahman, who had been in exile in Tashkent, as Amir, forbidding him to maintain foreign relations with any state other than Britain. But trouble was stirring in the south, where a rival leader Ayub Khan, son of Sher Ali, rallied tribal support from his base in Herat and in July 1880 attacked and trounced the British Kandahar garrison at Maiwand, a few miles west of Kandahar. Remnants of the garrison retreated to Kandahar, rescued from the enemy's siege by Roberts after an astonishing forced march of 300 miles in thirty days. How much better it would all have been by train. The disaster highlighted the inadequacy of communications between India and southern Afghanistan, the very route by which the British always feared an invasion. They must at all costs be improved.

Twenty years earlier the American Civil War had demonstrated the usefulness of railways in keeping an army mobile and adequately supplied when operating far from its base. As the Russian Transcaspian Railway edged through Central Asia to Marv, only a few miles from the Persian border and an easy march from Herat and Kandahar, British military strategists reckoned they should be building another railway, mile for mile, up to and beyond Quetta. General Annenkov was not to have everything his way. The frontier needed stern policing wherever it was drawn. Policing needed reliable communications. Communications meant railways. The Second Afghan War and the near tragedy at Kandahar proved their point.

Communications in northern India left much to be desired. The Indus was not a satisfactory river for steam navigation, its current too strong even for steamers, although the first steamboat in India, the *Snake*, was launched in 1820 and there was a fleet of Laird steamers on the river by the 1850s. Railways in India in general had been slow to take off due to lack of finance. The first serious proposals were not made until 1843 and it was ten years before the first stretch opened – 22 miles out of Bombay up the Western Ghats to Thana. It was all a question of the return on investment.

The campaign for a railway in the northern part of the country was led by the railway engineer William Andrew, an enthusiastic imperialist whose publicity echoed Waghorn's. Railways, he wrote, are 'the great civilising power . . . The railways do more for mass education than all the efforts of the Education Department' and he hoped 'to bind the vast population [of India] by an iron link to the people of Europe.'[7] Andrew had two links in mind, a railway along the Euphrates valley and another through the north-west of India and southern Afghanistan via the strategic cities of Kandahar and Herat. In 1855 he established the Scinde Railway Company in London to raise finance for a 108-mile line from Karachi along the Indus. By 1878 and the outbreak of the Second Afghan War the railhead was still a long way from the mountains of the north-west. There was little commercial enthusiasm for Andrew's wider visions but as far as the shorter lines were concerned he was rewarded during the war when *The Times* commented: 'if Andrew had been listened to, we should have been spared the ignominy of feeling that a British army [Stewart's in 1878] . . . has occupied five weeks in covering less than seventy miles.'[8] As many as 40,000 camels died in that campaign. At the time of the war the nearest railhead was at Sukkur on the Indus; even Rawalpindi, one of the most important strategic points in northern India, was not reached by train until 1880.

One of Lytton's first measures on reaching Simla in 1876 was to dispatch an army engineer, Major James 'Buster' Browne, to survey a railway route from the Indus across the Kach desert into the Bolan Pass. This is a forlorn and cruel desert, extreme in climate even by desert standards, scoured by burning winds for much of the summer. Many years later, in the summer of 1915, thirty-two soldiers died of heat stroke in a train which broke down in mid-desert. It is part of Baluchistan, the key to Lytton's forward policy; within a few months of his arrival he had signed the Treaty of Jacobabad with the Khan of Kalat, a vacillating and often violently inclined gentleman who controlled most of Baluchistan including the vital Bolan Pass. Under the terms of the treaty the British acquired the fort of Quetta guarding the northern entrance to the pass as well as permission to build rail and telegraph links. Quetta became a kind of listening post for Afghan and Central Asian affairs. Relations with the Khan and other tribal leaders of Baluchistan were maintained on a more or less even keel by Sir Robert Sandeman, a Scots frontier officer whose main job was to ensure that the Bolan Pass was kept open and safe.

No line had actually been ordered when the Second Afghan War broke out in September 1878. To facilitate the punitive expedition the Viceroy's Council immediately ordered the laying of a fairweather light railway from the Indus to the small outpost of Sibi at the foot of the Bolan Pass – most of it over the lifeless, treeless plain. The first rail was laid from the railhead at Sukkur on the Indus in October that year, by which time the worst of the summer was over, the last in Sibi 133 miles and a hundred days later. From Sibi onwards, however, into south-eastern Afghanistan the army was back to camels. Sir Donald Stewart's

40 James 'Buster' Browne,
builder of the Bolan Railway in
north-west India, now Pakistan

army invading Afghanistan from the south had to use its feet to get
there. 'There is nothing the weary traveller can see,' recorded Captain
Hoskyns of the journey, 'but the bare hill on either side, and the
detestable shingle at his feet.'[9] 'Huge stocks of winter clothing, medical
comforts, grain and the various requirements of an army in the field
had been brought by rail to Sibi and had there remained for want of
transport to take then on,' wrote Roberts.[10] Roberts was the most potent
advocate of railways, 'good civilisers as well as defenders of India's
security, vital to civil as well as military administration.'

The man responsible for extending the railway, James Browne, was
an impressive character, stocky and robust, a good raconteur according
to his subordinates, an admirable linguist and a bold and skilful
engineer. He was 'notably a ruler of men,' wrote his deputy, George
Scott-Moncrieff, getting the best out of his employees 'by absolutely
straight dealing. Nothing was more abhorrent to him than crooked
ways, nothing he liked so much as straight manly conduct.'[11] All these
qualities were essential if communications were to be improved over
such forbidding terrain. Engineering problems were made all the greater
by the government's determination to maintain uniformity of gauge with
the rest of India, modelled on the 'comfort, speed and steadiness' of
Brunel's Great Western Railway in England and established from the
outset at 5 ft. 6 in., costing a heavy £20,000 a mile. In later years, when
speed to meet military and famine demands was a prime consideration,

41　Hauling the guns up the Khojak Pass at the start of the Second
Afghan War

other gauges were introduced, including a metre gauge (before India went metric) so that horses could be carried crossways in the wagon. For Browne's railway all labour and their supplies would have to be imported. Beyond Sibi a line through the pass involved gradients of 1:25, constructed in the most inhospitable territory politically as well as climatically. Browne outlined a slightly easier route to the north over the Hurnai pass with 1:45 gradients but without even an existing cart track. A preliminary line was being laid there when the news of the Maiwand defeat came through. Troops guarding the works were immediately withdrawn and local tribes, 'not slow to take advantage of any retrograde movement,' attacked and massacred a group of workers at Kochali. Browne's biographer, J. Macleod Innes,[12] allows him not a moment of doubt about the project but he must have breathed a sigh of relief when the effect of Disraeli's defeat by Gladstone in 1880 was to call a halt to 'forward' projects such as strategic railways.

In Afghanistan defeat was turned into victory by Roberts' march from Kabul to Kandahar to come to the rescue of the beleaguered British force. His own description of the logistical problems of keeping his army supplied on that long summer march underlined the desperate need for improved communications if Britain was really to defend its Indian frontiers from intrusion. Only the personality of Roberts himself and the heroism he inspired kept the army from a disaster as great as in the First Afghan War. Lytton returned to England and Roberts withdrew from Kandahar, overtaking the regiments of his field force on their way home through the pass 'over the interminable boulders which made the passage of the Bolan so difficult and wearisome to man and beast.' 'Horses all lose their shoes when they come this way,' Conolly had written. Materials and men were withdrawn from Quetta; talk of railways died away. Masterly inactivity was again the keynote of frontier policy.

For three years the pass was left in peace. The Mervousness aroused by the Russian advance to Marv in 1883, however, revived the need for a swift, reliable route to the frontier. Any Russian invasion was thought likely to march south of Marv into eastern Persia, past Herat, across the relatively well watered Sistan plain to Kandahar and then, like so many before, through the Bolan Pass into India. Rail advances must meet rail advances, even though the Bolan presented a far greater challenge than the deserts of Turkestan. Secrecy was essential to any such scheme and in public the Bolan project was known as 'a road improvement scheme'. It was the first of several strategic lines built over the next forty years to reinforce the frontier. 'We were not permitted to use such facilities as any ordinary railway contractor would have insisted upon,' wrote Scott-Moncrieff, not even a line of rails for conveying stores and materials, only camels and men.

'It is not an every day experience,' commented the magazine *Engineering* upon completion of the 'improvement', 'to build a line of railway 223 miles long, climbing in 80 miles to an elevation overtopping the Mont Cenis, the St Gothard and the Arlberg and then crossing a summit of 6,600 feet . . . through a country on which nature has poured all the climatic curses at her command.'[13] Of the two possible routes to the frontier from the railhead and foot of the pass at Sibi, it was decided to concentrate on that through the Hurnai Pass as more suitable for broad-gauge heavy traffic, although it was about twice the length. Speed of construction rather than cost was the prime consideration though Browne was later accused of extravagance, and the more expensive broad gauge maintained because of links with the rest of India. 'What was wanted was not a piece of irreproachable engineering but a military appliance to pour troops into Afghanistan as rapidly as they could be brought up from India.'[14] In fact it cost about £10,000 a mile. The Bolan route, which would meet the Hurnai line just north-west of Quetta at Bostan, would be developed for a light railway only. Work began on both at the same time.

The Hurnai route was to run from Sibi through the mountains to Pishin, absorbed from Afghanistan in the Treaty of Gandamak, a few miles north of Quetta and Bostan. The slope of the Hurnai route was certainly more reasonable than that of the Bolan Pass. The geography, consisting of a series of cross rifts between steep-sided parallel valleys, was not. The line had to climb over 6,000 feet in 120 miles. The extremes of climate meant that work had to be carried out according to season – the lower reaches in winter, the higher, where winter temperatures of 18 degrees below zero could snap the rails, in summer.

The country is a rugged wilderness of rocks and stone with hardly a blade of grass, yet in certain places it turned out to be rife with malaria. Rivers deeply encased in gorges divide the plateau like a jigsaw puzzle. The region's few inhabitants ('thieves and cut-throats by profession [who] regard a stranger like a gamekeeper does a hawk – to be bagged at all costs') are and always have been a law unto themselves and they do not like strangers. Scott-Moncrieff, dispatched in midwinter to survey the route beyond Hurnai, went not exactly disguised but wearing a large local sheepskin coat to cover his European-style trousers. British officers dressed thus had been mistaken for Afghans in the wintry advance north of Quetta during the Second Afghan War, but the sheepskin was also good armour, difficult to pierce with the sword. 'Whether I was thus disguised or not, and thus safe, I cannot say, but the melancholy fact remains that the next Englishman who penetrated those regions a few months later, was murdered.'[15] Browne was forbidden to risk disturbing the locals by using local juniper forests for his sleepers, so incurred delays and expense acquiring timber from Kashmir. 'So serious were the difficulties, so great the breakdown in health . . . so wild the country and so unfit for large bodies of labourers or employees, so overwhelming the catastrophes that occurred, that the pluck and determination which carried it all through must seem beyond praise.'[16]

There were four main engineering problems. First was the 14-mile Nari Gorge and the Nari river, particularly dangerous in flood; the railway eventually crossed the river six times in the gorge alone. Next came the Gundakinduf Defile, about 8 miles long, with two tunnels and four bridges; a station here, now disused, was aptly named Tanduri, or 'oven'. Then the Chuppur Rift, a 300-foot chasm over two miles long in the higher reaches of the line; a river flows from the valley at the upper end, a mere trickle in summer, a dangerous torrent after rain. The line here, laid in a great semicircle in order to stay with the ruling gradient, involved a 'crowd' of tunnels and the magnificent Louise Margaret Bridge. Finally the summit portion, about 25 miles long, included 5 miles of the 'Mud Gorge' where a 'wild and precipitous glen' about 3 miles long is filled with slippery and treacherous mud, as hard as rock in dry weather but a heaving morass after rain.

Work began at both ends: at the upper Bostan end in summer, the Sibi end in winter. Everything had to be brought in – stores, tools, thousands of men and their food including 500 camel-loads of food a day, transported on herds of excellent Afghan camels. There was little useful material left over from the building of the Sibi line – a 'heterogeneous collection of rubbish' including dangerously decayed dynamite which had to be replaced; Browne ordered a hundred tons in all from Nobel's dynamite company. A batch of Browne's assistants came 'fresh from England'. There were sapper and miner battalions. Pioneer battalions furnished semi-skilled labour, including one group of Punjabi Sikhs – admirable soldiers 'accustomed to digging' but not easy to discipline. There were other battalions of sappers. Afghans, Pathans and Baluchis provided the manual labour. As George Stephenson said, the most difficult engineering is the engineering of men. Browne was everywhere, either on one of his three horses or on a camel 'with a wild dirty Beluch sitting in front of him'.

Cholera hit the work camps just as work was about to begin in the autumn of 1884. Of fifty-one officers on the line, twenty-two were invalided out. The Afghan workmen fled with one accord; new masons and bricklayers had to be recruited from the Punjab. The disease reappeared the following May, affecting engineers as well as workers; several of Browne's ablest assistants died. 'Whole classes of employees, such as the telegraph and post office clerks, fled in a body,' writes Browne's biographer. Malaria was a constant hazard, especially around Hurnai. In the summer of 1886 the gangs of plate-layers and girder erectors had to be renewed every two months 'as they melted away from fever, dysentery and scurvy. The whole line of the work is dotted with stones to mark the graves of the unfortunate wretches whom the high wages offered have attracted from their homes in India or Afghanistan.' Everyone was affected; many Europeans left with shattered constitutions and 'those that remain are all more or less worn out by sickness, fatigue and climate.'

Unprecedented floods in March 1885 coincided with the Penjdeh incident. The Russian confrontation with the Afghans at Penjdeh on the ill-determined north-western border of Afghanistan induced even Gladstone to call in Parliament for £11 million for what seemed inevitable war with Russia. The House of Commons was with him to a man and voted the money the same night. Twenty-five thousand troops were made ready to advance to Quetta. Orders went out to Browne to push ahead with all speed. Browne and Scott-Moncrieff sat up all night working out how they would march to Herat. It would not be easy. The weather was appalling, and one morning Scott-Moncrieff was woken by an orderly with a flood warning. 'Up I jumped and saw a sight such as I ... hope never to see again – a truly awful flood. Huge brown waves leaping and roaring, whirling timber and corpses spreading over everything.'

Nine inches of rain fell in April that year compared with the normal two to three inches. Floods washed away bridges, temporary roads and camp sites, particularly in the Nari Gorge. Workers refused to enter one of the more dangerous tunnels unless their wages were quintupled. The floods also made it clear that the bed of the Chuppur Rift was no place for a railway line, least of all with the local tribesmen looking on, 'notorious robbers who are restrained by the fear of neither God nor devil, much less of man.' From a trickle the river rose to a height of 30–40 feet. It is like a great crack into the heart of the earth; Scott-Moncrieff compared it with Gustave Doré's illustrations for Dante, 'a most formidable obstacle to the railway and, but that I knew my chief was a man of indomitable perseverance, I should have thought that the successful construction of a railway through it was impossible.'

Two lines of continuous tunnels were built either side of the rift, connected by an iron-girder bridge. The only way to excavate the tunnels was to let workmen down on ropes from the top of the cliff. The first man down had to carve a foothold by driving a crowbar into the perpendicular wall. Other bars could then be driven in and a platform built. Only at this point could blasting operations begin. Browne confessed to difficulties in recruiting volunteers for the job. The tunnels then had to be lined with bricks brought 230 miles by camel from the plains. A rock perforator was ordered to speed up the drilling but it weighed 11 tons and never left Sibi. Finally a lighter American machine was sent from New York and dragged to Chuppur by two elephants. The bridge, 250 feet above the river, with a vast central span of 150 feet, was manufactured in Britain, then transported to India where its erectors were known as 'meccano engineers'. It was named after the Duchess of Connaught, Louise Margaret, who opened it in 1887.

42   Ancient caravan track and modern railway through the Bolan Pass in north-west India, now Pakistan, the railway completed in 1886

The line eventually reached the Mud Gorge with its treacherous slips. 'That one bit of line has caused more trouble since than all the rest of the railway put together,' wrote Scott-Moncrieff, and Browne himself reported that it would be some time before the regime, or foundation, of Mud Gorge was thoroughly established. The soil was continually on the move in rainy weather and its instability was one of the main reasons why the Hurnai line was eventually abandoned. Speed was essential; tunnelling through the treacherous shale would have taken too long, so Browne laid his line on top of it. At one place, aptly named Puddle Hollow, the whole hillside slipped 300 feet, burying 1,000 feet of railway beneath a thick layer of mud. 'No engineer who has seen the place can withhold his tribute of admiration to the patient skill that has daily faced disaster,' wrote a correspondent in the *Pioneer*.[17]

Not surprisingly the authorities began to look more generously on the route of the light railway through the Bolan Pass. Browne had first surveyed the line, some 60 miles long and rising from Sibi to a height of 6,000 feet, in 1876. By 1880 it had reached the mouth of the pass and was used to transport troops and stores towards Kandahar at the start of the Second Afghan War. After the Penjdeh incident the government decided to take it on to Quetta with a 12-mile metre gauge stretch in the middle through the narrow Dozan Gorge where the line rose half a mile in fifteen miles. 'Goat tracks' were carved along the steep hillside so that labourers could carry rails, barrows, bricks and cement to the next spot ahead of the line; one false step and they would have fallen 200 feet. Cholera again devastated the ramshackle labour camps that summer, while winter floods swept away the piers carrying the line to and fro across the Bolan river. Nevertheless it reached Quetta in August 1886 and was continued to Bostan, where it met up with the Hurnai line. Engineers then tried to replace the central section with broad-gauge track but repeated floods and wash-outs led in the 1890s to a complete realignment of the route through the neighbouring Mushkaf valley. This 'good, sound, massive construction' opened in 1895 and the train runs over it today. Chugging down the steepest stretch, with a gradient of 1:33, with the points kept switched to sidings, the train has to demonstrate the efficacy of its brakes by coming to a dead halt and holding it for two minutes before the pointsman will switch over his points. In the upper reaches of the pass, where the train crosses the Bolan River nine times, one still glimpses the frail remnants of the old line, a bridge pier here, a stretch of rail ending nowhere, an eroded embankment there. This was one invasion the Bolan Pass did not let through.

Quetta itself is still some 70 miles short of the Afghan border. It is the military headquarters of much of Pakistan's army, an oriental Aldershot. Vendettas, espionage, communal or tribal violence stalk through its muddy bazaars, feeding on rumours from the latest round of the Great Game. Its extensive modern arsenal, accumulated for the long-awaited invasion from the north, is buried deep beneath a hillock crowned by the old fort. The town is ringed by mountains whose valleys strangers do not visit without a tribal go-ahead. Quetta was never envisaged as the terminus of the line; it must continue to the north, said the military authorities, where the land opens out towards Kandahar, even to Herat or Kabul. Russian manoeuvres in Transcaspia and Turkestan were still pressing on the nerves of the Viceroy and his Council, aggravated by the Transcaspian Railway which opened in 1888. Afghanistan must be made more accessible for the military.

And so the line was extended, optimistically renamed the Kandahar Railway although the Amir never allowed it that far. It runs through the Khwaja Amran mountains to the little border settlement of Chaman, swollen these days by Afghan refugees. The range is not particularly high but it is rugged and inhospitable, the familiar leafless, waterless scene inhabited by 'wild and bigoted' tribesmen. The main route through, known as the Khojak Pass, is inaccessible to wheeled vehicles. In 1839 at the outset of the First Afghan War the British army took five hard days to get themselves and their supplies over the pass, with heavy losses; it took nearly two weeks in the winter of 1878–9. 'The bullocks dragging the heavy batteries had their feet actually torn off,' recorded Hoskyns.[18] 'The cold and dearth of supplies were far more deadly enemies than the Afghan.' Guns had to be dragged up a 30-degree slope; the thousands of pack animals were caught in a log-jam in its narrow defiles. So another 'road improvement scheme' began inching over the plain north of Quetta in 1888, across territory acquired from Afghanistan in 1879, this time involving the longest tunnel in India. Curzon stood on the pass with Robert Sandeman as work on the tunnel was about to start and 'felt a thrill of satisfaction at being for the moment on the very uttermost verge, the Ultima Thule, of the Indian Empire.'[19] Local tribesmen picked up their spades and picks again; Hazaris were recruited from Afghanistan, Arabs from the Gulf, Zanzibaris, Punjabis, many coming from the seasonal migration of tribes from hills to lowlands. Browne asked for his 'favourite prescription', battalions of Pioneers. Sixty-five Welsh miners also arrived with experience of building the 4½-mile Severn Tunnel, opened two years earlier.

Many labourers died of pneumonia as a result of the bitter winds that scour the hills in winter. Eight hundred died from typhus in the winter of 1890–1. Parched on the surface, the hills in spring released torrents of water inside the tunnellings, which still cause problems today. The tunnel runs horizontally straight through the mountains but rises and falls, coming to a camel's hump in the centre. As a train nears the hump it sets off a gong to warn the driver he is about to begin the descent, rather steeper down to Chaman than coming up from Shelabagh on the Quetta side; it takes two locomotives to get the train up the incline and through the tunnel to avoid the danger of the engine driver being asphyxiated by fumes. The engineers originally installed ventilation shafts but the locals found it too tempting to drop rocks down on passing trains and the shafts were bricked up. The invention of gas masks in World War I came to the rescue of troops heading for the frontier in 1919 at the outbreak of another Afghan war; wearing their masks they could stay in the train instead of being obliged to get out and march over the pass. The first train steamed through the tunnel in September 1891.

Once a week an ancient locomotive still steams out of Quetta to Chaman. It is full of Pathans – beak-nosed men from either side of the border herding bewildered women and children from one makeshift home to another or the lucky ones to stark fortified villages buried deep in the highlands. Passengers have a laborious journey, the smoke and the smuts falling through the window before one has thought to close it, evoking sympathy for the Frontier Scouts taking their turn at the border post of Chaman, or indeed for the Amir Amanullah heading south for a durbar in 1927. This august person pulled the communication cord in mid-tunnel, intending to get out and walk the rest of the way; his party would have been asphyxiated by the smoke from four locomotives pulling the train but for a strong wind. Conceived in a mood of belligerence, the line turned out to have a more peaceful role to play, trundling fruit from Afghanistan down to the baking plains of India, thus countering the hostility of the Amir Abdur Rahman, who had likened it to 'having a knife thrust into his vitals,'[20] and the sang-froid of the Quetta stationmaster who when asked if the line would go on the remaining 60 miles to Kandahar replied: 'Well I don't think that 'ere 'hole was made through the 'ill to peep through.' He was right of course; Afghanistan was now within three days' train ride of the port of Karachi, itself only twenty-five days steaming from Britain. But the Amir remained implacably opposed to any extension of the route into Afghanistan, and the country to this day possesses no railway line.

43   Rope incline railway over the Khojak Pass near the Indo–Afghan frontier, to facilitate construction of tunnels under the pass, 1888

Despite its problems the Bolan Pass offered by far the most practicable route between Central Asia and India. The other principal route, through the Hindu Kush via the Khyber Pass, was much more inhospitable not only in the pass itself but also beyond, between Kabul and the Russian frontier on the Amu-Darya. The likelihood of a Russian advance on British India via this route was therefore more remote but plenty of scope remained for foreign agents to upset the uneasy peace on India's North-West Frontier, tying up British troops which were needed elsewhere. German agents tried to stir up unrest among the tribes during World War I, and after the assassination in 1919 of the firmly neutral Amir Habibullah, his son and successor Amanullah was persuaded to conduct his own *jihad* into India's northern provinces. These regions were, he was assured, ripe for revolution against the British. Invading the region in May 1919, he was soundly trounced by the British, partly with aircraft, partly with effective frontier forces. Nevertheless, weak frontier communications were highlighted by the invasion, subsequently known as the Third Afghan War. Railways came once more to the rescue.

As Viceroy in India from 1898 to 1905 Curzon had maintained a 'forward' policy of defending India against possible invasion right up against the frontier. The impracticability of maintaining troops of the Indian army along the frontier led him to establish a system of tribal levies for its defence. Local tribesmen were the main problem, a vengeful concoction of Afridis, Shinwalis, Mohmands and others who had been antagonised by an often ill-researched frontier laid down in 1893, the so-called Durand Line. Boundary commissions on the borders of Afghanistan were usually triggered by British or Russian panics or tribal incursions, 'drawing lines upon maps where no human foot has trod,' complained Lord Salisbury, 'only hindered by the small impediment that we never knew exactly where the mountains and rivers and lakes were'.[21] The tribes were to be contained by a series of lonely frontier posts dotted among the hills of Kohat, the Khyber or Waziristan where British frontier officers commanded Curzon's ramshackle and irregular tribal levies, known as *khassadars*, with a courage much romanticised by their contemporaries. Plenty of it was needed the moment one stepped outside the fort:

> With home-bred hordes the hill-sides teem.
>   The troop-ships bring us one by one,
> At vast expense of time and steam,
>   To slay Afridis when they run.
> The 'captives of our bow and spear'
> Are cheap alas! as we are dear.[22]

Concurring with Kipling, Curzon for his part declared that 'no school of character exists' to compare with the discipline of the frontier.[23] The little lines that skirted the hills were a useful back-up to this celebrated discipline.

Frontier railways in India, like the Transcaspian Railway and its tributaries in Central Asia, all grew out of an imperial rivalry that demanded rapid movement of troops over vast expanses of territory, some of it made hostile by its geography, some by its inhabitants. 'There is no such means of pacifying an Oriental country,' Curzon wrote in praise of the 'all-conquering influence of steam,' 'as a railway, even a military railway; and if for bullets and bayonets we substitute roads and railroads as the motto of our future policy to Afghanistan, we shall find ourselves standing upon the threshold of a new and brighter era of relations with that country.' The trouble was, bullets as well as bayonets were needed to make the railway safe.

The system was directed from Peshawar Cantonment, the British suburb of the old Pathan frontier town, once part of Afghanistan, afterwards part of the Sikh kingdom of Ranjit Singh, finally part of British India. Dusty, dirty, Peshawar is still crowded with Pathans loping through the bazaar, out-staring the stranger, and squatting on the pavement to smoke their hashish, while beyond the city the barren crags of the Hindu Kush leading to Afghanistan are as much a no man's land as they ever were in Curzon's time.

The railway had reached Peshawar from the Indus crossing at Attock in 1883. In 1901 it was extended 12 miles towards the Khyber Pass to Jamrud over which a daily train, 'the flying Afridi', clanked and groaned. But continuing further into the Khyber area presented problems. The terrain leading up to and over the Khyber Pass has always been more hostile than that of the Bolan or even the Khojak Passes and certainly more expensive to defend with a 'road improvement scheme'. For the same reasons it was a less likely invasion route than that through Baluchistan and thoughts of building a railway here arose only at moments of crisis. Kitchener arrived in India as commander-in-chief in 1902 and immediately ordered a system of lateral communications, a network of little narrow-gauge lines twisting in and out of the hills to Thal, Dargai and Bannu. One of Kitchener's lines lay along the Kabul River, reckoned to be a safer avenue into Afghanistan than the Khyber Pass. The Peshawar line was also extended a few more miles. But the signing of the Anglo–Russian Convention in 1907, ending some seventy years of mutual distrust, resulted in the abandonment of the project. During World War I border and railway energies were concentrated in Persian Sistan. Then, in 1919, Afghan incursions revived the cause.

The Khyber Pass was the last major trade route between India and Central Asia to be crossed by a railway, although its inspiration was war rather than commerce, the movement of troops not traders. Its principal engineer was Colonel Gordon Hearn. The route to be taken by the railway was dictated partly by topography but also by the attitude of

44   Ali Masjid, the most formidable of several Pathan fortresses overlooking
        the railway from Peshawar to the Khyber Pass, completed in 1925

those whose tribal territory overlooked the track. Digging started at the
further end, at Landi Kotal, to see how the tribes would react. A few
contractors were murdered. 'Only those with nerves of iron could
endure it for long,' a new contractor was warned.[24]

The main work of construction came in the laying of the 'formation'
or bed of the 30-mile line, including the drilling of innumerable short
tunnels. There were the usual problems with the weather: the notorious
Khyber wind often buffeted the theodolite, preventing accurate measurements for the tunnels; mirages caused distortions; freak storms
brought enormous downpours and wash-outs. Centuries of such storms
made tunnelling particularly hazardous; once again water, shale and
mud poured down on the wretched tunnellers as soon as they went
underground and all tunnels, most of them steep and curved, had to be
lined with bricks. And there was the perpetual danger of attack either
by tribal sharpshooters, only partly conciliated by labour contracts, or
by sandflies who delivered a particularly virulent type of fever. A chain
of fortified posts was built along the hills overlooking the line, the most

formidable at Ali Masjid, and stations were built as forts, with instructions on the drawings to 'combine Booking Office windows and Machine-Gun Loophole.' They were manned by *khassadars* who also guarded the line by day. But there was no antidote to the sandfly.

The Khyber Railway opened as far as Landi Kotal in 1925. A brigade was stationed there in a substantial frontier fort to bolster the morale of the railway staff. Over its 30 miles there are thirty-four tunnels and ninety-two bridges and culverts. There are four reversing stations; at a particularly steep stretch one station is directly below the next. A year later the Khyber Mail could descend the hill to Landi Khana, two miles short of the actual frontier; the preparations for its extension into Afghanistan can still be seen today, disappearing into the turbulent hills. Everyone came to see the amazing construction; 'there are two places in the world,' wrote one of the engineers, Victor Bayley, 'where, if you wait long enough, you can see everyone of any importance. One is Victoria Station and the other is Landi Kotal.'[25]

Fortunately perhaps, the train has never been very busy. Once a week two old engines reluctantly leave Peshawar and pull a train for four hours past cliff faces inscribed with the names of regiments that served on the frontier and those of their comrades who died there, through stations whose names evoke that frontier heroism Curzon so admired. It is even slower than Russian trains. Tribesmen used to be able to travel free; perhaps no one dared ask them for the fare. Its destination, Landi Kotal, used to be a thriving mart for goods smuggled from Afghanistan; now it is an empty frightened spot, its platform only momentarily rescued from habitual mistrust when the weekly train arrives.

The Ultimate Link

If we think of the Middle East and Central Asia as territorial crossroads, their equivalent at sea is the Indian Ocean, in particular that part of it known as the Arabian Sea. Criss-crossed like the land by ancient trade routes which in the nineteenth century were speeded up dramatically by the steam engine, it soon became as significant strategically as the land junctions. The British had been quietly policing the Arabian Sea for many years in their efforts to suppress the slave trade. The strategic significance of the waterways, however, was first brought to British attention by gun-running to India's North-West Frontier.

Disorder on the frontier had to be fed from outside. 'People are at last beginning to realise that if the arming of the Pathan belt continues, a frontier rising in the future will be an affair of infinitely more gravity than heretofore.' So wrote Arnold Keppel in 1911.[1] Tribal revolts had turned the frontier into a promising market for gun-runners; 30,000 rifles got through to Afghanistan and the frontier in 1907. They became most menacing when the frontier forces found themselves facing modern fast-loading Martini-Henry rifles discarded from the Boer War instead of the old *jezail*, a matchlock weapon capable of throwing a ball only 100 yards or so.

Where were they coming from? Land investigation was out of the question because of the hideous terrain over which it would have to be expensively conducted; instead the more economical navy was called in, to play the role of policeman in intercepting gun-laden Arab dhows that crossed backwards and forwards between the Arabian peninsula and the southern coast of Persia and thence to the fastnesses of Afghanistan. Gun-running in the Gulf and its suppression brought the British up against a newly aggressive Turkey, laying claim to long-ignored imperial fringes, and its main European ally, Germany.

The gun-runners were merely confirming ancient trading links between India and Mesopotamia via the Gulf that go back at least as far as 3000 BC. The British inherited and expanded them, their interest in the Gulf beginning with an expedition to Persia in 1615 by the East India Company looking for new markets for English woollens. No one in the Gulf itself wanted the woollens but the little settlements acted as entry ports to the Persian interior with roads leading from them to Isfahan and Shiraz. As Britain consolidated her possessions in India so her interest in the ancient role of the Gulf as a conduit to Mesopotamia developed, and it came to be viewed as another vital link between east and west.

So East India Company 'factories' were replaced by sun-baked Indian government residencies and agencies. Bushire on the Persian coast, a collection of mud houses at the end of a sand spit jutting out from the mainland, became the headquarters of a British Resident responsible for British maritime and trading interests in the whole Gulf area. These had been safeguarded in 1853 by the establishment of peace between Britain and the sheikhs of the so-called Trucial Coast of Arabia. Arab raids on shipping were suppressed; so, in theory, was slavery. Opium, horses and the foul-smelling asafoetida took their place in the markets of the area, often carried in 'the charmingly officered and well-found' steamships of the British India Steam Navigation Company (BI). The company had been established in 1862 by an enterprising Scotsman, William McKinnon, living in Bombay, and it developed out of a coastal trading service into one covering most of the Indian Ocean. Many of their vessels were now made of lightweight steel, rather than iron.

By 1900 the Persian Gulf was crowded with British and Indian shipping, Hindustani was the prevailing language and 'peace prevails everywhere.' 'As long as you are on the shores of the Gulf you are so to speak in India.'[2] The British presence on shore was understated, represented by a handful of officials who were paid in rupees, lived in bungalows, talked of tiffin and ate curry at every meal. They were appointed from the Indian Political Service and their quickest route to the Gulf from home was via Bombay. Links with civilisation were maintained by the fortnightly British India service. Cabin passage from Basra to Bombay on board these vessels cost around £20 including bed linen and furniture, food but not wine. Most of the passengers were Indian; most travelled deck class, their families camped round their possessions 'like a series of bored and exclusive picnic parties in Richmond Park on a crowded holiday.'[3] There was fast mail and slow mail, the carriage of mail being essential to the otherwise unprofitable route, the slow mail including 'umbrella stops' off the beaches of the least important settlements where an Indian clerk sat out on the shallow sandy shore to spot the funnel of the British India vessel. 'Unhealthy as was the climate of the Persian Gulf, and monotonous and dreary the life on that station,' wrote the naval historian Charles Low of Bushire, 'the younger officers ... managed to enjoy themselves fairly well' with hunting, cricket, fishing and pig-shooting.[4] But other settlements – Bahrain for instance, Lingeh and Bandar Abbas on the Persian coast, were lonely outposts of the empire and the funnels of BI a welcome relief on the horizon.

The gun-running business was first spotted during the Second Afghan War but up to 1897 the trade had been carried on mainly across the Gulf to Bushire and up into Persia, to arm the Bakhtiari tribesmen of Luristan against the central government, and of only minor strategic interest to the British. But in 1897 the Afridi revolt in the hills behind Peshawar attracted the attention of arms dealers, who began directing their trade to the south coast of Persia, the wild and desolate Makran. In 1907 some samples from a captured haul were forwarded to Simla and recognised as cast-offs from the Boer War. 'Dhows lurk in the innumerable inlets in this scantily populated wilderness,' Mr Lovat Fraser told the Royal Central Asian Society, 'and steal across to the Makran under the cover of the night.'[5] Even the British India steamers were caught carrying guns, to the embarrassment of their owners when their vessels were challenged by naval gunboats. Disconcertingly, the guns were also often made in Britain and handled by British firms. Military operations against the trade were ruled out because of the terrain of the Makran, the 'dread Gedrosia' through which Alexander had floundered when trying to head home from India. Instead gunboats of the Indian navy were dispatched to blockade the south Persian coast. 'Troubles grow apace,' wrote Arnold Wilson, a young political officer in 1910. 'Trouble over gun-running at Dibai. HMS *Hyacinth* landed a party: 14 killed and wounded on our side, 40 Arabs on the other.'[6]

The *Hyacinth* was one of several gunboats brought in to interrupt the trade. This was effective and inexpensive policing. They were small, manned by an officer and six to twelve 'bluejackets', with a group of several boats linked to a cruiser. Firepower and shallow draught (the largest possible gun in the smallest possible hull) made the gunboat the ideal vessel for denying the enemy the defences of inshore reefs and creeks. They were charmingly named – as well as the *Hyacinth*, there were the *Perseus*, *Sphinx* and *Lapwing*, the last famous for having seized a cache of guns aboard the steamer *Baluchistan* in 1898 – but left their crews 'more uncomfortable than any civilian in the worst prison or in an excursion train,' according to Arnold Wilson. They were known as 'bug traps', for obvious reasons.

The landlocked harbour of Muscat on the coast of Oman was the principal loading point for the weapons, with the names of British steamers painted on the rocks at the entrance to the harbour still visible today. Muscati traders had for centuries traded across the Indian Ocean from Zanzibar to the Makran coast and further and it was to insure this trade against European interference that the Sultan of Muscat, bowing to British pressure during the Napoleonic wars, excluded the French from Oman. The exclusion was reaffirmed in 1891 but came under French attack in the 1890s with the appointment of a French vice-consul, who asked the Sultan for permission to establish a coaling station. Potential for conflict was further enhanced by the availability of the French flag to local shipping, including the gun-running dhows.

Here were the makings of an international incident. Cables flashed along the Indo-European telegraph which the Sultan had kindly assented to have laid across his front door in the 1860s. The British were extremely jealous of their hegemony in the Gulf; the mere presence there of another power would unsettle India and the Sultan of Muscat was severely reprimanded for allowing the French their coaling station. He was after all supposed to be a British vassal, despite

45   The forts of Jalali and Mirani at the entrance to Muscat harbour, much
     frequented by arms smugglers in the early twentieth century

Muscat's propensity for running guns to Britain's opponents; he was firmly told to remove the French, and obediently did so. Muscat itself in the early 1900s 'bristled with rifle depots and stores', according to Keppel. 'Every other shop in the bazaar is a rifle shop', although when Keppel was there in 1911 the blockade had been so effective that 'there are now in Muscat itself at least 200,000 rifles and 3,000,000 rounds of ammunition for which a market cannot be found.'[7] Having reached the Makran, the guns were dispersed through Afghanistan, mainly to its eastern border with India.

Curzon as Viceroy attached great importance to keeping Britain's rivals out of the Gulf. At a durbar held in the Gulf in 1903, much criticised for its grandiloquence, he told the shaikhs assembled on his steam yacht, 'we found strife and we created order, we saved you from extinction at the hands of your neighbours . . . we are not now going to throw away this century of costly and triumphant enterprise . . . The influence of the British government must remain supreme.'[8] But not only the French were threatening the British hegemony. Already other European shipping lines, notably the German Hamburg–Amerika Line (Hapag), were inaugurating voyages direct from Europe to the Gulf. Germany, France and Russia were appointing consuls whose activities were not always friendly to the British. A British naval and military blockade of the Makran in 1911, after a particularly successful gun-running season, not only underlined the growing competition for access to a waterway – the Gulf – which the British had hitherto regarded as exclusively theirs, but also demonstrated how that exclusion could be undermined. 'You cannot mobilise a squadron and an expeditionary force and start out to conduct warlike operations, and then ask the rest of the world to be kind enough to look the other way,' observed Lovat Fraser.[9] The trade was brought temporarily under control by the establishment in Muscat in 1912 of an arms warehouse which regulated the trade. But it has revived whenever there has been upheaval in the area, and was to cause the British some unpleasant panics in World War I.

The British were now as much concerned by the activities of other European powers in the upper as well as the lower, arms-dealing, end of the Gulf. The commercial potential of the lower rivers of Mesopotamia had always aroused interest in Bombay. 'Baghdad from its matchless situation would, with the slightest fostering care, become a grand centre of English, Arab, Persian and Eastern commerce,' wrote W. P. Andrew, the great protagonist of railways, 'and nothing is wanting to distribute it widely and increase it greatly, but the establishment of steam.'[10] As so often happened, the commercial interest developed in the later nine-teenth century into the strategic: an infringement of the trade in this part of the Middle East was interpreted in India as an infringement of Indian defences, ultimately a potential threat to British maritime power.

The failure of Chesney's hopes for the Euphrates was no criticism of his chosen vessels, and four more iron steamers had been ordered from Laird's by the East India Company; these arrived in bits in Basra (having come via the Cape) in 1839. They were placed under the command of Henry Lynch, who on Chesney's departure for India had taken the *Euphrates* back up the Tigris to Baghdad and was now joined by the new vessels, manned by officers of the Indian navy, including a brother, Michael. At first Mesopotamia had been unkind to the Lynches, 'enterprising men, sociable and hospitable, as English mer-chants in distant and uncivilised lands almost invariably are,' wrote the archaeologist Henry Layard, basking in their hospitality after a long exploratory journey in 1840.[11] Another of Henry Lynch's brothers had been drowned when the *Tigris* capsized; Henry had to be invalided home later in 1840, and Michael died at Diyarbekir in 1841. Such misfortunes failed to discourage these staunch entrepreneurial imperial-ists and the same year that Michael died, another brother, Thomas Kerr Lynch, set up as a merchant in Baghdad.

Gradually the Lynch commercial empire expanded, to become in 1860 the Euphrates and Tigris Steam Navigation Company, running two of Laird's little steamers, the *City of London* and the *Dajlah*. With their coal-hungry low-pressure engines they could steam the 500 miles (only 350 by land, a point in favour of the later railway) from Baghdad to 'filthy, half-ruined and fever-stricken' Basra,[12] in 52–60 hours and return upriver in four to five days. At Basra they rendezvoused with the British India vessels, which then steamed down the Shatt al-Arab over the mud flats at Fao (like walking on the skin of a rice pudding according to a soldier stationed there in World War II) and out into the Gulf. This was the kind of progress to justify Chesney's forecasts about Mesopotamia's commercial potential – mainly for British cotton goods, in exchange for dates, liquorice and horses for India.

For many years the Lynches had a virtual monopoly of trade in the area, their 160-foot paddle-boats loaded with freight and passengers steaming past the occasional tribal fracas. David Fraser travelled downriver in 1908 aboard the sandbagged and bullet-pocked *Blosse Lynch*, shot at by riverain Arabs as hostile to outsiders as in Chesney's day.[13] Henry Layard as ambassador in Constantinople had tried to

46   A traditional dhow alongside an early oil tanker at Abadan, in the
Shatt al-Arab

persuade the Ottoman authorities to let the Lynches have more
vessels but without success, 'one of the many instances of that fatuous
short-sightedness which has brought the Turkish Empire to ruin,'
Layard wrote acidly. Even without them, however, the company
prospered.

The company also established itself at Muhammarah (now Khurram-
shahr) at the entrance to the Karun River leading into the Persian
interior and from 1908 helped with the exploitation of oil in south-west
Persia, discovered in commercial quantities in the same year. The
Karun became the object of 'special British solicitude' in the 1880s as
the trade route and avenue of approach to the great towns of the Persian
interior. In 1890, after visiting the river, Curzon could write that
'Central Persia, as far north as Isfahan, already derive the bulk of their
luxuries and almost the whole of their clothing, from Manchester or
Bombay; and each fresh town, we may say each new village, that is
brought into communication with the Persian Gulf, will thereby be
drawn into the mesh of the Lancashire cotton spinner or the Hindu
artisan.'[14] A succession of adventurous young naval officers had forced

their way up the Karun, including Lieutenant Selby 'of somewhat violent and impetuous disposition'. In 1842 Selby, with Henry Layard on board, had his vessel hauled over the rapids at Ahwaz but eventually landed in trouble by running aground in the heart of hostile Bakhtiari territory. Despite the physical problems posed by the river and the terrain through which it ran there was much talk in Britain of establishing a steamer service and building a railway line. The Lynches did manage a rudimentary steamer service but the Shah's opposition to railways put paid for the time being to a railway.

By the turn of the century it appeared to many British politicians that the seemingly natural extension of British hegemony of the Gulf to Mesopotamia and south-west Persia was about to be threatened by Germany's railway plans. In 1889 Kaiser Wilhelm II came to pay his respects to Sultan Abdul Hamid of Turkey on board the imperial paddle yacht *Kaiser Adler*. A keen sailor who liked to put on a good show for his grandmother Queen Victoria at Cowes week, the Kaiser was still feeling his way when it came to relations with the Ottoman Empire. The *Kaiser Adler* was a suitable vessel for a young man with few pretensions and a warm regard for the sea. Or so perhaps he tried to reassure Chancellor Bismarck, who saw no good reason to jeopardise

47   Loading a boiler on to a dhow in the Karun River to transport it to the Anglo–Persian oilfields

a carefully developed relationship with Russia by over indulgence towards Turkey.

The Kaiser was cool towards what he viewed as an old order that stood in the way of German aspirations to rival the industrial and commercial empires of other European powers. While the Sultan was looking for military and technical assistance and more mobility for an army already being trained by the Prussian General von der Goltz, the Kaiser was looking for a corridor for German expansion into south-west Asia. 'The Orient is the only territory on earth which has not yet been taken possession of by some aspiring nation,' wrote the German orientalist Aloys Sprenger in 1886, adding with an echo of Peacock, 'it offers the finest opportunities for colonisation and if Germany . . . should act before the Cossacks come along, she would, in the division of the world, get the best share.'[15] The Kaiser dismissed Bismarck the year after that first visit to Constantinople and when he returned to the Ottoman capital in 1898 it was in a very different guise.

In the interval a strong friendship had developed between the Ottoman Empire and Germany. German merchants and industrialists saw the empire as a promising market for German goods; German soldiers were busy training Turkish soldiers. This time the Kaiser steamed through the Dardanelles on board a new yacht, the *Hohenzollern*, a steel vessel, 375 feet long, weighing 3,700 tons and capable of a speed of 21 knots. This was a more imposing vessel than the old paddle yacht, symbolic of a more prosperous but also more aggressive Germany. Socialists in the Reichstag had opposed the appropriation of funds for a replacement for the *Kaiser Adler* so the Kaiser had his designers draft him a twin-screw naval dispatch vessel, built in the Vulcan shipyard at Stettin, whose ram-shaped bow, more suited to a fighting vessel, added an unusual expression of professional determination to what was intended as a pleasure boat. Behind the glistening façade of the Yildiz palace on the Bosphorus the Sultan was supposed to take heart as he followed the *Hohenzollern*'s course through the grey November waters. Here was a new, more indulgent ally for the beleaguered Turks. Abdul Hamid disliked the British hectoring and lecturing (especially by Gladstone, who had called him the Great Assassin) quite as much as the British disliked his wayward despotism.

On his second visit to the Sultan the Kaiser was more explicit about his plans for a revitalised Ottoman Empire under German tutelage. His trip included an extended visit to the Holy Land and Syria but the linchpin of the revitalisation was to be a railway connecting Constantinople with Baghdad and the Persian Gulf, reopening Darius' ancient

Royal Highway between Persia and the Mediterranean and reaching to the outer limits of the Ottoman Empire. The ambition was borne on a flood of inspiring rhetoric, uttered with aplomb by the Kaiser. Throughout the trip, organised by Cook's, he delighted in an embarrassingly Messianic role – 'Deutschland über Allah,' sneered *Punch* – that had him allegedly issuing orders that no one should be forbidden to gaze on him. He nearly entered Jerusalem by the celebrated Golden Gate, which legend says will not be opened until the second coming of the Messiah. The legend was recalled only just in time and 'Cook's Crusader' redirected through a new gate, deliberately cut for the occasion. More to the point, the visit confirmed German interest in Anatolian railways, in particular their extension into Mesopotamia.

Long-distance rail travel was now all the rage in Europe, the most triumphant example being the Orient Express. Constantinople had been in direct communication with Berlin since 1885 with the completion of a network of lines through Hungary, Serbia and Bulgaria. Many of them ran along well-worn trade routes, a fact not lost on the Kaiser and his expansionist advisers. In 1889 the first through express, the Orient Express, ran from Paris to Constantinople just before the Kaiser's first visit to the Sultan; one wonders why he failed to avail himself of such a symbol of what railways might achieve. The express, steaming through Germany, Austria-Hungary, Rumania and Bulgaria, was a victory of commerce over politics, most of the time following old Nordic and Roman roads. Its founder, the Belgian banker Georges Nagelmackers, was determined to overcome that familiar resistance of border officials and civil service bureaucracies to any infringement of their blockading powers. Despite avalanches and the occasional attack by Balkan bandits passengers revelled in the bliss of sleeping and eating on a heated train, steaming through borders and stations at the dead of night, enchanted by that curious sensation of not quite knowing where one is; then staggering stiffly out of their plush compartments into the lofty grandeur of the Pera Palace Hotel in Constantinople:

> There is every sort of light – you can make it dark or bright;
> There's a button that you turn to make a breeze.
> There's a funny little basin you're supposed to wash your face in
> And a crank to shut the window if you sneeze.[16]

Nagelmackers' triumph raised all manner of enthusiasm for Channel tunnels, advocated as a cure for seasickness, Alpine tunnels (including the 8-mile Mont Cenis completed in 1871 and the 9-mile St Gothard completed in 1881) and, once again, those short cuts to India. A railway eastwards from Constantinople seemed a natural extension for the Orient Express.

In the latter part of the nineteenth century increasing debts tempted the Ottoman authorities into mortgaging the finances of the state in return for concessions of raw materials. The hope was that economic development would alleviate the cultural and political strains that were pulling the empire apart. Railways would be the cure-all, essential to the extraction of Anatolia's riches. German industrialisation had really only taken off in the 1870s, after unification; now Germany was also anxious to secure and develop sources of raw materials and markets for her manufactures similar to those her European rivals had already found overseas. Railway building in the Ottoman Empire may have been driven by commercial logic, but it was seized on by both Kaiser and Sultan for their political ends.

Although the river route through Mesopotamia had proved too problematic, the concept of steaming east by land had been attracting more and more attention for some time. As early as 1742 an imaginative Irish manufacturer named William Paine had suggested an Atlas Railway passing through Mesopotamia and terminating eventually in Peking. The advent of railways and steam locomotives and their rapid progress through Europe brought new commercial and political force to the concept, adding to the chronic anxiety of the foreign ministries of rival European powers. For many years the railway engineer William Andrew, with long experience of Indian communications, was the principal British protagonist of the eastern route. In 1857, for instance, he called on Palmerston together with a respectable queue of fellow engineers, several of them former members of Chesney's Euphrates Expedition (including Chesney himself as chief consultant engineer for the project) and a selection of prominent Russophobes who saw a Euphrates railway as the best way to forestall Russian threats to India. The route would promote commerce, civilisation and Christianity, in that order, but without forgetting the strategic factor: 'the advancing standard of the barbarian Cossack would recoil before these emblems of power and progress, the electric wire and the steam engine and his ominous tread would be restrained behind the icy barrier of the Caucasus.' 'Who is to say,' wrote Dr J. B. Thomson, quoted by Andrew, 'but that even in our own day we may not hear of excursion trains to Palmyra, Baghdad and the Tigris, by the Great Eastern Orontes and Euphrates Valley line of Railways, the stupendous aqueduct of ancient Seleucia forming a terminus, with branch lines to Baalbek and the Plains of Issus – the battlefield of Alexander and Darius.'[17] But despite

Palmerston's enthusiasm, which stemmed at least partly from his opposition to the proposed Suez Canal, Andrew was never able to raise the necessary finance. Before long the canal was seen clearly as the more promising route, and was secured finally by the British occupation of Egypt in 1882. But the British continued to worry about the Euphrates approach to India and Mesopotamia was considered, despite its depressed economy, to be the key to oriental trade.

Certain railways in the Ottoman Empire had been built in the 1860s and 1870s, but were limited to opening up Turkey's coastal fringe. Despite generous capital return guarantees from the Ottoman government British investors had taken ten years to build a difficult 80-mile line from Smyrna inland through the Menderes valley and over the Azizieh Pass to Aydin. This opened in 1866 and was subsequently extended in 1888. Another small line linked Mersin and Adana on the south coast. The French had built a 90-kilometre line from Smyrna to Turgutlu and had various small lines planned or built in the Levant linking Beirut and Damascus, and Jaffa and Jerusalem. Another line between Haydar Pasha on the Bosphorus ('a railway station, not an old gentleman, as sometimes supposed in political circles', according to David Fraser) and the nearby port of Ismit opened in 1873 to take the Sultan to a favourite hunting lodge. It was leased to British operators but German rather than British entrepreneurs took up the concession and offered to extend it to Ankara as well as to Konya. This was the first railway venture into the tricky topography of the Anatolian highlands, often so inappropriately described as a plateau.

The company that took it up was the Anatolian Railways Company, established at the instigation of Dr Georg von Siemens of the Deutsche Bank in 1888. The foundation of the company heralded a burst of railway construction, opening up the country to the ideas as well as commercial demands of Europe and paving the way for the acceptance of change and revolution in a region which had hitherto been far removed from such dangerous influences. The company moved fast and the 444-kilometre line from the Bosphorus to Eskişehir was complete by 1893 thanks to Italian engineers and local labour and despite raids by local brigands (one of whom was later converted to being a stationmaster). It remains a deliciously slow climb through wild gorges and past rushing torrents – every excuse for the fact that most trains belie the optimism of the timetable and arrive hours late at Eskişehir. In this town, made Crewe-like by the railway, ancient steam locomotives still valiantly shunt only slightly younger rolling stock from siding to main line and thankfully back again.

By the time of the Kaiser's second visit a Baghdad railway was common talk. Steam was recognised as the great reviver of trade, more easily envisaged as such because the tracks were often laid along ancient trade routes. Historians joined politicians in pointing out that armies had moved along the routes as easily as caravans. Every European power wanted access to the commercial potential of Mesopotamia and south-west Persia, all the more so because of the newly evaluated oil reserves; an Austro-Russian combine envisaged a line from Tripoli in Syria to the Gulf, French financiers suggested a similar route (backing their proposal with a present to the Sultan of a handsome watch decorated with a bejewelled map of the Ottoman Empire showing the projected line), and the British revived their Euphrates Valley scheme. 'Asia Minor, and its natural dependency, Mesopotamia,' declared *The Spectator* in 1898, 'are among the most desirable places on the earth's surface.'[18] 'Babylonia,' countered Sprenger to a more receptive audience, 'is the most promising field for colonisation in the present.' German academics preached a pan-German crusade, but despite *The Spectator* there was little interest or money forthcoming from Britain and the British were out of favour with the Sultan; the occupation of Egypt still rankled and Gladstone had been, in Turkish eyes, particularly intemperate in his denunciation of Armenian massacres.

The German project to link Constantinople with Baghdad through Anatolia was the most attractive to the Turks. Troops as well as trade could be moved along this line, though heading south and east from Konya rather than Ankara because of Russian objections. The line would follow the traditional trading and invasion route to Syria and Mesopotamia through the Cilician Gates of the Taurus to Adana, over the Amanus mountains to Aleppo and the fertile Syrian hinterland, and then eastwards via Nisibin to the Tigris, Mosul and Baghdad. The site of the terminus was left open because of British objections to the use of Kuwait, geographically by far the most suitable place. The line would link up with existing or planned lines in Syria and also with Khaniqin on the Persian border. The Turks were quick to see its military as well as commercial advantages, recalling all too vividly the problems in 1877 of moving troops from Syria to fight a war with Russia in eastern Anatolia. The same year as its line reached Ankara, the Anatolian Railway Company was given permission to extend a line from Eskişehir to Konya, round the edge of the highlands.

The news, a year after the Kaiser's grandiose parade through Ottoman dominions, that a Baghdad Railway was to go ahead was at first greeted with equanimity by the British. There was some concern about the fact that it trespassed on the natural line of extension for the Smyrna–Aydin line, but at least it did not appear to impinge on British maritime supremacy. The very concept was magnificent, as hyperbolic in its scope as anything from the early days of steam, an enterprise bound to do justice to the vision of the early railway builders. The idea of twentieth-century locomotives hurtling over ancient camel tracks was attractive enough to quell any incipient jealousy. 'Imperial carpet-bagger,' scoffed *Punch*, but at least someone was keeping the Cossacks at bay. 'Thus the prosaic locomotive whistle is destined to echo through the desert places of the cradle of the human race, and to awaken the land from its sleep of centuries,' wrote *The Scientific American* with an approval echoed in most corridors of power.[19] 'A sensible idea,' agreed *The Times*, as good a short cut to India as Suez although it should be noted that it was a short cut from Hamburg not London.[20] 'We wish to cooperate,' said Germany's Foreign Minister in the Reichstag in March 1908, 'in awakening from a sleep of a thousand years an ancient flourishing civilised region.'[21] Construction of the Baghdad Railway seemed largely a question of raising the finance; its investors and advocates, principally German but also British and French, were concerned with its commercial potential and on that basis spent the next four years trying to increase their numbers. Government guarantees to pay a certain amount per kilometre to make the line viable were supposed to decline as the takings rose.

Reactions were rather different at the far end of the proposed line. That other imperial link, the Indo-European Telegraph, whose 1,400 miles of cable were laid up the Gulf from Karachi in 1862, buzzed with apprehension when in 1899 a vessel of the German Hapag Line appeared in the Gulf and steamed up to Kuwait to investigate the harbour potential of this prospective terminus. It had the great advantage of being outside the mud flats exposed in the low season at the entrance to the Shatt al-Arab. It had the great disadvantage of being part of what Britain regarded as her Gulf hegemony. Hearing as early as 1899 of the German plans, Curzon had acted swiftly, instructing the British agent in Bushire to make a secret agreement with the Ruler of Kuwait assuring him of British protection. Under no circumstances would another foreign power be allowed to acquire property rights in this British preserve and no other foreign emissaries were to be allowed to call. British hackles had also been raised by the appearance of German commercial vessels, agents and even consuls in various Gulf ports. A German merchant, Herr Wonckhaus, set up shop at Lingeh on the Persian shore of the Gulf in 1896, hoping to exploit red oxide deposits on the island of Abu Musa; he was given very short shrift by British gunboats. The Hapag Line began a regular service to Gulf ports in 1906; Russia and France also sent occasional war vessels to the Gulf, teasing the British like a game of Tom Tiddler's Ground, with the excuse of looking for coaling depots. This threat to British maritime interests aroused much more animosity than movements eastwards by land, and a venture which started as a commercial undertaking thus acquired a political dimension alarming as well as obstructive to German railway entrepreneurs.

By 1903 the Anatolian Railway Company had failed to find international backing for its venture and the Ottoman authorities substituted for its concession the Baghdad Railway Convention. The company and the Deutsche Bank remained the principal interested parties, although both often complained of too much German government interference. The convention set up the Société Impériale Ottoman du Chemin de Fer de Baghdad, theoretically a Turkish–German company. Though named after Baghdad the line would terminate further south, either at Basra or preferably – avoiding that Fao rice pudding which could be crossed only at high tide – at Kuwait, still under consideration despite being a red rag to the British bull. There was a suggestion, however, that the British should build the Baghdad–Basra section to protect their interests. The plan was to finance the railway partly by raising import tariffs, much resented by Britain as Turkey's main trading partner, partly by generous kilometric guarantees. Under this scheme the Ottoman government guaranteed a certain amount of revenue per kilometre of line; because of the government's anxiety for the line to be built, it often gave guarantees far in excess of likely revenue, on the basis that in due course the line would generate more traffic than it actually did, thus leading to long-term debt problems. Substantial concessions were made by the Ottoman authorities to the Germans to give the project some viability. Grants of public lands, forestry, tax exemptions, permits for industrial development, even concessions for exclusive mining rights 20 kilometres either side of the line and archaeological rights 10 kilometres either side were designed to attract German investment. The terms of the concession were to be valid until 1987.

Political moods in Europe changed rapidly in the highly charged atmosphere at the turn of the century. The Russians, sitting well to the west of their present borders in Anatolia, were unenthusiastic about a railway running through an area which they viewed as peculiarly their own. They were also anxious to develop their own Caucasian network to link up with any Mesopotamian line. The French were ambivalent because of their alliance with Russia, and also because French bankers, expert in railway financing, were involved in Siemens' fund-raising. British opposition was slower to develop but was suddenly touched off by the recognition that the line was intended to terminate at Kuwait. This above all was an invasion of the British 'zone of influence' in lower Mesopotamia and the Gulf, a zone all the more jealously guarded in the wake of the discovery of commercial quantities of oil.

Terms of the Baghdad Railway Convention were leaked to the British press in advance of actual publication. Germany had now replaced Russia as the British bogey; pan-German ambitions gave the British plenty to think and write about and the German press had had the nerve to criticise British policies and actions in the Boer War. In April 1903, the British government led by the Prime Minister, Arthur Balfour, suddenly found itself under violent attack for even considering participation in a scheme so obviously to Britain's disadvantage, one which confirmed every suspicion that Germany was out to undermine and eventually replace Britain as the pre-eminent power in that part of the world. Balfour, who argued that it was better to help build the line rather than have it built without Britain, was helpless before the outcry. 'Whether the English government assist or do not assist,' he said plaintively in the Commons debate, 'it is undoubtedly in the power of the British government to hamper and impede and inconvenience any project of the kind; but that the project will be carried out, with or without our having a share in it, there is no question whatever.'[22] Not good enough, answered a growing section of British public opinion mobilised by such old Mesopotamian hands as the Lynches. Mesopotamia and the Gulf were a British preserve and in no circumstances – not even the generous offers of participation made by the railway company – would Kuwait be the terminus.

As it turned out the topographical obstacles were at least as great as political ones, and expensive to deal with; even today the irrationality of timetables, or rather the inability of the trains to keep to them, highlights the problems faced by the German and Swiss engineers and their multinational gangs of navvies as they toiled through Anatolia to meet the strategic deadline of their employers. For by the time the Baghdad Railway was heading south from Konya, its main function was to move Ottoman armies and their supplies (and, by implication as far as the British were concerned, German) to protect the outer limits of the Ottoman Empire and to threaten British interests in Mesopotamia and down the Gulf. And of course in India. Russian opposition to the line was withdrawn after the Potsdam agreement with Germany in 1910, which recognised Russia's sphere of influence in northern Persia. The Russians agreed to obtain from the Shah permission to build a line south from Tehran to Khaniqin on the Mesopotamian border to link up with a branch from the Baghdad Railway.,

Though the strategy behind the line was German, the builders and administrators came from all over Turkey and Europe: David Fraser in 1909 was surprised, after all the palaver at home, to find French and Turkish the languages spoken and the officials he met, from top to bottom, were Turkish, Greek or Armenian, almost never German. From Eskişehir to Konya and on to Ereğli the line was simple and cheap to build – 'miles and miles of bare plain, with here and there cowering villages which merely emphasise the extreme desolation.'[23] Not far from Ereğli the foothills of the Taurus begin; for a while the train takes some lavish diversions to avoid the obstacles but soon the bare hills crowd in. At Bulgurlu they brought the train to a standstill in 1904 and there it rested for the next six years. Finance was a constant headache; including the tunnel stretches the cost was working out at £40,000 a mile. Beyond the Taurus lay another barrier, the Amanus Mountains, running north to south across the route. They could have been circumvented had the line been directed along the coast from Adana to Iskenderun (Alexandretta) but that, said the Ottoman government, would leave the line exposed to attack from vessels out at sea. It must therefore go through the mountains as indeed it eventually did, but not until after the outbreak of war.

Otherwise the line was completed up to and beyond the Taurus by 1912, joining up with the existing French line over the Cilician plain between Adana and Mersin before reaching the Amanus Mountains. Down on the Cilician plain construction ran into one of its nastiest and all too frequent problems: Turkish massacres of Armenians, in this case in Adana in 1909. Many of the middle rank of labour, the semi-skilled, the semi-official, were in fact Armenian or Greek, both persecuted in the mood of Turkish nationalism which was beginning to emerge in the heartlands of the Ottoman Empire. Beyond these mountains the line went down to Aleppo to meet up with the railway heading south through Syria to the Hijaz, before turning eastwards to meander slowly over the rolling pastures of Kurdistan past countless tumuli, tumbled walls and ancient tombs to the village of Akçakale, now on the Turkish–Syrian border, when World War I began.

The railway was also interrupted by a change of government. In 1908 the Young Turks returned from their various homes in exile to rise in revolt in Constantinople against Abdul Hamid. The Sultan kept his position for another year before abdicating in favour of his younger brother, Mehmet V, and going into exile. In the wider empire the revolt had few implications beyond heightening the sense of a disintegrating administration. Throughout Syria and Mesopotamia that summer and again in 1909 sporadic raids and rebellions created a general disorder in the region that was hardly conducive to the building of railways. Stations east of the Euphrates, as in the Hindu Kush, became fortified buildings with loopholes for the defenders; a visiting army engineer was glad to note that wells were set inside enclosed courtyards. Germans and Turks squabbled over priorities on the truncated track and the problems of finance. Unpaid construction gangs rioted in Mesopotamia in the summer of 1914 and barricaded their German managers in their houses. 'The banks of the Euphrates echo with ghostly alarms,' wrote Gertrude Bell in 1911, 'the Mesopotamian deserts are full of the rumour of phantom armies; you will not blame me if I passed among them *trattando l'ombre come cose salde*.'[24]

As for the Baghdad end, the British swallowed their pride in July 1914 and in the 'Baghdad peace', so short-lived and never ratified, finally accepted the German suggestion that they should build the line south from Baghdad; none of it was serviceable, however, when Indian troops landed at Basra in the autumn of 1915. The Mesopotamian campaign was mostly conducted by river steamer. The line was also being laid north of Baghdad, but only 78 miles of it were finished by October 1914. The two ends were 400 miles from meeting.

So Europe went to war, much of it fought in the Middle East. Whose tactics the railway line should serve led to frequent breakdowns in the German–Turkish alliance, with the Baghdad Railway Company badgered by both parites to fill gaps in a line that could be vital to either. The Turks at first wished to use it to attack, then to defend their interests in Arabia, the Germans to transport soldiers and their supplies through Mesopotamia towards India, hoping to force the British to transfer troops from the Western Front. This was not 'a fairy tale adventure,' wrote old Marshall von der Goltz who was to die in the Caucasus campaign in 1916. What Alexander, Tamerlane and Nadir Shah had done so could others 'with the perfected means of the modern age.'[25] Under German pressure the Turks initiated a crash building programme, rushing narrow-gauge equipment to the gaps; the material was ultimately paid for by the Germans, anxious that the Turkish army should keep British troops pinned down in Mesopotamia.

The Taurus Mountains are magnificent at any time of year, best on a sparkling winter's day with the whole snow-capped range in view. 'About half an hour before I reached the plain at the foot of this mountain,' wrote the archaeologist Charles Fellows in 1851, 'a view burst upon me through the cliffs, so far exceeding the usual beauty of nature as to seem like the work of magic. I look down from the rocky steps of the throne of winter, upon the rich and verdant plain of summer ... This splendid view passed like a dream; for the continual turns in the road, and the increasing richness of the woods and vegetation, soon limited my view to a mere foreground.'[26] Fellows' ecstasy was the railway engineer's nightmare, although the German railway builders displayed astonishing bravado in marching up to such mountains and saying, 'I will go through!' They were not the first: the railway line for the most part follows the ancient invasion and caravan route through the Taurus and a careful eye can detect a few remaining stretches of an old Roman road – no Nobel dynamite in those days. The generations of Persians, Greeks, Arabs, Turks and Crusaders who used it often reported an uneasy passage, vulnerable to ambush and wasted by thirst.

The defeat of Serbia in 1915 eased the transport of railway materials; even so the Taurus stretch took two years to build. The line, plotted by a Greek engineer named Mavrogordato, goes through the heart of one of Asia's most strategic and dramatic passes, the Cilician Gates, plunging 4,700 feet in 68 miles between the little stations of Belemedik and Durak. The Gates themselves are a deep fissure in a mass of rock blocking the ravine, below which lies the fertile but malarial plain of Cilicia. Much of the time the line clings to precipitous limestone banks of the Chakrit River, with no foothold apparent for man or beast. The train often disappears into tunnels, thirty-seven of them, unfortunately for the passenger, sitting in smoke- and smut-filled carriages in the days of steam. One tunnel collapsed during construction, trapping fifty tunnellers, but by means of a lateral passage driven in from the hillside all were rescued within forty-eight hours. Even building a service for the line was an achievement. All the labour had to be imported to this deserted, inhospitable region and came from everywhere – expert tunnellers from Italy, Austria and Switzerland, less expert manual labour from other parts of Turkey, from Greek silver mines and from northern Syria. In charge were the tunnelwise Swiss. Special military railway units arrived from Germany. Anti-Armenian mania upset the morale of local labour gangs, the Turks replacing deported Armenians with Russian prisoners of war. British prisoners of war, dispatched north after the British defeat by the Turks in Mesopotamia in 1916, arrived in too wretched a state to be of any use and were pushed on to camps in central Anatolia. Malaria and cholera attacked the work camps as they had those in the Bolan Pass.

But by August 1917 a narrow-gauge track had been laid through the Taurus and a standard-gauge track through the Amanus, both operative as long as there was fuel. By 1917 this was in very short supply and nearby hillsides were denuded. From January 1917 little Décauville trucks were running through the tunnels six times a day, driven by fireless locomotives.* They were loaded with troops, supplies and ammunition for the Palestine and Mesopotamian campaigns that had previously been transported over the mountains by lorry. Standard-gauge locomotives from Germany were also transported through the tunnels, like David carrying Goliath – the boiler on one Décauville truck, the frame, cylinder and wheels on the other. Another fourteen tunnels had to be drilled out of the Amanus Mountains to let a narrow-gauge track through; the main tunnel – the Bagtche tunnel – was nearly 5 kilometres long. It took six years to complete, not helped by the discovery of a 2 metre stratum of porphyry in the middle; at that point drillers could only progress about 10 centimetres a day. And where the train emerged into daylight came bridges, the grandest of them the 300-metre meccano-like Here Dere Viaduct near Rajou, from whose lofty heights passengers gazed down on the distant plain like conquering heroes come. On October 9th, 1918 a standard-gauge track through the Taurus opened, giving an uninterrupted run to trains from the Bosphorus to Aleppo. Three weeks later Allenby's troops marched into Aleppo. The war was over, new frontiers would be devised and the railway planners' vision would forever be constrained by the prevarications of governments, down to the most subordinate customs official.

Abdul Hamid also made use of railways to strengthen the Ottoman hold on the Arabian periphery of the empire. Here were the two holy cities of Mecca and Madina, the control of which the Sultan and his successors viewed as vital to the imperial rule that had been reimposed in 1845 after more than a century of semi-independence. As Caliph of all Muslims the Sultan had initiated his plan for a railway to take pilgrims – and, more to the point, troops – to the holy places of Islam. In April 1900 Abdul Hamid announced to the faithful his intention to build a line from Damascus to Madina and Mecca, appealing to the Muslim world for funds. They responded magnificently and by 1904

* The boiler of a fireless locomotive was heated before entering the tunnel and the furnace detached. The steam generated was sufficient to get the locomotive through the tunnel without further heating.

$3.5 million had been collected. More unfairly, civil and military servants of the Ottoman Empire were subjected to a compulsory levy of 10 per cent on their salaries. British strategists eyed the line apprehensively as another potential threat to their approaches to India, running far too close to the Suez Canal for comfort.

From the engineering point of view the laying of the line presented few headaches to its chief engineer, the likeable and indefatigable German, Heinrich Meissner. Most of it ran across the semi-arid plains and hills of Jordan and Palestine and the desert of what is now northern Saudi Arabia, the route marked by wells and caravanserais used since the time of the Prophet Muhammad by the thousands of pilgrims on their way to and from Mecca. It also followed the ancient incense route, but instead of frankincense and myrrh camels were now loaded with water for the labour gangs and railway battalions, filling their water bags at Roman and Islamic cisterns.

The Hijaz Railway linked with a number of branch lines between the interior of the Levant and the coast, several of them built by the French.* European rivalries expressed themselves in the Levant in competition for railway concessions; the building, management and control of a railway was often decisive in establishing a sphere of influence and the outline of the post-war Anglo–French partition of the Levant and Mesopotamia can be seen in their railway concessions there before the war. A branch line was also constructed from Deraa to Haifa which included some spectacular engineering over the Yarmuk gorge. For reasons of speed and economy it was decided that the line should be metre gauge, the commonest in the area, although the foreign builders of Ottoman railways seldom concerned themselves with the uniformity of gauge that would be essential to an efficient use of the lines in war. The links added a touch of commercial sense to the Hijaz Railway as it moved steadily forward, two or three kilometres a day. A new stage was opened each year in September on the anniversary of the Sultan's accession, the final stage to Madina on September 1st, 1908. 'The Pilgrimage made easy!' claimed *The Illustrated London News*. 'The railway is by no means the only modern thing that has reached the sacred city'; electric light had also been switched on in the mosque housing the Prophet's tomb.[27]

* Other Levant railways were from Jaffa to Jerusalem, 1892, (metre gauge); Haifa to Deraa, 1905 (1.05 m.); Beirut to Damascus, French built, 1894 (partly Abt rack, the rest metre gauge); Damascus to Aleppo, French built, 1906 (standard gauge from Rayak). The French lines were run by the Chemins de Fer Damas-Hama et Prolongements (DHP).

48 The inauguration of the Hijaz Railway at Madina, September 1st, 1908

49 *A Miscarriage*, showing T. E. Lawrence in Arab disguise, plotting the
dynamiting of the Hijaz Railway

Throughout the construction of the line Meissner's greatest problem
was the chronic hostility of local Arabs. The great annual pilgrim
caravan had always been viewed by local tribes as fair game (in 1828
20,000 pilgrims were killed in a single season) but in Meissner's case
and in that of many of his best foremen, who were mostly Italian, the
problem was the fact that local enmity was aroused also because they
were Christian. Fundamentalism is not new to Islam or to Arabia, and
had been revived at the end of the eighteenth century by Muhammad
Abd al-Wahhab. Wahhabism is still the dominant influence in Saudi
Arabia, while Mecca and Madina have always been jealously guarded
against 'infidel' intrusion. Even the telegraph had at one time been
prohibited between the two holy cities. Meissner and other Christians
were forbidden to survey beyond the ancient caravan city of Madain
Salih, but there were no trained Muslim substitutes until the arrival of
some Egyptians. Railway working parties were regularly attacked by
armed bedouin who referred to the line as the 'riding donkey of the
Sultan'. No one dared stray from the immediate vicinity of the camp as
the line worked its way south. Arab raiding parties covered huge
distances, 60–70 miles in a day, and they were as well armed as the
Turks. The problem was eased as Muslim technicians gradually

replaced Christian but the railway never reached Mecca nor, more significant for the prosperity of the region, the Red Sea port of Jiddah.

Arab unrest immediately gave the line a military validity as well as a religious one. However, according to one Major Maunsell sent to report on it in 1911, it was not an efficiently run line, its faults supportable for pilgrims but less so for armies.[28] Muslim engine drivers had 'fatalistic ideas unsuited to such a profession'; coal supplies were erratic since the best still came from Cardiff and the Turkish alternative was smoky and of poor calorific value; and 'scanty workmanship' on its mainly Belgian and German locomotives shortened their lives and landed too many of them too often in the workshops at Aleppo, Damascus or Maan. Most passengers, holy or martial, were expected to travel in great discomfort: 'the covered wagon is the most useful vehicle for the conveyance of troops as it gives some shelter from the summer sun and cold winds in winter, while the peasants are accustomed to lying on the floor,' wrote Maunsell. The troops were to discover its discomfort all too soon as they were trundled over Anatolian and Levantine tracks to within 200 miles of the Suez Canal.

The Hijaz Railway, so romantic to British nurtured on *Seven Pillars of Wisdom*, had a short life. Its death knell came in 1917 at the hands of a British archaeologist in fancy dress, who later published a highly coloured account of his wartime activities in *Seven Pillars*. 'Meanwhile the Ageyl were measuring out gelatine,' T. E. Lawrence wrote with glee of an attack near Maan, 'and soon we lit their charges and destroyed a culvert, many rails and furlongs of telegraph.'[29] A few months later near Deraa – 'from the watercourse we could look about. The explosion had destroyed the arched head of the culvert, and the frame of the first engine was lying beyond it . . . The second locomotive had toppled into the gap, and was lying across the ruined tender of the first. Its bed was twisted. I judged them both beyond repair.' Lawrence actually managed to blow up twenty-five bridges. Some locomotives were luckier and survived to a worthy old age but south of Maan the line was never repaired and a lone engine near the great Nabataean ruin of Madain Salih rests amongst iron girders twisted by Nobel's gelignite. Poor Herr Meissner.

Poor visionaries of the Baghdad Railway too; not until 1940 did a train run all the way from Haydar Pasha to Baghdad. The last stretch was a three-quarter-of-a-mile tunnel south of Mosul. Another war was in progress and this train's epochal passage from Istanbul to Baghdad in three days with another fourteen hours to Basra went almost unnoticed. Politics has always sat heavily on the line and in consequence passengers needed the patience of a saint (several of whom spent years atop pillars in the vicinity of its route) to survive the border crossings and customs delays that play havoc with its timetable. Thanks to modern politics very little of the Baghdad Railway is accessible today.

14

Aftermath

World War I saw the steam communications of the previous ninety years used to maximum advantage. Steam turned an essentially European conflict into a global one, with fleets and armies moved swiftly from one battle zone to another. British and Indian troops steamed through the Suez Canal and the Mediterranean and round the Cape to Flanders, Gallipoli, Egypt and Mesopotamia; German troops steamed into Anatolia and Transcaucasia; Russian troops also steamed into Transcaucasia and into Persia; Turkish troops steamed much of the way to Mesopotamia and Palestine. Yet there remained a gap in the pattern of steam communications, a hollow space between east and west that defied the politicians and the engineers: Persia and Afghanistan. No railways were built in either country before World War I and the war itself hardened hitherto shifting lines separating nations whose existence had once exercised only map-makers. Thereafter railways were laid within countries for their internal benefit. And as the barriers rose so the great steam crusade – with its optimism about the sublimity, the energy, the civilising force of engines shunting over continents – gave way to disillusion. For all the hyperbolic jargon of geopoliticians and aspiring engineers, it has never been possible to steam all the way by land from Europe to India. Even more than Afghanistan Persia (now Iran) was, and is, the principal stumbling block. The geographical reasons are obvious: the country is too large, too underpopulated, its few large towns spaced well apart round the perimeter of a boomerang-shaped desert 800 miles long and 150–200 miles wide. Distances between centres of population are enormous. But there were also political reasons. Persia existed as a nation, in a way that neither the Ottoman Empire nor India had, and a nation which since the fifteenth century and its adoption of Shiah Islam as a national religion had had very little taste for foreigners. Shahs of Persia, particularly in the nineteenth century's age of imperialism, were faced with the problem of trying to maintain the unity of a country which was fissiparous by nature but also resistant to foreign exploitation. Railways could have been of enormous benefit in uniting the country but were expensive and encouraged exploitation; the finance would have been available but most of it would have come from the two powers most threatening to Persian independence – Russia and Britain.

Britain had been concerned about Persia ever since Napoleon sent emissaries there in 1807 to try to instigate an invasion of India, and throughout the nineteenth century tried to prevent the Russian government from establishing a secure route through Persia to a warm-water outlet on the Indian Ocean. Various sweeping suggestions were made to cover the country from north to south with railways but all foundered on this distrust between Russia and Britain, each concerned to see that the other acquired no special advantage. Russia's Asian railways – the Transcaucasian and the Transcaspian – had aggravated the menace to India but the British were able to counter this by tightening their hold on the Gulf, hence the strong British opposition to proposals for a Caspian to Gulf railway through Persia. An agreement for such a line, the first stage of which, from the Caspian, was even surveyed, was part of the huge Reuter concession granted by Shah Nasir al-Din to Baron Julius de Reuter, a naturalised British subject, in 1872. The British government was not enthusiastic, however, and Russia was equally hostile to any non-Russian building such a line, pressing the Shah into cancelling the concession a year later. In fact the Russian authorities hoped to be allowed to build a far easier line via Tabriz, particularly after the Russo–Turkish war of 1877 placed eastern Anatolia under their control. But this the Shah was adamantly opposed to: it would make it far too easy for a Russian army to enter Persia. The Russians contented themselves with building railways across the Armenian highlands from Tiflis to their great fortress at Kars and south to Erivan in Armenia and Julfa on the Persian frontier. British officialdom was content as long as they went no further.

In the early years of the twentieth century, Britain and Russia patched up their quarrels in the face of the growing German menace and in the Anglo–Russian convention of 1907 effectively divided Persia into Russian and British spheres of influence – much to Persian indignation. Russia's zone extended south to include Isfahan while Britain accepted a smaller share in the south-east that nevertheless safeguarded communications up the Gulf. Thanks to the agreement some railway enthusiasts, even in Britain, thought a trans-Persian line might at last be feasible. It would 'make North India the halfway house of a vast railway system directly connecting Central Europe with Central China,' Colonel Yate told the Royal Central Asian Society in 1911.[1] The 1,600

50 Nasir ud-Din Shah landing at Dover, June 18th, 1873. This first visit of a shah to Britain highlighted the gulf between industrialised Europe and Persia.

miles of track from the Caucasus to the Indus would cost no more than £21 million to build (actually, at £13,000 a mile, not exactly cheap), and the 5,700 miles between London and Bombay could then be travelled in seven days for no more than £40: 'In time,' Yate continued, 'when a round dozen or so of railway termini are touching his frontiers, he [the Amir of Afghanistan], will be unable to resist their seductive conveniences, and then Kabul, Kandahar, Herat and Mazar-i Sharif will appear in Bradshaw's Continental Guide, and lines formerly closed to the British traveller will enable Indian officials to make the most of their privilege leave.' Not so, indicated both Shah and Amir, their resistance to such encroachments abetted by lack of finance. At the outbreak of World War I, the nearest approach to a railway line in either country

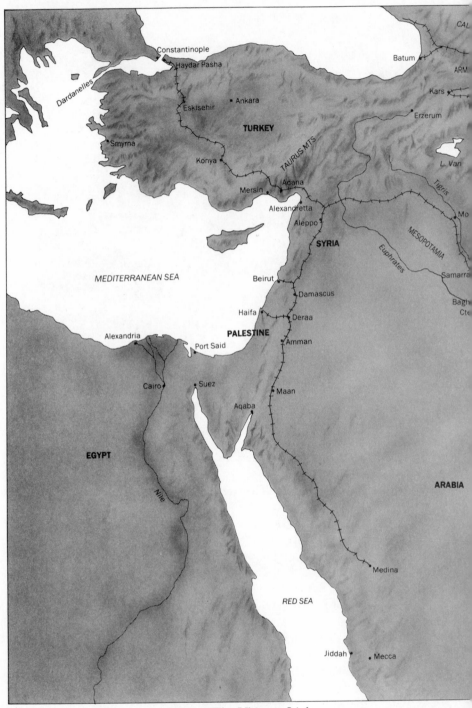

Map 9   The Ultimate Links, 1914

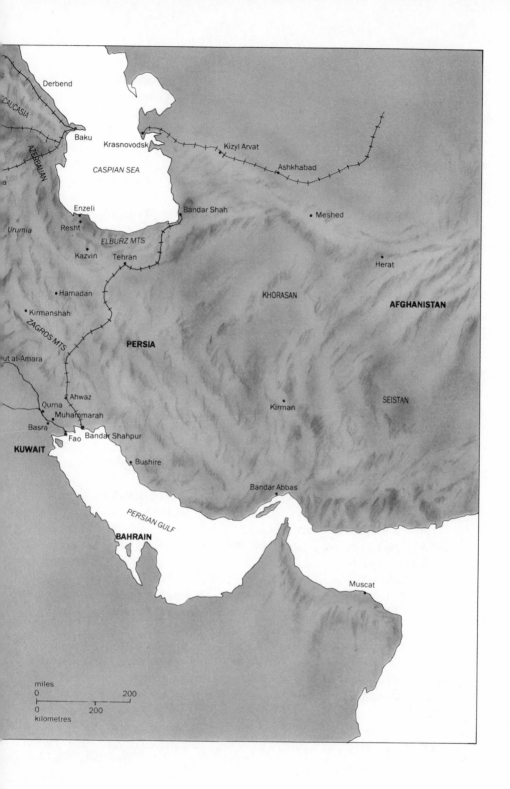

miles
0   200
0   200
kilometres

were some rails imported from Belgium for a proposed line from Resht on the Caspian over the Alburz Mountains to Tehran. The rails had a complicated journey to their destination – via the Volga to the Caspian and Resht, thence by camel to Tehran – but they were eventually only used for a little 6-mile metre-gauge line from Tehran to the shrine of Shah Abd al-Azim just outside Tehran. The line continued to run until the 1960s – not quite the threat to India which any other line might have turned out to be.

Persia was thus an abhorrent vacuum in the protective shield that Britain had erected around India. This included Egypt, Aden, the Gulf and lower Mesopotamia, but was dependent on maritime rather than land links. With Indian as well as British forces needing to be concentrated in Europe during the war, Britain was hard put to maintain that protection. The defence of oil installations was also important, with the British navy now steaming on oil rather than coal. Troops were dispatched from India to Bahrain even before war was officially declared but the ensuing Mesopotamian campaign was severely handicapped by the army's dependence on river transport. Thanks to British opposition to the Baghdad Railway and the reluctance of the Indian government to spend money on track that would have no profitable purpose after the war, there was no railway between Baghdad and the head of the Gulf. Troops had to be transported by river boat up the Shatt al-Arab to Basra (with little resistance from the Turks) and then on towards Baghdad. The further north the British advanced the more over-extended their supply lines became.

The Tigris was, moreoever, an unsatisfactory alternative to rail, its course meandering drunkenly through the flat lands south of Baghdad. Traffic was constantly being sabotaged by treacherous shoals, especially in the low season and especially over the critical stretch between Kut al-Amara and Baghdad. 'One steamer firmly aground in mid-stream might hold up all traffic for days,' wrote an army chaplain. 'It is not at all an enviable experience to be held up on a mud bank from four to six days.'[2] The Turks, on the other hand, despite the unfinished state of the Baghdad Railway, could use large stretches of it to transport and supply their troops. Having pushed the Turks as far back as Ctesiphon, just south of Baghdad, the British were immediately forced to fall back, their retreat covered by little gunboats dodging in and out of the low season shoals. The main body of the army was on land, the wounded on river boats. At Kut al-Amara, some 70 miles from Baghdad, they dug in, withstanding a five-month siege before falling to the Turks in April 1916. Those still able to walk were dispatched north by the Turks to be put to work on the railway then drilling its way through the Taurus and Amanus Mountains.

The Russian army was much more easily moved to the eastern front. The Transcaucasian network had been considerably expanded in the pre-war years for just such an emergency and a branch line to Julfa on the Persian border was now extended to Tabriz, the great market centre of Persia's north-west. A side line ran off to Lake Urmiyyah. Another line ran from Tiflis through a deep rift in the Caucasus plateau to Alexandropol (Leninakan) on what is now the border with Turkey and on to Kars; it was extended 40 miles to Sarikamish, on the 1878

51　*The Trouble in Persia*: a Russian Caucasian regiment marching through Tiflis to entrain for the Persian frontier, 1908

Russo–Turkish border and some 60 miles from Erzerum, just before the outbreak of war. Erzerum was the Turks' frontier headquarters, scene of the denouement of John Buchan's *Greenmantle*. All these lines came into use during the Caucasus campaigns of the war and gave the Russian forces the mobility, flexibility and lines of supply which the Turks so desperately lacked. Russia's campaigns in the area, to prevent Turkey or Germany reaching the Baku oilfields, were fought over the mountains of the 'Little Caucasus' and the Armenian highlands, windswept uplands inhabited by semi-nomadic Kurds – a bitterly hostile region in winter, the season chosen by the Turks to open their campaign in 1914.

Turkey entered World War I almost by mistake, the government being at first undecided which side, if any, to support. Poor tactics by Britain and some swift action by Germany thrust Turkey into the war on the side of the Central powers and immediately opened up Britain's flank in India and Russia's in the Caucasus, where the Turks were initially at a grave disadvantage due to their lack of railways. The nearest railhead to Erzerum was Ankara, some 600 miles to the west. The Russian army on the other hand, under the command of General Yudenich, was a well-organised, well-equipped 'railway army', conducting its operations over a network of Décauville lines. Yudenich was able to forestall a Turkish advance into the Caucasus and eventually to capture Erzerum in February 1916.

Russians and Turks also joined battle in northern Persia. The most recent Shah, Ahmad, had come to the throne in 1914 and declared Persia's neutrality in the war without being in a position to defend it. The only effective armed forces in the country were the Cossack Brigade, trained and officered by Russians to keep order in the northern provinces, and the Swedish Gendarmerie, an internal security force. Persia favoured Germany out of distaste for her Russian and British 'protectors'. Her neutrality was already violated by a section of the eastern front running from Trebizond via Lake Van and Kurdistan through Persian territory in the north-east to a point near Hamadan. It was a mobile front, with the Russian army making as much use as possible of the railway lines now extended to the frontier zones of the Caucasus, the Turks slogging on foot through the mountains of Armenia and Kurdistan. Nevertheless, by mid-1916 Russia's military energy was exhausted, to a large extent because the overworked railways could no longer keep her armies supplied. The winter of 1916–17 was particularly harsh. In the new year, while Britain in Mesopotamia was reversing the fortunes of war, capturing Baghdad from the Turks in March 1917, the Russian front had come to a standstill, the army's morale undermined by poor food, worn-out equipment and lack of respect between officers and men.

It was common knowledge as the winter snows began to thaw in the spring of 1917 that the war was bitterly unpopular in Russia. Food and fuel shortages were aggravated by military monopolisation of the railways. Those who worked the railways had been notorious for many years for their notions of revolutionary socialism: railway workers had been heavily involved in the 1905 revolution, and the murder of Rasputin in February 1917 was the signal for sporadic strikes among railway workers all over the country. Drivers, guards, oilers and mechanics were often Bolsheviks but their influence was seldom given much weight. Few were prepared for the violence with which the general discontent burst into revolution in March 1917, let alone for the speed with which the news was carried by railway throughout the length and breadth of Russia and its empire, releasing hatred and passions all the more rampant for the effectiveness with which Tsarist rule had suppressed them for so long.

The revolution forced a new range of strategies on the Allies, arising from the likelihood that the new Russian government would make peace with Germany. Not only did it reopen the Great Game; it also created the possibility of a Turkish or German advance on India via the Caucasus and Transcaspia or via Persia, where hitherto the Russian army had blocked the way. Russian armies in north-west Persia now refused to obey the orders of their Tsarist officers. In Tehran 'mischievous Bolshevik propaganda' played on public opinion, already confused by German propaganda calling for a *jihad*, or holy war, against the infidel British. It was hoped such a war would spread to Britain's Muslim subjects in India. German agents succeeded in virtually destroying British influence in south-west Persia, and their propaganda converted Bolshevik committees as well as many Persian politicians to anti-British activities. Afghanistan and Baluchistan also remained unpredictable trouble spots. Gun-running through southern Persia and western Baluchistan had been contained by 1912 but picked up again during the war. In his *Raiders of Sarhad*, published in 1921, General Reginald Dyer vividly described his expedition to suppress the gun-runners; 'those who were carrying torches,' he wrote, 'must be kept away from the loose powder along the Indian frontier.'[3]

Throughout a swathe of Middle Eastern territory the menace from north of the Caspian seemed all the greater because of the dearth of British influence in the area. Political and military strategists dislike a vacuum as much as nature does, and in the case of the Middle East this led to the mounting by the Indian government of several small, rashly inspired and ill-coordinated expeditions in Central Asia and the Caspian basin. By the autumn of 1917 Bolshevik influence was widespread and well organised in many parts of the Russian Empire, but a strong groundswell of nationalism had also swiftly developed in the remoter areas of the empire. This encouraged the British, both in India and in London, to aim at reinforcing that protective shield around India by including in it a number of Central Asian and Caucasian states that by 1918 were trying to hold off a Bolshevik takeover. Such a policy would help counterbalance the Persian vacuum. In the Caucasus it was

complicated by separate Turkish and German advances on Baku, both
allies hoping to gain control of the oil, though Turkish efforts were also
partly inspired by Enver Pasha's dream of a Pan-Turanian empire
ultimately to spread eastwards over most of Central Asia. Georgians,
Armenians and Turkomans were setting up committees whose rival
socialist and nationalist claims compounded the confusion that British
strategists were desperately trying to elucidate. Sir Harry Luke, British
chief commissioner in the area, compared Transcaucasia in 1919
(equally applicable to the 1990s) to 'that toy of my childhood which was
composed of minute fragments of coloured glass in a box, the pattern
of which changed as you shook it this way and that. But there was this
essential difference. The pictures presented by the kaleidoscope were
invariably pleasing.'⁴

From the Black Sea to the Indian frontier of Afghanistan German
agents made the most of the confusion, stirring up trouble among the
Jangali tribesmen of Persia's north-west frontier and threatening to
penetrate a joint Russian–British 'cordon' set up in eastern Persia in
the early years of the war to keep such agents out of Afghanistan. The
situation grew even more inflammable with the signing in March 1918
of the Brest–Litovsk Treaty between Russia and Germany, releasing
Turkish and German troops for the penetration of Transcaucasia.
'Intervention through Persia towards the Caucasus, Transcaspia and
Turkistan is essential to protect the tranquillity of our Empire in India,'
Lord Milner, Secretary of State for War, wrote in a memo the same
month. 'If we continue to neglect north Persia, it will be only a matter
of weeks till the Germans send an armed party to Kabul ... the only
way of safety appears to lie in a forward policy in Persia, to be pursued
at once and with the utmost vigour.'⁵ Central Asia was viewed as
particularly vulnerable to the Pan-Turanian dreams of Enver Pasha,
because its various peoples are mostly Turkish-speaking. Such fears
were immediately linked to Afghanistan and Baluchistan. Yet Britain
was ill-equipped to handle them given the almost total absence of land
links.

Nothing daunted nothing gained: in 1918 four British expeditions
were directed by land to counter the threat. British forces in India had
been depleted by the dispatch of troops to the western front. It was
essential to make the best use of those that remained by well-planned
sorties into that swathe of territory of doubtful loyalty. One, under
General Lionel Dunsterville ('consisting of a few Englishmen of the
right type'⁶ and referred to as Dunsterforce), was dispatched from
Mesopotamia to Enzeli on the Caspian with a view to destroying the

Baku oil facilities in the likely event of a Turkish or German victory in the Caucasus. Another, under General Wilfrid Malleson and known as Mallmiss, was directed from India through eastern Persia to the Transcaspian Railway at Ashkhabad; railway workers at Kizil Arvat had rebelled against the Tashkent Soviet and now set up their own provisional government much in need of support to hold off the Bolsheviks. The third, under Commodore David Norris (giving the navy a share in the adventure), was detailed to establish a flotilla on the Caspian to control most, according to Admiralty instructions, if not all of that vast inland sea, and back up both Dunsterville and Malleson. A fourth, under Colonel Frederick Bailey, was an intelligence operation dispatched to Tashkent. All expeditions except Bailey's used Persian territory as a base for their operations. The Shah was not consulted.

None was particularly successful. Geography was as much against them as fluctuating politics, affecting supply lines and communications. Mountains, deserts, harsh winters and broiling summers were not conducive to the conduct of war, any more than they had been to the development of those communications in time of peace.

The East Persian Cordon used by General Malleson's mission was a road extension through the Persian provinces of Khurasan and Sistan to the railway that by 1914 ran from the Kandahar Railway just south of Quetta to Duzdab (now Zahidan) a few miles into Persia. The line was used intermittently by pilgrims and traders, but most effectively by General Dyer in his 1916 expedition against gun-runners. As early as the 1870s Sir Robert Sandeman had called for a Sistan railway to control the Baluchi route from Persia. Sistan is in the south-east of Persia, much of it semi-desert but easily crossed, or so it seemed to those British familiar with frontier conditions, by an invading force despite arctic winters and stifling summers. Sistan's border with Afghanistan and Baluchistan had been redrawn in 1903 'to secure respect for Great Britain's power in a region of growing importance to our Imperial interests,' said Valentine Chirol,[7] but deserts as frontiers had begun to lose some of their terror and their strength; 'like the loftiest mountains, like the stormiest oceans, they have yielded to the all-conquering influence of steam,' said Curzon.[8] General Browne had built the extension as far as Nushki, and a road on to the Persian border despite 'the pessimism of adverse critics, who croaked about the waterless deserts to be traversed, the intolerable heat of the summer and the bitter cold of the winter, which no caravans would dare face.'[9]

The need for vigilance on the Sistan border lapsed after the Anglo-Russian Convention, and British and Russians joined hands in 1914 to ward off any German attempt to infiltrate and destabilise Afghanistan. Physical conditions were grim: the British press, discussing what to do with the Kaiser after the war and hearing of east Persia's climatic extremes, recommended it as a future place of residence for this august personage, most particularly a spot with the unenticing name of Murkhi Surkh. Beyond Dalbandin in Baluchistan creeping sandhills, 'huge mounds of earth, of a crescent shape, impelled forward by wind and possibly other satanic influences,' according to the principal engineer on the project, Major W. E. R. Dickson,[10] might in the course of a night completely envelop the vital railway track. From Duzdab, just south of the great salt desert, a motorable road headed northwards. Dickson favoured a railway, for the excellent reason that 'it is so easy to stuff extras into railway carriages or vans but to do so on road transport means breakdowns.' By now, however, the internal combustion engine was all the rage and towards the end of 1917 Malleson was motoring 630 miles north up to Mashhad, ordered to do everything in his power to interrupt the Transcaspian Railway, build up the defences of the apparently moderate Transcaspian government and prevent thousands of tons of cotton (used for munitions) falling to the enemy. The cordon was rendered ineffective by the Russian collapse, although Turkish and German propaganda still called for a *jihad* into India along that route. Any Axis advance would be facilitated by the thousands of Austrian and German prisoners of war released or escaped from camps in Central Asia after the Revolution.

Dunsterforce was ordered into north-west Persia at about the same time, to recruit and train anti-Turkish units in Persia, Armenia and Transcaucasia. Unfortunately there was no 'cordon' to help the general with his communications. The troops' progress up the Tigris had been trailed by an army of engineers laying tracks in a confusion of gauges, using rails and sleepers torn up from Indian branch lines and shipped to Basra.* These included a track from the Baghdad Railway to Khaniqin, intended for extension to Hamadan, Kirmanshah and eventually Tehran, an ancient and well-worn trade route. But the engineers had to contend with Indian government parsimony regarding strategic railways, as well as with the Zagros Mountains, rocky and

---

* Kut to Baghdad: metre gauge; Baghdad to Baquba, 2′6″; Sumaika to Sadiya, 2′6″; Basra to Qurna: metre gauge; Baghdad to Falujah and Baghdad to Musaiybi 4′8″, the same as the Baghdad Railway which was extended north as far as Tikrit by September 1918.

barren, passable for donkeys and camels but never yet for trains. The track reached the barrier of Jabal Hamrin on the border and there it stopped. Thereafter Dunsterforce was dependent on lorries and vans, struggling through a countryside devastated by four years of war and swarming with rebellious tribesmen incited by German agents to oppose the British advance. Consisting of some 1800 officers and men with others spread out to defend the road through to Mesopotamia, it was far too small a force to meet the grandiose objectives of a War Office with little idea of what was happening on the ground. 'We cannot help feeling from Dunsterville's telegrams that possible failure is uppermost in his mind,' the War Office cabled GOC, Mesopotamia. 'He should be removed if he lacks the necessary determination to see this difficult situation through.'[11]

Despite such misadventures Dunsterforce – 'all very tired men'[12] – eventually reached Baku in stages from Enzeli, only to find the local administration in total disarray. Baku still had its Tartar and Armenian millionaires, furriers and carpet dealers, excellent hotels and the best restaurant in Transcaucasia. But its population also contained an inflammable mixture of races, aggravated by poor labour conditions and intrusive foreign influence. The first labour uprising in 1901–2 was partly organised by a young Georgian named Dugashvili, alias Stalin, and Baku socialists had been in the forefront of the 1905 uprising, leading later that year to communal massacres and the destruction of oil facilities. Now, in 1918, the population once again turned on each other. Moreover the local Tartar labour force in the oilfields had no intention of allowing the British to destroy their means of livelihood. Dunsterville found local troops too involved in nationalist politics to offer any resistance to the Turks, who captured the city in September 1918 just before the October armistice. By some careful subterfuge and with the help of Norris' Caspian flotilla Dunsterville managed to evacuate his force to Enzeli. From here he was redirected to Krasnovodsk, headquarters of the British effort to gain control of the Caspian, which Dunsterville was now supposed to garrison.

Dunsterville's failure to prevent the Turks capturing Baku increased the importance of Mallmiss, with the government in India facing a Bolshevik repetition of the old Tsarist threat to invade India. Malleson was now ordered across the Russian frontier to Ashkhabad to prevent the Transcaspian Railway being taken over by German, Turkish or Bolshevik forces. Despite the havoc caused to the railways by war and industrial action, Russian communications were such that the Bolsheviks had seized power in Tashkent only seven days after the revolution broke out in Petrograd; and a major reason for the ultimate Bolshevik victory was their control of the railway network. The revolution was taking its toll of the rolling stock, however, and Malleson's survival in Central Asia was at least partly due to the Tashkent government's running out of supplies. It was also due to a most efficient intelligence network, with agents covering a 1,000-mile radius. 'There was hardly a train on the Central Asian railway which had not one of our agents on board, and there was no important railway centre which had not two or three men on the spot.'[13]

Armoured trains proved to be 'the mainstay and pivot of manoeuvre of either side, since they alone could carry guns through the sandhills and dunes of the desert,' wrote Captain Blacker, himself a member of Bailey's expedition to Tashkent the same year.[14] The Austrians had been the first to use armoured trains, in Vienna in 1848, and they were also used during the American Civil War and by the British in the Boer War; Churchill was taken prisoner off one in South Africa. Some were used to patrol the Suez Canal in World War I, bullet-proofed by hammering on old steel plates and running on military tracks. They had their problems, however, a speciality being that the opponent could pick up tracks ahead of the train and re-lay them at a wider gauge. 'Next time the Bolshevik train advanced, the engine driver found himself bumping along the sleepers with his wheels still between the rails.'

But perhaps the most ambitious expedition of the three was that of Commodore David Norris, ordered to the Caspian in the full heat of July 1918 to establish a seaplane base at Enzeli.[15] Go and command the Caspian Sea, he was told; seize all hostile shipping; bomb the oil wells in Baku; and capture anything you can and arm it. Control of the Caspian was viewed as essential back-up for Dunsterforce but also, once Baku was in Turkish hands, as preventing Turkish, German, or in the event Bolshevik, emissaries infiltrating either Afghanistan or Baluchistan.

'People at home [who order such expeditions] use a very small scale map, which is often a delusion as regards distances. In Mesopotamia we had to supply by river from Basra to Baghdad and thence by road to Enzeli. It was much the same as if you had to supply by a river the size of the Thames at Staines, going at 6 mph as far as the Firth of Forth, and thence by Ford vans to Christiansen [Oslo].'[16] Norris had to take his tiny force of officers and ratings – on loan from the East India squadron – over the mountains together with their naval guns, transported by lorry. A small pre-revolutionary flotilla of four lightly armed gunboats was already on the Caspian, and some 200 merchant vessels with which Norris was supposed to link up. Their crews turned out to be unreliable and disinclined to obey either their officers or the British. Norris fitted out a merchant flotilla by commandeering Nobel's tankers and collecting whatever bits of scrap he could lay his hands on, mostly by wandering round railway yards at Krasnovodsk and Kizil Arvat. Injured almost immediately in an accident, he was replaced by Captain Basil Washington who telegraphed headquarters, as winter set in in 1918, that he was ready to secure complete control of the Caspian, rather more sweeping an achievement than was desired.

Winter ice clamped down on the flotilla's activities in the northern half of the Caspian. By the time of the March thaw the equation had changed again: the Turks were leaving Transcaucasia while the Bolsheviks were pressing relentlessly on Transcaspia. In Baku, where the British fleet was wintering, opera companies were performing, White Russian hostesses entertaining and crowds promenading on the seaside boulevards; but the price of bread was rising, labour unrest growing, and the Russian crews of the British vessels were increasingly unreliable. In February the flotilla was augmented by six motor coastal boats brought over the Transcaucasian Railway from the Black Sea, now under British control (exercised from London rather than from India). For a brief period travellers from the Caspian to Constantinople through the Caucasus could sleep in a British mess every night.

But Bolshevik pressure on Transcaspia had already begun to have an effect, taking advantage of political disagreements among the rival parties in the region. Ultimately the more ruthless Bolshevik organisation, backed by its control of the railway network radiating from Moscow, won the upper hand. By September 1919 the British government in London had finally come to the conclusion that intervention in Transcaspia was out of the question. Mallmiss was evacuated to Persia, and Transcaspia and the Caspian were soon in Bolshevik hands. By 1920 all British troops had been withdrawn from Persia.

Yet the Persian communications vacuum still existed and still worried the British government. Even after the war the British government still had hopes for its inclusion in that protective shield essential to the defence of India. In April 1919 Curzon, as chairman of the Foreign Office committee on Persia, advocated and tried to impose on the Shah a treaty of independence reflecting that 'forward' thinking so conditioned by Curzon's memorable visit in 1891. The treaty included not only a clause allowing for British military and financial advisers but also a blanket undertaking by the British to develop Persian railways. In the event Persia still held off the rival threats and blandishments of the

British Empire and the Soviet Russia. Churchill was right when he wrote in his *Aftermath*, 'I do not see how anything we can do within the present limits of our policy can possibly avert the complete loss of British influence throughout the Caucasus, Transcaspia and Persia.'[17] Opposition to the treaty was led by a determined military officer, Reza Khan, who in due course persuaded the National Assembly to repudiate it.

Ironically the creation of a Persian railway system was ultimately a German accomplishment. Reza Khan, who ousted the Shah in 1923, enthusiastically employed German engineers to build the Trans-Iranian Railway, starting in 1927. Its route is curious: it runs from the little-frequented eastern corner of the Caspian at Bandar Shah to an even less frequented sand spit in the north-east corner of the Gulf at Bandar Shahpur. Reza Shah wanted to remove its termini as far as possible from anyone's sphere of influence. In the circumstances this was not easy but both British and Russian governments were sufficiently irritated by his ploy to justify it in the Shah's eyes. The greatest obstacle was the Alburz Mountains, which involved some remarkable engineering. German firms and technicians helped supply this, with a German company building the Bandar Shah to Shai sector in 1928 and German engineers employed in the Scandinavian consortium Kampsax which took over the construction in 1933. German factories supplied locomotives and rolling stock, including a 'parlour train' for the Shah.

Despite German assistance, however, the railway was essentially Persian, or Iranian as it more accurately came to be called after Reza Shah decided to revive memories of former glories by imposing the ancient name. The railway was an internal affair, though extremely useful as a supply line to the Soviet Union in World War II. Neither terminus was of strategic or commercial interest to the two powers who had hung over Persia's destiny for so long. Other lines have been developed since then, and the main line extended to Kirman in south-east Iran in 1977. But it has never linked up with the British-laid line from Baluchistan, which still ends just inside Iran, at Zahidan. In the north, it is many years since a train crossed the border at Julfa.

'The British Empire is pre-eminently a great Naval, Indian and Colonial power': so ran a famous dictum around the time of World War II.[18] It was not, despite the modern enthusiasm for the steam locomotive, despite the early Stephenson initiative, a great railway power. Robert Stephenson returned from a visit to France and Germany in the early 1840s to warn railway developers that they were in danger of falling behind their continental colleagues. Nevertheless the insular British preferred, for obvious reasons, to back maritime communications and by extension naval defence. Despite the efforts by such railway enthusiasts as W. P. Andrew and Chesney to encourage steaming to India by land, the British as a nation, revelling like Kipling's McAndrew in the purr of those triple expansion engines, felt safer relying on links with India by sea. Thus the Suez Canal and the Cape of Good Hope became part of the great hymn of empire sung ever louder by political troubadours in the fifty years before World War I. The British consolidated their hold on India by alliances and annexations assisted by land communications as we have seen, but the extension of that hold into the Middle East depended on maritime rather than land communication. Resistance to railways under the Channel, however effective a remedy against seasickness, has the backing of tradition.

Dreams of transcontinental railways – Atlas, Calais to Karachi, London to Delhi or Peking – sank in the aftermath of war, as frontiers hardened into walls and chauvinism flourished in the fertile soil behind them. Asian borders, once open to the passage of men and goods, also recognise the passage of armies, to the detriment of the modern traveller; a question for the future will be whether governments can ever accommodate the far-ranging and not necessarily illusory visions

52 Locomotive at Bandar Shahpur on the Trans-Iranian Railway, linking the Persian Gulf with the Caspian, 1936

of the nineteenth-century engineer, so skilled at crossing geographical barriers but ultimately defeated by political ones. As the fires were extinguished in locomotive furnaces so were the imperial enthusiasms of Europeans, their self-confidence, once symbolised by the 'orchestra sublime' of the steam engine, eroded by world wars which faster travel had helped to stimulate. Persia's resistance to the blandishments of steam only preceded by a few years its demise and the departure of those magnificent vehicles of commercial and political imperialism to the wreckers' yards of the industrial underworld.

Traces of the achievements of those engineers can still be seen on weed-invaded railway sidings and in silted harbours: great rusting engines seeming pacific enough, like elephants tamed into submission only to be discarded when no longer useful. An engine waits patiently in a wrecked shed in the Hijaz, a few hulks rot on a Caspian shore. Some still shunt over the rugged Anatolian plateau or along Pakistan's northern frontiers, a far cry from their days of belligerence; one or two steamers still stutter up and down the Nile but would be of little use to a modern Kitchener conquering the Sudan. A lucky few are nostalgically cosseted by steam enthusiasts.

And yet it had been so easy, in the heyday of steam, to use it to power the themes of empire so beloved of nineteenth-century politicians. Nathaniel Hawthorne's hero Clifford, in *The House of the Seven Gables*, predicted that railways would return man to a nomadic state.[19] 'They gave us wings; they annihilate the toil and dust of pilgrimage; they spiritualise travel!' he exlaimed to a disbelieving ticket collector. Later enthusiasts the world over have tried to sustain this romanticised vision of steam technology. On a more commercial, even political basis, it is interesting to speculate whether railways may yet take on a new lease of life, as those walls erected after World War II are undermined.

53 *The Dardanelles Lock*: *Punch* cartoon of 1903, commenting on German
friendship with the Ottoman Sultan, seen as to Britain's detriment

Notes

Chapter 1   *The Power of Steam*

1 Thomas Babington Macaulay, *The History of England* (5 vols), 1858–61, Vol. V p. 250.
  John Ruskin, *Praeterita*, 1885–9, Vol. III p. iv.
2 Fanny Kemble, *Records of a Girlhood*, 1878: 'from a letter to a friend, August 26th, 1930.'
3 Charles Kingsley, *Letters and Memoirs* (2 vols, edited by his widow), 1877: to Mr Ludlow, autumn, 1848.
4 W. S. Lindsay, *The History of Merchant Shipping* (4 vols), 1874–6; Vol. IV 1876, p. 65.
5 Ibid.
6 Rudyard Kipling, 'McAndrew's Hymn ', 1893.
7 Anthony Trollope, *Dr Thorne*, 1858, Ch. 9.
8 Terry Coleman, *The Railway Navvies*, 1965.
9 R. M. Ballantyne, *The Iron Horse, or Life on the Line*, 1871, p. 101.
10 *Calcutta Review*, LV, 1858, p. 46.

Chapter 2   *High Seas to India*

1 Dr Samuel Johnson, entry for March, 1759, in Boswell's *Life of Johnson*, 1791.
2 Thomas Twining, *Travels in India A Hundred Years Ago*, 1893.
3 William Hickey, *Memoirs*, 1768.
4 Alexander Macrabie, MSS. Eur. E.25, India Office Library.
5 James Wathen, *Journal of a Voyage to Madras and Calcutta in 1811*, 1814, p. 5.
6 Rev. George Trevor, MSS. Eur. E.25, India Office Library.
7 Harriet Atkinson, MSS. Eur. A.25, India Office Library.
8 Lord Valentia, *Voyages and Travels in India etc* (3 vols), 1809, Vol. I p. 4.
9 Marquis of Wellesley, *Despatches*, 1836; letter of October 6th, 1800.
10 Quoted by James Nasmyth, *Autobiography*, (ed. Samuel Smiles), 1883, p. 130.
11 *Asiatic Journal* O.S. XV, 1822, p. 477.
12 See H. L. Hoskins, *British Routes to India*, 1928, p. 90.
13 James Taylor in *Bombay Courier*, March 6th, 1825.

14 *Oriental Herald*, IV, 1825, p. 395.
15 G. F. Davidson, *Trade and Travel in the Far East*, 1840, p. 101.
16 *Bombay Courier*, March 27th, 1825.
17 Davidson, op. cit., p. 116.

Chapter 3   *The Overland Route*

1 Joseph Field to Parliamentary Committee., Parl. papers 1834, no. 478.
2 Charles Dickens, *Household Words*, 1850, Vol. I p. 494.
3 George Baldwin, *Political Recollections Relevant to Egypt*, 1801, p. 79.
4 James Capper, *Observations of the Passage to India*, 1783, p. xiv.
5 Mrs Lushington, *Narrative of a Journey from Calcutta to Europe*, 1829.
6 Sir Nicholas Waite, 1706, quoted in S. M. Edwardes, *The Rise of Bombay*, 1903.
7 See Hoskins, *British Routes*, p. 214.
8 Waghorn to the Court of Directors, quoted in *Asiatic Review* O.S. XXVII, 1826, p. 218.
9 Quoted by John Sidebottom, *The Overland Mail*, 1948, p. 18.
10 *Asiatic Journal*, N.S. XXVIII, 1829, p. 103.
11 James Taylor, *Bombay Courier*, March 6th, 1825.
12 Sidebottom, op. cit., p. 32.
13 Thomas Waghorn, *Overland Journey to Bombay*, 1831, p. 15.
14 The voyage is described in *Asiatic Journal* N.S. XIV, 1834.
15 Wilson to Parliamentary Committee, Parl. papers 1834, no. 478.
16 Ibid.
17 *Bombay Courier*, March 31st, 1832.
18 *The Times*, January 7th, 1833.
19 Parliamentary Committee, Parl. papers 1834, no. 478.
20 Emma Roberts, *Notes on an Overland Journey . . . to Bombay*, 1841, p. 2.
21 Waghorn, *Egypt As It Is In 1837*, 1838, p. 24.
22 Samuel Bevan, *Sand and Canvas*, 1849, p. 16.
23 Dr R. R. Madden, *Egypt and Muhammad Ali*, 1841, p. 2.
24 William Makepeace Thackeray, *Notes of a Journey from Cornhill to Cairo*, 1845, p. 177.
25 Dr R. R. Madden, *Travels in Turkey . . .* (2 vols), 1829, Vol. I p. 224.
26 John Carne, *Letters from the East*, 1826, p. 76.
27 Quoted by Sidebottom, op. cit., p. 75.
28 Edward Robinson, *Biblical Researches in Palestine* (3 vols), 1841, Vol. I p. 224.
29 Waghorn, *Egypt*, p. 27.
30 Emma Roberts, op. cit., p. 170.
31 Quoted by Sidebottom, op. cit., p. 110.
32 Quoted by Sidebottom, ibid, p. 113.
33 Ferdinand de Lesseps, *Recollections of Forty Years*, Vol. I p. 203.

Chapter 4   *High Road to India*

1 Francis Chesney, *Expedition for the Survey of the Euphrates and Tigris 1835–37* (2 vols), 1850, Preface.
2 James Capper, *Observations on a Passage to India*, 1784, p. 42.
3 Chesney, op. cit.
4 Quoted by Carl van Doren, *The Life of Thomas Love Peacock*, 1911, p. 222.
5 Parl. papers 1834, no. 478.
6 Ibid.
7 Ibid.
8 Quoted by Partick Kinross, *Between Two Seas*, 1968, p. 34.
9 C. P. Nostitz ed. (Mrs Helfer became Countess Nostitz by a second marriage), *Travels of Dr and Mme Helfer in Syria* (2 vols), 1878.
10 W. S. Ainsworth, *Personal Narrative of the Euphrates Expedition* (2 vols), 1888, Vol. I pp. 218–9.
11 Ibid, pp. 390 ff.
12 David Fraser (a journalist who went to investigate the Baghdad Railway in 1909), *A Short Cut to India*, 1909, p. 259.
13 Ibid, p. 295.

Chapter 5   *Tender Loving Care*

1 Parliamentary report, 1837, no. 539.
2 Harriet Tytler, *Memoirs*, ed. Anthony Sattin, 1986, p. 48.
3 William Makepeace Thackeray, *Notes of a Journey from Cornhill to Cairo*, 1845.
4 Ibid, p. 29.
5 Harriet Martineau, *Eastern Life, Present and Past* (3 volumes), 1848, Vol. I p. 5.
6 Quoted by Michael Bird, *Samuel Shepheard of Cairo*, 1957, p. 160.
7 P.&O. journal, 1842.
8 Ibid.
9 See Boyd Cable, *A Hundred Year History of P.&O.*, 1937, Ch. 12.
10 Quoted by Cable, ibid, p. 22.
11 P.&O. advertisement, P.&O. papers.
12 Douglas Farnie, *East and West of Suez*, 1969.
13 Quoted by Farnie, ibid., p. 33.
14 George Parbury, *Handbook for India and Egypt*, 1842, p. 311.
15 *Morning Post*, September 1853.
16 *Birkenhead Advertiser*, September 1853.
17 Quoted by G. S. Graham, *Great Britain in the Indian Ocean 1810–50*, 1967, p. 397.
18 William Adamson's manuscript diary is among the P.&O. papers.
19 Tom Taylor, *The Overland Route*, 1853.

Chapter 6 *War*

1 For instance by A. J. P. Taylor, William Langer, and J. A. R. Marriott. See bibliography.
2 Quoted by Gerald Morgan, *Anglo-Russian Rivalry in Central Asia*, 1981, p. 15.
3 Harriet Martineau, *The Westminster Review*, 1853.
4 Karl Marx, *The Eastern Question*, reprint of letters written 1853–6, 1897, p. 533.
5 W. S. Lindsay, *A History of Merchant Shipping*, Vol. IV p. 97.
6 Farnie, op. cit., pp. 29–31.
7 G. Toudouze, *Histoire de la Marine*, 1934, Ch. 14.
8 Ibid., p. 346.
9 *Bentley's Miscellany*, Vol. XXV, 1854, p. 359.
10 Admiral L. G. Heath, *Letters from the Black Sea*, 1856.
11 Fanny Duberley, *Letters*, 1855, this one dated November 11th, 1854.
12 William H. Russell, *The Seat of the War in the East* (2 vols), 1855–6, Vol. I p. 559.
13 E. A. Pratt, *The Rise of Railways in War and Conquest*, 1915, p. 206.
14 Quoted by Terry Coleman, *The Railway Navvies*, 1965, p. 186.
15 Quoted by Coleman, ibid.
16 General James Outram, *Outram's Persian Campaign in 1857*, 1860, p. 220.
17 Quoted by Cable, *P.&O.*, p. 193.

Chapter 7 *'A Dismal but Profitable Ditch'*

1 Joseph Conrad, *An Outcast of the Islands*, 1896.
2 Dr R. R. Madden, *Travels in Turkey, Egypt, Nubia and Palestine* (2 vols), 1829, Vol. I p. 230.
3 See Hoskins, *British Routes*, p. 294.
4 Arthur Anderson, *Communications with India, China etc. via Egypt*, 1843, p. 14.
5 Lucie Duff Gordon, *Letters from Egypt*, 1875, letter dated November 14th, 1865.
6 W. H. Russell, *A Diary in the East*, 1869, p. 71.
7 J. Charles-Roux, *L'Isthme et le Canal de Suez* (2 vols), 1901, Vol. I Annexe, p. 13.
8 Ferdinand de Lesseps, *Recollections* (2 vols), Vol. I p. 290.
9 J. C. Jeafferson, *Life of Robert Stephenson* (2 vols), 1864, Vol. II p. 148 .
10 Ibid., p. 143.
11 George Delane, *The Times*, December 16th, 1859.
12 Sir Henry Bulwer, Bulwer Papers, 1862.
13 Percy Fitzgerald, *The Great Canal at Suez* (2 vols), 1876.
14 Sir Robert Colquhoun, in Foreign Office records, FO 78/1796.

15 Fitzgerald, op. cit., Vol. I p. 202.
16 Russell, op. cit., p. 433.
17 *Spectator*, November 27th, 1869.
18 *Saturday Review*, November 13th, 1869.
19 *Illustrated London News*, November 20th, 1869.
20 Eugène Fromentin, *Voyage en Egypte*, 1869.

Chapter 8   *Posh*

1 Sir James Elphinstone, *Journal of East Indian Association* V, 1871, p. 40.
2 P.&O. papers.
3 Holt, Institution of Civil Engineers, minutes of proceedings 1877–8.
4 Sir Charles Dilke, *Greater Britain*, 1868, p. 569.
5 Quoted in John Marlowe, *The Making of the Suez Canal*, 1964, p. 304.
6 Robert Blake, *Disraeli*, 1967, p. 559.
7 Quoted by W. S. Lindsay, *Merchant Shipping*, Vol. IV p. 445.
8 Quoted by Angus Davidson, *Edward Lear*, 1938, p. 222.
9 W. J. Loftie, *Orient Line Guide*, 1889, p. 3.
10 *Punch*, January 14th, 1903, p. 31.
11 J. Johnston Abraham, *The Surgeon's Log*, 1911, p. 82.
12 Rudyard Kipling, *The Light that Failed*, 1913, p. 25.
13 André Chevrillon, *Romantic India*, 1897, p. 20.
14 Lindsay, op. cit., Ch. 9.
15 John Steele, *The Suez Canal, its Present and Future*, 1872, p. 20.
16 Abraham, op. cit., p. 46.
17 W. H. Seward, *Travels Round the World*, 1873, p. 527.
18 Captain J. M. Mackenzie, *Report on Egypt and Arabia*, 1837 Foreign Office papers, FO 78/3185.
19 Rudyard Kipling, 'For to Admire', from *A Choice of Songs*, 1925.
20 J. C. Parkinson, *Ocean Telegraph to India*, 1870, p. 61.
21 Arnold Wilson, *South-West Persia; a Political Officer's Diary 1907–14*, 1941, p. 231.
22 P.&O. papers.
23 Kipling, 'A Song of the English', from *In Seven Seas*, 1896.

Chapter 9   *The Capricious Stream*

1 W. H. Russell, *A Diary in the East*, 1869, p. 322.
2 John Keats, 'Ode to the Nile', published in H. B. Forman's edition of Keats' poetic works, 1883, Vol. II p. 254.
3 Major Charles Head, *Eastern and Egyptian Scenery*, 1833.
4 Quoted by Jean Marie Carré, *Voyageurs et écrivains français en Egypte*, 1956.
5 Percy Bysshe Shelley, 'To the Nile', 1818.
6 James Leigh Hunt, 'The Nile', in *Poetical Works*, 1832. According to Keats,

he, Hunt and Shelley sat down on February 4th, 1818, to write a sonnet on the Nile.

7   Victor Hugo, 'Le feu du ciel', from 'Le Nil' in *Orientales*, 1841.
8   W. H. Bartlett, *Gleanings on the Overland Route*, 1851.
9   Thackeray, *Cornhill to Cairo*, 1845, p. 168.
10 Madden, *Travels*, Vol. I p. 208.
11 Queen Victoria, *Life in the Highlands*, 1868, p. 52.
12 Russell, op. cit., p. 277.
13 De Lesseps, *Recollections*, Vol. I p. 136.
14 Ellen Chennells, *Recollections of an Egyptian Princess*, 1893, p. 52.
15 Lucie Duff Gordon, *Letters from Egypt*, 1865.
16 Sir John Wilkinson, *Manners and Customs of the Ancient Egyptians* (3 vols), 1837–41; and *Handbook for Travellers in Egypt*, published by John Murray in 1843.
17 *The Excursionist*, 1870.
18 Amelia Edwards, *A Thousand Miles up the Nile*, 1877.
19 Théophile Gautier, *L'Orient* (2 vols), 1877, Vol. II p. 209.
20 Quoted by Amelia Edwards, *A Thousand Miles Up the Nile*, 1877, p. 159.
21 *The Times*, October 9th, 17th, and 25th, 1888.
22 An interview in the *Pall Mall Gazette*, January 1884.
23 Quoted by Julian Symons, *England's Pride*, 1965, p. 238.
24 Ibid., p. 122.
25 Lady Gwendolen Cecil, *Life of Robert, Marquis of Salisbury* (3 vols), Vol. III 1921.
26 Winston Churchill, *The River War* (2 vols), 1900, Vol. I p. 125.
27 Ibid., p. 290.
28 Ibid., p. 290.
29 Ibid., p. 292.
30 Pierre Monteil, *Souvenirs vécus*, 1924, p. 65.
31 G. N. Sanderson, *England, Egypt and the Upper Nile*, 1964, p. 1.
32 W. W. Stead, *Pall Mall Gazette*, November 15th, 1898.

Chapter 10   *Through Caspian and Caucasus*

1   Marvin described his journey in *Regions of Eternal Fire*, 1884.
2   Quoted in J. N. Westwood, *A History of Russian Railways*, 1964.
3   Alexandre Dumas, *Impressions du voyage* (3 vols), 1841, Vol. III p. 235.
4   It was also quoted by Count Lobanov-Rostovsky, *Russia in Asia*, 1933, p. 76.
5   Valentine Chirol, *The Middle East Question*, 1903, p. 25.
6   Robert Young, *Timothy Hackworth and the Locomotive*, 1923, p. 277.
7   John Maxwell, *The Czar, his Court and People*, 1848, p. 125.
8   Xavier Hommaire de Hell, *Travels in the Steppes of the Caspian Sea*, 1847, p. 297.

9 J. F. Baddeley, *Rugged Flanks of Caucasus* (2 vols), 1940, Vol. I p. 39.
10 Sir Robert Ker Porter, *Travels in Georgia etc 1817–1820* (2 vols), 1821–2, Vol. II p. 519.
11 W. P. Andrew, *Memoir on the Euphrates Valley*, 1857, p. 61.
12 Charles Marvin, *The Russians at Merv and Herat*, 1883, p. 412.
13 A. T. Cunynghame, *Travels in Eastern Caucasus*, 1872, p. 316.
14 W. P. Andrew, *Indian Railways*, 1884, p. 138.
15 Robert Weatherburn, several articles in *Railway Magazine* in 1913 and 1914.
16 George Curzon, *Persia and the Persian Question* (2 vols), 1892, Vol. I p. 60.
17 Gabriel Bonvalot, *Through the Heart of Asia* (2 vols), 1889, Vol. I p. 20.
18 Quoted by Westwood, op. cit., p. 33.
19 Captain Frederick Burnaby, *A Ride to Khiva*, 1877, p. 20.
20 This and the following quotations are from Marvin, *Regions of Eternal Fire*.
21 *Railway Magazine*, July 13th, 1913, p. 46.
22 Curzon, *Persia and the Persian Question*, Vol. I p. 65.
23 Chirol, op. cit., p. 21.

Chapter 11   *Not for Trafficking Alone*

1 George Curzon's account, *Russia in Central Asia*, was published in 1889.
2 Ibid., p. xii.
3 Arminius Vámbéry, *Travels in Central Asia*, 1864, p. 103.
4 Count Pahlen, *Mission to Turkestan 1908–9*, 1964, p. 23.
5 See Gerald Morgan, *Anglo–Russian Rivalry in Central Asia 1810–95*, 1981.
6 Annenkov, quoted in Charles Marvin, *The Russians at Merv and Herat*, 1883, p. 38.
7 James MacGahan, *Campaigning on the Oxus*, 1874, p. 5.
8 Quoted by Seymour Becker, *Russia's Protectorates in Central Asia 1865–1924*, 1968, p. 17.
9 MacGahan, op. cit., p. 425.
10 Curzon on Skobelov in *Russia in Central Asia*, 1889, pp. 86–92.
11 Coined by the Duke of Argyll, *The Eastern Question* (2 vols), 1879, Vol. II p. 371.
12 Quoted by Marvin, *The Russians at Merv and Herat*, pp. 4–63.
13 George Dobson, *Russia's Railway Advance into Central Asia*, 1890, p. 281.
14 Gabriel Bonvalot, *Through the Heart of Asia*, Vol. II p. 213.
15 William Curtis, *Turkestan, 'the Heart of Asia'*, 1911, p. 35.
16 Robert Weatherburn, 'Leaves from a Locomotive Engineer', *Railway Magazine*, 1913.
17 Described in Curzon's *Russia in Central Asia*.
18 Curtis, op. cit., p. 69.
19 Matthew Arnold, *Sohrab and Rustum*, 1853.
20 J. T. Woolrych Perowne, *Russian Hosts and English Guests*, 1898, p. 123.

21 Curzon, op. cit., p. 233.
22 Quoted by B. H. Sumner, *Tsardom and Imperialism 1880–1914*, 1940, p. 7.
23 Perowne, op. cit., p. xi.

Chapter 12   *Road Improvement Schemes*

1 Arthur Conolly, *Journey to the North of India* (2 vols), 1834, Vol. II p. 219.
2 Henry Bellew, *From Indus to Tigris*, 1874, p. 3.
3 George Curzon, *Russia in Central Asia*, 1889.
4 Both men quoted by Robert Blake, *Disraeli*, 1967, p. 627.
5 Quoted by Mary Lutyens, *The Lyttons in India*, 1979, p. 135.
6 Disraeli, speech at the Mansion House, 1878.
7 William Andrew, *Indian Railways*, 1884, p. xvi.
8 *The Times*, October 13th, 1879.
9 Quoted G. R. Elmslie, *Life of Sir Donald Stewart*, 1903, p. 216.
10 Frederick Roberts, *Forty-one Years in India*, 1897.
11 George Scott-Moncrieff in *Blackwood's Magazine*, May, 1905. Scott Mon-crieff also wrote on the railway in greater detail in 'The Frontier Railways on India', *Professional Papers of the Royal Engineers*, Vol. XI, 1885, p. 213.
12 J. Macleod Innes, *The Life and Times of General Sir James Browne*, 1905.
13 *Engineering*, April 13th, 1888, p. 368.
14 Scott-Moncrieff, op. cit., *Blackwood's*, p. 616.
15 Ibid., p. 612.
16 Innes, op. cit., p. 243.
17 *Pioneer*, May 3rd, 1893.
18 Quoted Elmslie, op. cit., p. 217.
19 Earl of Ronaldshay, *Life of Curzon* (3 vols), 1928, Vol. I p. 130.
20 S. B. Wheeler, *Abd al-Rahman*, 1895, p. 199.
21 Quoted by G. J. Alder, *British India's Northern Frontier*, 1963, p. 183.
22 Kipling, 'Arithmetic on the Frontier', *Departmental Ditties*, 1892.
23 Curzon, Romanes lecture on 'Frontiers', Oxford, 1907.
24 Victor Bayley, author of *Permanent Way Through the Khyber*, 1934, p. 16.
25 Ibid., p. 242.

Chapter 13   *The Ultimate Link*

1 Arnold Keppel, *Gun-running and the Indian North-West Frontier*, 1911, p. xi.
2 Percy Sykes, *Ten Thousand Miles through Persia*, 1902, p. 87.
3 Commander Somerville, *Blackwood's Magazine*, June and July, 1920. Somerville was appointed in 1907 to survey suitable harbours on the Persian coast of the Gulf.
4 C. R. Low, *History of the Indian Navy* (2 vols), 1877, Vol. II p. 95.
5 Lovat Fraser, *Proceedings of the Royal Central Asian Society*, May 17th, 1911.

6 Sir Arnold Wilson, *South-West Persia, a Political Officer's Diary*, 1941, p. 130.
7 Keppel, op. cit., p. 125.
8 Quoted by Ronaldshay, *Life of Curzon*, Vol. II p. 316.
9 Lovat Fraser, op. cit.
10 W. P. Andrew, *Memoir on the Euphrates Valley Route to India*, 1857, p. 84.
11 A. H. Layard, *Autobiography* (2 vols), Vol. I p. 330.
12 A. H. Layard, *Early Travels* (2 vols), Vol. II p. 180.
13 David Fraser, *A Short Cut to India*, 1909, p. 250.
14 Curzon, 'The Karun River and the Commercial Geography of South-West Persia', *Proceedings of the Royal Geographical Society*, 1890, p. 514.
15 Aloys Sprenger, *Babylonien, das reichste Land in der Vorzeit*, 1886.
16 T. S. Eliot, *Old Possum's Book of Practical Cats* ('Skimbleshanks: the Railway Cat'), 1939.
17 Quoted by W. P. Andrew, op. cit., p. 87.
18 *Spectator*, October 22nd, 1908.
19 *Scientific American*, Vol. 51., 1901.
20 *The Times*, October 28th, 1910.
21 Quoted by E. M. Earle, *Turkey, the Great Powers and the Baghdad Railway*, 1923, p. 101.
22 Hansard, Parliamentary debates, House of Commons Vol. 120, 1903, p. 1,247 etc.
23 David Fraser, op. cit.
24 Gertrude Bell, *Amurath to Amurath*, 1911, dedication to Lord Cromer.
25 Quoted by Ulrich Trumpener, *Germany and the Ottoman Empire*, 1968.
26 Charles Fellows, *Travels and Researches in Asia Minor*, 1852, p. 130.
27 *Illustrated London News*, October 10th, 1908.
28 Report by Major Maunsell RA, July 1907, to the War Office (in the India Office Library L/P &S/10/12).
29 T. E. Lawrence, *Seven Pillars of Wisdom*, 1926.

Chapter 14 *Aftermath*

1 Lt. Col. Yate, *Proceedings of the Royal Central Asian Society*, February 1911, p. 15.
2 William Ewing, *From Gallipoli to Baghdad*, n.d., p. 234.
3 Reginald Dyer, *Raiders of Sarhad*, 1921, p. 89.
4 Sir Harry Luke, *Cities and Men* (3 vols), 1953–6, Vol. II p. 160.
5 Milner MSS, 'The Middle East Theatre', March 1918.
6 Quoted Elizabeth Monroe, *Britain's Moment in the Middle East*, 1963, p. 46.
7 Valentine Chirol, *The Middle East Question*, p. 280.
8 Curzon, Romanes lecture on 'Frontiers', 1907.
9 W. E. R. Dickson, *East Persia – a Backwater of the Great War*, 1924.
10 Dickson, ibid., p. 50.

11 Milner MSS for 1918, p. 113.
12 General Dunsterville's account of his expedition is in his *Adventures of Dunsterforce*, 1920.
13 General Malleson, *Proceedings of the Royal Central Asian Society*, 1922, p. 101.
14 Captain C. V. Blacker, *Proceedings of the Royal Central Asian Society*, 1922, p. 12.
15 Captain David Norris, *Proceedings of the Royal Central Asian Society*, 1922.
16 Ibid., p. 217.
17 Churchill to Curzon May 20th, 1920, quoted in Churchill's *The Aftermath*, in *World Crisis*, 1929, p. 414.
18 Quoted by Lord Hankey, *Supreme Command 1914–18* (1961), p. 46
19 Nathaniel Hawthorne, *The House of Seven Gables*, 1841, Ch. 5.

Select Bibliography

This bibliography contains secondary sources used in my research; other contemporary sources will be found in the chapter references. All are published in Britain unless otherwise stated. I have also consulted some of the following documents:

Parliamentary debates, in the British Library
Parliamentary papers, in the British Library
Foreign Office records, in the Public Records Office
India Office records, in the India Office Library
Milner MSS, in the Bodleian Library
P.&O. papers in the National Maritime Museum.

Books

Alder, G. J., *British India's Northern Frontier 1865–95*, 1963.
Alexander, J. E., *Cleopatra's Needle*, 1879.
Allen W. E. D., *Caucasian Battlefields*, 1953.
Antier, J-J, *Au temps des premiers paquebots à vapeur*, Paris, 1982.
Avery, Peter, *Modern Iran*, 1965.
Baddeley, J. F., *The Rugged Flanks of Caucasia* (2 vols), 1940.
Barton, W., *India's North-West Frontier, 1939*
Bayley, Victor, *Permanent Way Through the Khyber*, 1934.
Beatty, Charles, *De Lesseps of Suez*, 1956.
Becker, Seymour, *Russia's Protectorates in Central Asia: Bukhara and Khiva 1865–1924*, Cambridge, Mass. 1968.
Berridge, P. S., *Couplings to the Khyber*, 1969.
Bird, Michael, *Samuel Shepheard of Cairo*, 1957.
Birkenhead, *Description of Birkenhead Iron Works*, 1874.
Blackwell, William J., *The Beginnings of Russian Industrialisation* (2 vols), 1968.
Blake, Robert, *Disraeli*, 1967.
Cable, Boyd, *A Hundred Year History of P.&O.*, 1937.
Carré, Jean Marie, *Voyageurs et écrivains français en Egypte* (2 vols), Paris, 1956.
Charles-Roux, J., *L'isthme et le canal de Suez* (2 vols), Paris, 1901.
Charuikov, N. V., *Glimpses of High Politics*, 1931.
Chesney, Louisia, *Life of General F. R. Chesney*, 1885.
Chevrillon, André, *Terres mortes*, Paris, 1897.

Chirol, Valentine, *The Middle East Question*, 1903.

Churchill, Winston, *The River War*, 1900.

Churchill, Winston, *The Aftermath*, in *World Crisis*, 1929.

Clapham, J. H., *Economic Development of France and Germany*, 1936.

Coleman, Terry, *The Railway Navvies*, 1965.

Cookridge, E. H., *The Orient Express*, 1978.

Davidson, Angus, *Edward Lear*, 1938.

Davies, Cuthbert, *The North-West Frontier 1890–1908*: Vol. V of H. H. Dodwell, *The Indian Empire*, 1932.

Doran, Carl van, *The Life of Thomas Love Peacock*, 1911.

Earle, Edward Meade, *Turkey, the Great Powers and the Baghdad Railway*, 1923.

Farnie, David, *East and West of Suez*, 1969.

Fitzgerald, Percy, *The Great Canal at Suez*, 1876.

Fraser, Douglas, *A Short Cut to India*, 1909.

Giraud, Hubert, *Les origines et l'évolution de la navigation à vapeur à Marseilles*, Marseilles, 1929.

Gottlieb, W. W., *Studies in Secret Diplomacy During World War I*, 1957.

Graham, G. S., *Great Britain in the Indian Ocean 1810–50*, 1967.

Grant, Christine, *The Syrian Desert*, 1937.

Greaves, R. L., *Persia and the Defence of India*, 1959.

Hankey, Lord, *Supreme Command 1914–18*, 1961.

Harwood, R. A., *Cleopatra's Needle*, 1978.

Henry, J. D., *Baku, an Eventful History*, 1905.

Henry, J. D., *35 years of Oil Transport*, 1907.

Hickey, William, *Memoirs 1749–1809* (4 vols) 1923–6.

Hopkirk, Peter, *The Great Game*, 1989.

Hopkirk, Peter, *Setting the East Ablaze*, 1986.

Hoskins, Harold, *British Routes to India*, 1928.

Hughes, Hugh, *Middle East Railways*, 1981.

Hughes, Hugh, *Steam in India*, 1977.

Hyde, F. E. *A History of Alfred Holt & Co. 1865–1914*, 1956.

Innes, J. Macleod, *The Life and Times of General Sir James Browne*, 1905.

Issawi, Charles, *The Economic History of the Middle East, 1800–1914*, 1966.

Jeafferson, J. C., *The Life of Robert Stephenson* (2 vols), 1864.

Jennings, Humphrey, *Pandemonium*, 1985.

Joby, R. S., *The Railway Builders*, 1983.

Kinross, Patrick, *Between Two Seas*, 1968.

Klemm, Friedrich, *A History of Western Technology*, 1959.

La Varende, *Les Augustin-Normand; sept generations de constructeurs de navires*, Paris, 1961.

Lambert, Andrew, *Battleships in Transition*, 1984.

Landes, David, *Bankers and Pashas*, 1958.

Langer, William, *The Diplomacy of Imperialism*, (2 vols), 1935.

Lewis, Bernard, *The Emergence of Modern Turkey*, 1961.

Lindsay, W. S., *The History of Merchant Shipping* (4 vols, esp. Vol. IV), 1874–6.

Llewellyn, Briony, *The Orient Observed: Images of the Middle East from the Searight Collection*, 1989.
Longrigg, Stephen, *Oil in the Middle East*, 1954.
Low, C. R., *History of the Indian Navy 1613–1863* (2 vols), 1877.
Lutyens, Mary, *The Lyttons in India*, 1979.
MacGeorge, G. W., *Ways and Works in India*, 1894.
Magnus, Philip, *Kitchener, Portrait of an Imperialist*, 1966.
Malik, N. B. K., *A Hundred Years of Pakistan Railways*, Islamabad, 1962.
Marlowe, John, *The Making of the Suez Canal*, 1964.
Marriott, J. A. R., *The Eastern Question*, 1917.
Marston, T., *Britain's Imperial Role in the Red Sea 1800–78*, 1961
Moberley, F. J., *History of the Great War 1914–18*, Vol. IV, 1927.
Monroe, Elizabeth, *Britain's Moment in the Middle East*, 1963.
Morgan, Gerald, *Anglo–Russian Rivalry in Central Asia 1810–95*, 1981.
Ochsenwald, William, *The Hijaz Railroad*, Charlottesville, 1980.
Parker H. and Bowen F. C., *Mail and Passenger Ships of the Nineteenth Century*, 1928.
Penrose, Boies, *Travel and Discovery in the Renaissance*, 1952.
Pratt, Edwin A., *The Rise of Rail Power in War and Conquest*, 1915.
Pudney, John, *Thomas Cook*, 1953.
Robbins, Michael, *The Railway Age*, 1962.
Rogers, H. C. B., *Troopships and Their History*, 1963.
Rolt, L. C., *Victorian Engineering*, 1970.
Ronaldshay, The Earl of, *Life of Curzon* (3 vols), 1928.
Sanderson, G. N., *England, Egypt and the Upper Nile*, 1964.
Sandes, E. W. C., *The Military Engineer in India*, 1933.
Sandes, E. W. C., *The Royal Engineers in Egypt and Sudan*, 1937.
Satow M. & Desmond R., *Railways of the Raj*, 1987.
Searight, Sarah, *The British in the Middle East*, 1980.
Sidebottom, J., *The Overland Mail*, 1948.
Singer C. et al, *The History of Technology*, 1958, Vols IV & V.
Sumner, B. H. *Tsardom and Imperialism 1880–1914*, 1940.
Sykes, Percy, *A History of Persia* (2 vols), 1930.
Symons, Julian, *England's Pride*, 1965.
Taylor, A. J. P., *The Struggle for Mastery in Europe*, 1954.
Toudouze, G., *Histoire de la marine*, Paris, 1934.
Trumpener, *Germany and the Ottoman Empire*, 1968.
Villiers, Alan, *The Indian Ocean*, 1940.
Wadia, R. A., *The Bombay Dockyard and the Wadia Master Builders*, Bombay 1955.
Waterfield, Gordon, *Sultans of Aden*, 1968.
Westwood, J. N., *A History of Russian Railways*, 1964.
Westwood, J. N., *Railways at War*, 1980.
Wiener, Lionel, *L'Egypte et ses chemins de fer*, Cairo, 1962.
Young, Robert, *Timothy Hackworth and the Locomotive*, 1923.

Index

n. = note   s.s. = steamship   s.y. = steam yacht